Strangers
in Paradise

The Christensen children seated by the entrance to
Jean François Millet´s studio at Fontainebleau
near Paris prior to our first trip to the south of France.

Strangers
in Paraⸯise

A Memoir of Provence

Paul Christensen

San Antonio, Texas
2007

Strangers in Paradise: A Memoir of Provence © 2007 by Paul Christensen

Cover painting, "Yellow Painting" © 1997 by Andrea Belag.
Courtesy of Mike Weiss Gallery, New York.
Photos between pages 154-155, "Images of Provence," by Paul Christensen.
Frontispiece and photographs on pages 30 and 204 by Cathy Christensen.

First Edition

ISBN-10: 0-916727-28-9
ISBN-13: 978-0-916727-28-4

Wings Press
627 E. Guenther
San Antonio, Texas 78210
Phone/fax: (210) 271-7805

On-line catalogue and ordering:
www.wingspress.com
All Wings Press titles are distributed to the trade by
Independent Publishers Group
www.ipgbook.com

Library of Congress Cataloging-in-Publication Data

Christensen, Paul, 1943-
  Strangers in paradise : a memoir of Provence / Paul Christensen.
     p. cm.
  ISBN-13: 978-0-916727-28-4 (alk. paper)
  1. Provence (France)--Description and travel. 2. Provence (France)--Social life and
customs. 3. Christensen, Paul, 1943---Homes and haunts--France--Provence. 4.
Poets, American--20th century--Biography. I. Title.
  DC611.P958C54 2007
  811'.54--dc22
  [B]   2006033592

Contents

Chapter I: Herbes de Provence   3

Chapter 2: In the Sacred Precincts   17

Chapter 3: Of Work and Dreams   31

Chapter 4: Jack Rabbit   47

Chapter 5: Pagan Dust   59

Chapter 6: "J'ai Un Crayon"   71

Chapter 7: Changelings   87

Chapter 8: Of Faucets and Cock Crows   99

Chapter 9: Spring Hath Sprung   109

Chapter 10: A Hole in the Wall   127

Chapter 11: A Home of One's Own   145

Photographs: Images of Provence   *following* 154

Chapter 12: Deaths and Entrances   163

Chapter 13: Belonging   181

Chapter 14: Weaving and Unraveling   193

Epilogue   205

Strangers in Paraɗise

A Memoir of Provence

To my three children,
Maxine, Signe, and Cedric,
who took the journey with me.

Chapter One

Herbes de Provence

There was thyme in the air, pungent and teasing. Lilacs and wisteria drooped their lazy blossoms along the garden fences. Every windowsill bore some splash of red geraniums among the green shutters and stone walls. Sunlight poured like dark honey from the sky. Women shuffled alongside the roads bearing small bundles, crinkle-eyed, leathery, like little demigods half turned into trees. They were gypsies hurrying back to camp. The roadside parks were full of caravans of gypsies working the cherry harvest. On higher ground roamed long, puffy green rows of new lavender, not yet spiked with purple tassels. The magpies swooped and quivered on the electric lines, little Fred Astaires in immaculate black and white tuxedoes, with piercing cries out to the sleeping meadows. It was our first day in Provence. June 1, 1986.

And here we were, unpacked, milling around in our little stone house, with the thick, almost chewy sunlight burnishing everything to a gilded luster. I saw my wife Cathy holding her hands up to the window to admire them. They had a deep ivory sheen, creamy as soap stone in the pure light. We were all staring at things with the excitement of painters.

No matter where you looked the colors bore a startling unfamiliarity. Is it possible, I wondered, for a wooden fence to be so beautiful? There it stood in my neighbor's yard undulating its six or seven shades of green, from avocado to jade to tawny olive, each hue velvet and fruity, shifting tone under the passing clouds. Down a slope of stony earth was a tapestry of wild flowers – blood red poppies among purple alfalfa blossoms, and little yellow buds thrust up like pointillist dots, all waving together in a shimmering Persian rug of colors. My three children had gone out to play under a thatched roof of ivy and black berry vines that had once served as a potting shed. The two girls, Maxine and Signe, set up house under the golden flakes of sunlight, and were cooking dinner over the flower pots, while my four-year old son, Cedric, stood around kicking small blue pebbles in the road.

We had rented a *gîte*, as they are called, a country house, for the month of June, before heading up to Paris for the rest of the summer. We had the corner house in a little row of stone cottages in a place called Croagnes, pronounced "crone" by the locals, a tiny hamlet with two other rows of cottages, a dusty, unused chapel, several farm houses with gardens, and an old manor set off on walled grounds above us. The Romans had made a settlement here, a fort with a garrison, which offered the strategic advantage of a look-out over the meandering valley below. At one time, according to the *Dictionnaire des Communes Vaucluse*, my guide in such matters, the hamlet swelled to three hundred inhabitants in the 1700s. Almost every village in the Vaucluse was crammed with people at that time, both the heyday of Provence and a time of plagues that swept over the towns and left many of them half-empty or even abandoned thereafter. Now it had the air of a sleepy Texas ghost town.

A few kilometers to the right stands the town of Gordes, where the rich concentrate in showy, expensively restored village houses, or in cliff-hanging villas, each with a swatch of putting green grass and a glittering opal pool. Behind this craggy outcrop of houses lies the Cistercian Abbey de Senanque, where the monk poet, Thomas Merton, spent part of his early years. Like most Cistercian abbeys, this one lies at the bottom of a steep canyon, with the rich alluvial soil growing grapes and lavender, and a luscious kitchen garden. Years later, we would drive to Senanque on Christmas Eve and on summer week ends to hear the monks chanting Greek Orthodox hymns. I have never known such clear, silvery voices, such basses as I heard on those Spartan afternoons of July and August, the monks gathered in a circle to intone, or, at night, to sing antiphonals from the choir pews.

To the left of Croagnes is the sun-bleached village of Saint Saturnin, topped by the ruins of a castle, moat intact, a few walls still weathering the sandy winds. Behind us, over the jagged ridges of canyons and escarpments, rises the bald granite peak of Mt. Ventoux, the western-most alp. The rest of the Alps roam off to the east, snowbound and remote.

We were in the heart of the Vaucluse, the summer playground of wealthy Parisians and tourist hordes, a quiet and, until recently, unsung region of the lower Rhone that is beginning to rival the Riviera as a leading resort. Everyone talks about the Luberon villages, the "five towns," though there are more than five. These ancient hilltop towns had endured the Roman Empire, Saracen counter-crusades, bitter religious wars, and now braced for an onslaught of wealthy vacationers storming their green hills and craggy slopes, which run from Apt in the east to Avignon in the west. Edging into the pine and oak woods are new villas and swimming pools tucked into clefts of rock, or squeezed between vineyards and orchards.

Above them rise the long shaggy hillsides of *garrigue*, the foliage of stubby junipers stark as Giacometti figures standing among spikes of grayish brown weeds, which we call chaparral in Texas. It all looked like cowboy country, the sort of landscape John Ford's camera lingered over in his western films. No cowboys here, just hares and lizards, and the upturned earth plowed by a boar's tusks.

It was my job to go find groceries after the unpacking; Cathy didn't want to drive yet. It was her first time in Europe and she seemed to think Europeans went by some other driving rules. She had been a bit daunted by the right-handed driving in London, where we had stopped briefly on the way over. I asked our New Zealand landlady, Pip, who lived next door, where I might go for food on a Sunday afternoon. She was a slender woman in her late forties, with cool, gray eyes and low blood pressure. We stood in the breeze with the beaded curtain clacking against her big double-doors as she pondered my question leisurely. Finally, she sent me off to St. Saturnin, where an *épicerie* might still be open, but she doubted it.

I climbed into our little Renault 5, still stale from the long car trip down from Paris, and headed up the valley road, which unraveled among cherry orchards, almond groves, vineyards and melon fields, until it climbed onto the slopes of St. Saturnin. I parked in the village square just below the statue of the truffle gatherer, a white plaster figure kneeling in slouch hat, cupping a black truffle in his hands. The *épicerie* was still open, with stands of vegetables lining both sides of the doorway.

It was obvious I was a tourist; I brought no shopping bag or cart with me, and simply went around piling things in my arms and lugging them over to the counter. The smell of earth rose from the eggplant I just prodded. The tomatoes were large and fiery red, ripe to perfection. Their smell was heavenly: rich, pungent, still warm from the sun. My tongue curled at the thought of biting into one.

I piled up a great quantity of food under the admiring gaze of *la propriétaire*. She smiled at each choice, and jotted down the price on a small notepad. I would go off and pinch cucumbers and hear her whispered encouragement behind me, and feel guilty when I passed something up. There were brown eggs heaped up in a basket, and as I selected a few she rushed beside me and began rolling them in strips of newspaper. I chose a dozen and they were whisked over to the counter. I held up the lanky, sprawling body of a *pintade*, a blue-skinned guinea fowl with head and scaly yellow feet intact, which was eased from my hand onto the weight scale. One kilo and 600 grams, almost three pounds. I chose six large peaches and a dozen small green apples, as things were taken from my arms and put into bags. I need only begin sniffing the wheels of cheese in a cooler to know my good lady would be standing beside me, cheese wire in hand. I chose a wedge of brie, half a globe of aged *mimolette*, two or three crusty little *crottins* of goat cheese. I could have gone on shopping like this for another hour or so if the suspicion hadn't crept into my mind that these things might be expensive.

I had a bag of ground coffee, some filters, thick slices of bacon, a small bag of black olives, two bottles of local wine, a pile of other bags containing artichokes, potatoes, carrots, cheese, the works. After everything was weighed and added up, I didn't quite catch the total. I looked a bit bewildered, I suppose. She scribbled the amount on a scrap of paper and handed it to me – I forget the exact figure, but it probably came to sixty or seventy dollars. I grimaced; the same things would have cost me thirty at a food store in Texas, but this was life abroad, I told myself, and unfolded the five hundred franc note and handed it over. She seemed very pleased as she counted off the change into my palm. Then she darted over to the cucumbers I had passed up, took two large ones, ran a cloth over them, stuffed them into my plastic sack, and fetched down a dusty bottle of wine, gave it a rub, and presented it to me with a wide, appreciative grin.

I was happy. It all seemed right to me, even the prices. These were things I hardly ever noticed back in Texas; they were just groceries to me, stuff you watched go into the bags and then carted home to dump into a refrigerator drawer. You never smelled them or admired their color, you just ate them. But here, in the bags that rattled in the back seat, were dark, stringent aromas, beautiful heavy objects still alive, potent with nature, lying there in a great profusion of colors: dark reds, cool greens, the lush almost black skin of the cucumbers, dimpled and moist where they had tumbled onto the seat. The peaches were erotic little spheres, warm, bruised, dripping a gold sap from their swollen skin. I could hardly drive for the logy air I breathed.

When I got back the sky had blurred to a rusty sunset. The wind was whipping the cherry trees, and turning up the gray undersides of the grape leaves. There was a noise of clapping and long sighs as the wind rolled over the tiled roofs. Our own beaded curtain swished and clattered against the glass doors like the fronds of a car wash. Puffs of dust rolled into the dark living room with each gust. It was exciting, as if at any moment gobbets of rain would thud down onto the dusty road out front. There were cool currents among the gusts, like slivers of winter still loose on the spring air. It was lovely, and smelled of rosemary, mint, the dankness of wells.

Cathy and I stood in the tiny kitchen and worked furiously, rinsing off vegetables, dicing, chopping, turning things over in the skillet as the chicken spluttered away in the oven. I had uncorked the bottle of wine that Pip had given us when we first arrived. It was breathing on the dining room table. When I came in to pour a glass, the room had already absorbed the thin, moldy tang of the wine. I took a sip and fumbled for a chair. My mouth flooded with memories – the taste of my grandmother's pasta, smells of winter kitchens, cob-webbed cellars, the jangling flavors of baked apples. It all came back, fleetingly, merging and disappearing as I swallowed. It was a glass of tangled memories, confused, yet sharp, haunting, a few painful to recall as they tumbled through my mind. I understood now why alcohol is called "spirits." It comes from the land of the dead, the underworld. Monks often planted their vines in grave yards to prevent theft – and the graves imparted their lonely world to the best of the wines, making us ache who drank them.

Cathy joined me and we sat in the darkness of the room, the kitchen yellow as a sunflower through the narrow door. The wind was a mournful presence, as if winter had come out of the ground and rolled over the housetops, while we drank last summer in the glass. I thought keenly of my deceased brother, who had left a hole in my life; he shimmered over the twilit air and seemed almost to touch my face as I raised my glass.

It was hard getting up. Night was upon us and we were hungry; the kids had come back and were upstairs putting their toys around, staking their territories. I pulled the roasted chicken out and carved it; the limbs fell away at the slightest pressure of the knife. The meat smelled of roasted nuts. I had quartered an onion and a lemon and stuffed them inside, along with sprigs of thyme and rosemary needles. The meat was flavored with them. We ate ravenously. I cannot recall tomatoes ever receiving so much praise. They were sliced and dusted with herbs and slivers of garlic, and drowned in olive oil and lemon juice, and we each had our own impression of their taste. Our lips shined, our eyes were merry with eating. I continued to sip wine hoping some new memory would arise from the past.

That was our first dinner, our initiation into the mysteries of Provence. We had passed under a kind of lintel into its gardens, its bottomless depths. We had tasted things that bewildered our tongues, as if the ancestors had come into the vegetables and trudged over our taste buds. We had taken communion with the strange, historic earth, and it made each of us go inward and chew with absorbed privacy. Even my son seemed dreamy and preoccupied, his cheeks bulging with potatoes, his eyes vague and reflective.

By the time we washed up and came into the living room, the evening had turned cool. Wind pounded the roof in long growling gusts and soot drifted in the air. We crowded into a corner of the living room near the hearth, wedged ourselves onto a small sofa and bench to listen to the storm brewing overhead. It had a sorrowful rage to it, as it bowed down trees and thrashed the high grass. The vines rattled, and the ivy came loose and swung around like tentacles in the dark. Rain pattered on the tiles occasionally as wind rolled and slid off heavily to the valley below. It was a great power loose in the world; we could do nothing but listen to it. It was free and we were its witnesses. By eleven, eyes drooped and we went to bed, to lie awake under the moaning storm roaming the hillsides and canyons like a throng of grieving widows.

I woke in the morning as if I had dropped ten years from my life. I felt fresh and vigorous, thirty-three once more. I felt good. Perhaps it was the fresh food, or even the wine! Though I felt a slight pain in the back of my head, and a certain rawness when I gulped down my first cup of coffee. I breathed deep, slapped my stomach smartly, and did a few jumping jacks beside the bed. I wanted to stretch every joint, and go running out into the vineyards. The storm had passed, but the horizon bore its traces – a vague, sandy light along the hillsides where dust had not yet settled. I could smell the sand still lingering in the air; behind it came the salad breath of the grass, already warm by nine. The little clumps of thyme would begin to heat and send off pungent charges of scent. I could sniff them already.

It was the first whole day for me. I knew what my duties were, my pleasures, I mean. I would set up my typewriter on the small table by the window, and get out my books and papers and start a journal. I had letters to write; the list of people was in my notebook, which I threw onto the pile. I would sit down in the first little freshets of air, where the morning shadows stood, and begin typing, thinking, dreaming while the steam rose from my coffee cup. It had been a long time since I felt this good.

I had spent the last twelve years teaching at Texas A&M University in Texas. No doubt you've heard of it, or of its famous football team. I had gone through all the routine promotions and published the required books and monographs, and was now – though I didn't realize it yet – approaching the long plateau of mid-career. The time when raises slow down and committee assignments grow tedious, and the things one didn't do grow alluring and important. For the first time in all those years of teaching I asked for one of those "summer abroad" courses, in which you squire round a group of students in pursuit of some loosely defined subject matter. In my case, a tour of cities where American expatriates lived and wrote their novels and poems.

So what if the passages were mainly used as background? *The Sun Also Rises* begins in the *Closerie des Lilas* on Boulevard Montparnasse. Would it not, I reasoned vaguely, make the scene more compelling to see the actual restaurant? The psychology seemed a bit rough, but perhaps all tours depend upon similar ruses in logic: see Provence as Cezanne did before he painted the fields outside Aix. Perhaps there is something to be learned about the difference between life and art. So, onward to tour T.S. Eliot's London, and Henry James' Rome, and all the other European settings of American literature. In truth, I couldn't say what purpose would be served by such a tour. The kids would gawk at the usual sights, shop, get boiled at the local pubs, and grind out a report for me at the end. But then Europe intervened as the book, and I was delighted to have thought up my little scheme. I got my quorum of twenty students and was given plane tickets, my summer salary, with work to begin next month when we moved to Paris.

I confess it was Paris, not Provence, that was the hub of our summer plans. I wouldn't have picked Provence at all had it not been for my difficulties finding an apartment in Paris for June. There were none, thanks to the new rent control imposed by the socialist government of François Mitterand. And those that were available were going for extortionary rents. The agent arranging our lodgings talked me into a June in Vaucluse, but not without a fight lasting several phone calls. I didn't know a thing about Provence, had never even gone beyond the edges of Paris, and I certainly had no desire to waste part of our summer in the *south* of France, when I had spent too many summers roasting in the Southwest! I wanted the Gothic north, with cement skies and cold mornings; I wanted city life, with its granite canyons and dusty, bonging cathedral bells.

"Where is this place," I asked the agent.

"In the Luberon," she said.

"The *Luberon?* Sounds like a motor oil. Who lives there?"

"It's famous as a place for writers, painters, composers, some of France's greatest artists live there. Lots of American actors, too," she said.

"Poets?"

"Oh yes, books about Provence are endless. You could write one, too."

I was beginning to take the bait. "Would I like it, do you think?"

"You won't want to leave."

So there we were, signed up for a month in the Vaucluse and at a reasonable price, at that. Around six hundred francs, or about one hundred dollars for the entire month.

To my surprise, Provence seduced us on our first encounter. My son could not stop muttering of his delights at this great sloping pasture below us, or that marvelous oak tree full of galls and hollow places. The girls were swept away by their little arbor, where they labored over rock salad and mud pastries, and flower sprays they collected from the fields. They seemed lost in their dreams out there, where the gold light fell in trembling flecks on their clothes, and they cooked up potions of wild parsley, prim rose and almond shells in the clay saucers they uncovered in the undergrowth. And Cathy? She stood out on the blinding terrace outside our bedroom, where the bees dangled over her head, and drank in sunlight. She gazed long moments over the tilting landscape, entranced by the scale of things, the savagery and beauty fused there.

We were typical Americans, typical *middle class* Americans. Both of us were academics, Cathy a part-time instructor and me a literature professor. Our children went to private schools in the town. We lived in a wooden house behind Bryan's doddering, abandoned Main Street. That was our most eccentric quality – the big, clapboard house with its Greek-revival angles and its big porch. Next door was the local madhouse, shortly to move into the suburbs to a new, one-story facility. Down the way lived Latinos and blacks, and a heavily fortified convenience store with two gas pumps out front. Behind the house was a little studio where I wrote and occasionally printed chapbooks of poetry on two Chandler & Price platen presses. Not so unusual that we ran into any trouble with the community. We were okay, we were northerners, out-of-towners who just happened to like Texas ways and got along with the neighbors.

At work it was different. We taught some of America's future engineers and ranchers, and gave them a dose of high culture and some literacy along the way of their becoming white collar technocrats. The university sprawled out like a vast factory, crammed with mainframe computers and slick laboratories, and retinues of Asiatic postdocs following some mighty geneticist to his institute. I worked next to the cyclotron, housed in a thick mausoleum of a building whose rounded end was the only clue that something whirled around inside at terrifying speeds, splitting off the scales from a human hair or draining the dust out of a drop of mercury. It was all part of the great arcanum of modern science, and we were on the distant edge of it – clinging to a few quaint humanistic truths.

My students were cheerful, blond and blue-eyed specimens of the post-Enlightenment. They had mathematical brains and a vast tolerance for facts, reams and reams of them. Their books were crammed with tables and graphs and equations, and it was all soup and doughnuts to them. They were heading into the radiant new dawns of America with gleeful hearts. I taught a kind of reluctant and brooding survey of the past, and an hour with me struck them as a trek through a dark forest. But they understood me well enough, and read literature with a raised eyebrow. I was surprised to discover they didn't *need* literature any more; they needed other spiritual comforts perhaps, but already they were passing beyond the age of literacy to something more cybernetic, more tuned to virtual reality. They wanted heavier trips with fantasy than a page of print could yield. They saw what science was up to, and they wanted literature to catch up or to give way to some art form that was more "with it."

So on we toiled, we last survivors on a cultural ice floe in time. I didn't want to burst into the future; I wasn't interested. I read the papers and was fascinated by all the developments sweeping us out of nature's gravity into the artificial cosmos. I half-wished I could be more sympathetic to all these dreams, wished – as a poet no less – I could screw down my VR helmet and tune in cybernetic utopias and walk around in my feely-suit as if truly *there*, as some of my brighter students described the experience. But I couldn't get into it. I was stuck in the printed word, still languishing after verbal paradises, such as you find in a few good poems and novels. Beyond that, well, let the transistors bake and the little gold wires find their niche in a printed circuit; as far as my eye balls were concerned, they weren't for frying under an electronic hat.

I gave up the notion there were any real paradises left. There were a few villages in the mountains of Mexico which we sometimes went off to, but the long trek across Texas and over the desert to San Miguel de Allende or further to Cuernavaca was too much to bear. We came back from such jaunts exhausted, sun-burned, broke, looking for the next bathroom up the road. It was glorious and it was devastating. And it weren't paradise. Paradise was something you *made up* in your idle moments while hiding in Prague, for example, or doing time in some little death row in Turkey. You couldn't find such a place on the map, only in your head. That is, until you went to Provence.

For someone who has dawdled his life away in air conditioned offices, with telephones and computers at the ready, I now found it difficult to concentrate. The tools of my trade lay before me, the paper waited for some drop of learned ink. But I sipped my coffee, crept down to the kitchen for more, found myself whispering audibly to myself about the long green hind legs of a grasshopper on the doorjamb, marveling at the pattern of shadow dappling the pebbles of the drive way, to wit any and all sensual pleasures luring me from work. I was regressing; I would soon be a child again. How I loved it.

Is it possible to bathe one's mind in sunlight? Already my eyes were clearer, tuned to minute shadings and hues, the variations of seemingly monotonous surfaces. I don't know how, but my eyes grew in intelligence. I feasted on splintery sills, the little terraces of light building up on the keyboard of my typewriter. I was back at the station, but drooped over like one of my football students – absorbed in some primal activity of the body, like chewing gum, tuned out utterly to the drone of learning.

It would take more work, I decided, to get back to the grind. I must be patient. I must accept the fact that the ground here was saturated with pagan lust; its vapors had seeped into my brain. I was besotted with pleasure – even hearing, though this is the thinnest sense in Provence. But here and there one could make out the dull tremolos of some little field bird tucked under the gnarls of the *garrigue*. The night jar in the shaggy chestnut tree up the hill filled the night air with that forlorn double-toned contralto, just as the moon peeped over the Luberon's crest. It moved my heart, and slid me uneasily down a slope of my own dark-ness, to feel the aching presence of some unnameable reality I had never confronted before. It was there in the rustle of the brittle weeds as a hare made his furtive move toward a patch of new grass.

I am terrible at the names of flowers and birds, a wastrel who squandered his brains on everything but the lore of nature. Which, I am now willing to admit, bears some of the purest poetry we have. Amaryllis, *rosier, noix,* even *aspidistra* – these are melodious syllables. Onyx, jasper, *le chêne* (oak), *passe-rose* (hollyhock), and my favorite, *coquelicot* (red poppy), druid and gnome: all seemed exquisite, a mysterious syllabary of Provence. Not everything fit, but the music certainly did. Sound? Was it so thin here? What of all the lush harmony that has poured out of religious mouths through sixteen centuries of French Christianity? Or of the chanting that has gone on forever among shepherds, pilgrims, vagabonds, and gypsies; or the neighing, bleating, barking and cheeping among the wild fauna of these hills? The low, guttural grunts of a boar are out of some wellspring from which Beethoven himself took the cello's voice in those late string quartets – the bass note of earth itself, rooting in the dark moist pebbled clay of the remote dark. I take it back: sound is as lush and thick and tangled among the hills as are sight and smell.

Suddenly I felt gaps in my experience, a hole in the floor of my certainty now that there was a landscape I *needed*! Even loved! It stretched out below my culture, my definitions of the world; it was redolent, pungent as garlic and wild onion, full of birds singing in a great distant cacophony, an ode to spring welling up out of the things I hadn't learned. I was raging, I told myself. Two days is not enough to fall in love with anything. It takes time. Besides, Paris is my first and only love. It must not be adulterated with small country pleasures. But when I looked out over the tiles of my neighbor's roof, to the gray hills rising into morning light, my heart ached. I longed to be there, walking among the rocks and rattling bushes, smelling the scent of crushed herbs underfoot. What a feeling to be walking in the footsteps of the Celts, on the same path nomads roamed long before there was a Greece or a Sumeria. And before that, the pioneers who had begun agriculture in southern France, as early as 6000 BC, long before the northern part ceased its hunting and gathering. This field represented some eight millennia of growing crops, and of honing points to kill the wild animals that ate from a farmer's field.

In all the pocked and dented hills are stone-age workshops for making tools out of the rich seams of quartz – choppers, hide scrapers, arrow heads, spear points. Their debris litters the ground even now. And on the ancient promontories, one can find amulets and coins from early pagan days – when goddesses were worshipped and given charms by girls about to marry or by older women asking for someone's health to be returned. All this abounds on the hills and crests, and I could barely keep myself from leaping into the fields slanting up to the Vaucluse Plateau.

But there was my conscience to salve. Hadn't I agreed to this little stay as a time for work before giving my guided tour of Europe? Yes, I said firmly, turning off the typewriter and bounding down the steps. It was time for a walk, I declared. Who will come with me? It was right and proper to go exploring; it would Rolfe the spirit and comb out the knots and tangles of our neglected souls.

So off we went, a train of us, my wife beside me, the kids dancing along behind, climbing the little mountain road above the manor house and along the cherry orchards. The boughs were laden with red fruit, inviting us with a shake of their leaves to come and pick. And we loaded our mouths with the soft, hot fruit, coughing out the pits as we chewed and bubbled and gulped our way along under the heavy limbs. I wanted it all, the fruit, the roads, the low-hanging sky, the heavy, syrupy light of the noon sun, to cram all the hills and gray-green valleys down my throat.

The road went on and on, slowly climbing a long escarpment forming one side of a crumbling canyon. I noted how often in Provence villages stood on some promontory between great gullies and draws, as if the wind were less vigorous here or the escape routes more numerous with two faults beside you. We lurched along with our bellies full of cherry pulp and began to feel the midday heat. It was late spring, and the sun was powerful overhead. The sky cloudless and serene, slightly pale along the edges where the heat lay. Now and then a breeze roamed down the hill and tickled our skin. But long years of idleness in the Texas heat caught up with us. Our group was slowing; we needed other diversions on this walk, but the fields were drifting off and the *garrigue* closed in.

Wild boar crept through the stubby oaks and briars, and a few jackrabbits scampered along tunnels in the thicket, but not much else was stirring. The magpies had all found shady roosts. We were quite alone in our stone hills. Finally, someone muttered a complaint and the rest chimed in. We stopped, our passion spent, and turned around. It was getting on to lunch, I thought, with a tinge of guilt. I was hungry, and I should be working. I was eager for a mouthful of olives and cheese, a sip of cool, dark wine, some crusty bread, and . . . oh dear, I was already lurching for the kitchen.

After a long lunch, I went up with fresh coffee to sit before my typewriter again. I liked my window; it was an unread book, page after page of Provençal language lying outstretched to the horizon. I read it eagerly, forgetting all about the keys lying under my finger tips. If anyone looked in at me, they would swear I was hard at work. But there I sat, eyes probing the countryside, ears drinking in the ticking and creaking, the chirps in the ivy. My nose was off somewhere running with the stoats and the badgers, crashing through undergrowth, sniffing up whole clumps of sage and wild lavender. I was everywhere but in my chair; even my knees felt good, stroked by a little breeze playing around the sill.

The writer is, for the moment, at his window, day dreaming over his hollyhocks and primroses, sniffing breezes as they waft up out of the hot fields. He can't put down a single word he is so in love with this modest, unassuming country, this place where everything is strangely familiar, haunted by its own boundless history, mingling a fragile present of waving grass and bird cries with all the eternal truths of Mediterranean life. For once in his life, he'll look and learn, and not make it up or think it up or intellectualize his emotions.

That was many years ago, a world ago from where I now sit, at another window a few miles east of Croagnes, writing this all down as I remember it. The family is scattered as far as Paris and west to Avignon, but I can hear the clinks of the pebbles and the girls' voices coming from the arbor. My wife is talking to Pip down below. It's there and vanished simultaneously. That rare and delightful memory of first coming here, turning the head to look with that rush, that flutter of the heart, that wakening to the natural world. It had been such a long and tedious pilgrimage before then. That is what this book is about – the way an American falls in love with a foreign country.

I know of few books, in fact, in which an American goes off to another country and sinks some roots. It's rarely done. Everyone heads for America as a new home. That's the grand narrative; the reverse is an unwritten page in which the Yanks go emigrating back to the Old World. It may be time, it may be the dawning of an era in which one's own prom- ised land seems a little crowded, a little ripe, a bit too habitual and set, a bit too frantically civilized to hold down another restless generation. But we are not heroes or pioneers, or worldly-wise travelers. "Just folks," as my Bryan neighbor used to say of himself.

As my wife tells it, the time came when one of our children asked from the back seat of the car, "What is it this time, Mom? The super- market or the gas station?" Is that all we ever did, she wondered? She told this story to friends over dinner one evening in our big wooden house in Bryan, and I listened with a frog in my throat. Were my little scions going to be small town kids? Had I bequeathed this strange gift to them? What could they do with it? How would they raise their own children from such knowledge? Small towns are all right, I suppose, but they lost some of their shine a few decades back, when franchises replaced the mom and pop stores, and farming became an "industry." Nowadays, one got into the car and dragged off to, well. . . to the supermarket or the gas station. Sometimes to a movie, but not often. Sometimes to a dinner party, but they got boring. Sometimes on a trip, but that wasn't too frequent. So what is it mom, the supermarket or the gas station? Try Provence, kid.

I did it for them, I like to think. But there was always myself to rescue. I wasn't too happy shuffling committee papers and grading tests, I confess. My life was parceled out among office chores and my time as a poet. The two seemed patched together in the same suit, but the voices in my head went on bickering through the years, not getting along too well as I hit forty and began blowing out birthday candles with a certain dread. After a childhood growing up in places like Beirut, Manila, and Saigon, where my father worked for the State Department, I had settled down to a placid academic career. And now I was middle aged, settled in, growing round and gray in my ordinary world. Forgive me, but the itch came back, the sound of foreign cities rang thinly in my ear, I began to look longingly into the photographs of the *National Geographic*, wondering what it would be like to disappear down that little side street in the corner of the page. O how I longed to get up, go out to the lawn, look at the house and slip away in a car to some airport, get out into the noisy, odorous clutter of some tropical town and live a second life!

I mulled these things over considerably before I landed my guided tour of Europe. Now that I had my chance, there, at the window in Provence, my eyes scanning the landscape, I could feel the powerful tug of the land. I knew I was being lured, but in my mind, or in my heart, I heard a voice say, take me, take me. Let me know desire again, give my soul a shake. Yes, I said, yes. And my eyes leered and ogled and flirted with the olive groves, the magpies coming out from their long noontime nap, the dogs barking at a herd of creamy sheep coming down the hill. Yes, to the shadows turning blue and purple under the cherry trees, yes to the wind picking up and blowing a veil of red earth down through the smoldering green vineyards.

What follows is a tale of years of summers and quite a few winters in Provence, from borrowed houses and rented cottages to buying a house in a village, learning how to live a Provençal life, and driving down to Apt with the kids chirping away in rich, twangy southern French. A tale that traces that mysterious, unmeasured progress of children into adults, for all three of my kids have now grown up and taken their freedom. One to a life of the artist in Avignon, another toward a Ph.D. in French literature at Brown and the Sorbonne; a third, my son, to a masters in political science in Paris, and a career in some ministry in South America. And a tale that puts more white hair on my head and my wife's, but no loss of love for this great swath of blue-green earth and hills. As I write this memoir of a life turned inside out, France has voted against the European constitution by a margin of almost 60%. The bankers are rubbing their heads in disbelief; Chirac is deeply wounded by the rejection of his own people to a dream of a United States of Europe. But that voice, deep down and as wide as an ocean in this little country, spoke against dilution, change, the abstract promises of modernization, and my heart joins their dances at the Place de la Bastille, in Toulouse, Marseille, celebrating French will, French love of their own ways. I am as rooted in that faith that the past is wise and a guiding spirit as any of the farmers now. But don't let me summarize; that's the academic way out. There is a story to tell, day by day, summer through summer, with the bees dotting my i's and the magpies crossing all my t's.

Chapter Two

In the Sacred Precincts

at r ay m rnin   Sounds of the bead curtain whipping the glass panes of the door. The wind picked up before dawn and was blowing down hard on our little hill. Our fire had gone out; the grate was cold. I threw a few twigs and pine cones into the ashes, lit a newspaper, and got a flame going. Cathy was in the kitchen figuring out how to work the espresso pot we found in the cupboard. Croissants were warming in the oven. The flame caught onto the logs finally, and smoke trickled up the chimney, curled around in the darkness, then blew down again into the living room. I stood sipping coffee with tears running down my eyes, batting smoke back up the flue with a magazine. It was hopeless; each gust rolled all the smoke back into my face, and snapped the beads against the panes with a cracking sound. I thought the glass would break. Outside, a strange rusty glare filled the sky, colored by ochre dust from the hills.

Pip came over to apologize for the weather. We were in for it, she said; it's a mistral. After all the muggy spring days of Texas, we loved the cold, the need for fires. It was cozy in our stone house, behind its thick walls. The kids were up, going out to stand in the wind, watching trees double over at each powerful gust. The branches howled and loose twigs went clattering over the roof tiles. It was a spectacle outside: everything trembled, shook, broke loose, fluttered wildly, rolled along paths and across meadows and vineyards. It was a spring cleaning, all right.

The wind died down by noon. The rooms were sour with wood smoke and covered with a film of ash and dust. We could taste it in the bread and cheese, the wine we drank. The house looked like it had been tumbled in a washing machine.

There are thirty-two different winds that hammer these jagged hills. The farmers know them all by name; they can look up into the trees and tell what each will bring into the valley: rain, a hard freeze, hot muggy weather up from Spain, dry, biting winds off the Sahara, hail from the Alps. After a good blow from the Sahara winds, called the *auro bruno* and the *auro rousso* from the color of the air, you find a reddish sand from the Arabian desert on all the furniture, their calling card.

The winds today were from two directions, and we were caught in the tangle of their currents as they shook trees down to their roots. There was the *travesso* from the west, coming off the Atlantic from Bordeaux, with the cold sea air in it; and the *mango fango*, slightly northwest, that dropped the soot of English chimneys on us. And the mistral, no need to italicize this master of storms, which came down on us from the north.

The mistral is a legendary wind, a cousin to *Santa Anas* and *simooms*, the *bora* of Trieste, and the *foehn* that sweeps down the Alps over Innsbruck. It's the big one, the father of all winds, and brings the tooth of winter into the house, chills marrow, sets teeth on edge, ages the patriarchs, tells you life is frail and momentary. It has a big soul and any-one who bears its name confers magic and power onto himself. Take, for example, the 19th century poet Fréderick Mistral, who looked a bit like Walt Whitman with his full beard and rough peasant clothes. He wanted to be known as the spirit of his place, and bore its greatest symbol in a surname reaching back to the Middle Ages. If Whitman had lived here, he too would have wanted this name; it was the proper title for a poet, master of winds. Mistral launched the *Félebrige* movement to save *Provençal* culture from the leveling forces of nationalism coming down from Paris.

There's a good story there – for Provençals (like their counterparts in all southern places) never did see themselves fitting into some other region's idea of a "nation." They had too much history of their own. Their blood had been woven to the oak and the silver creeks, and the wild wind to be treated as a marginal culture. The southerner still privately disavows there is a capital to the north, crafted out of granite and glass, where men sit in lofty chairs making all the decisions. Their resilience runs deep and shows up in polls and voting patterns; they go with almost anyone who opposes Parisian policies, or the "liberal" bent of mind. They get in trouble with racist issues and with their own parochialism, as they have recently with their allegiance to the *Front National* and its leader, Jean Marie Le Pen, whose motto is France for the French. Diminished in recent elec-tions from what seemed a threatening start at power, he now sits on the sidelines and offers critiques even the national newspaper, *Le Monde*, quotes avidly, as it did the other day when Le Pen pronounced Jacques Chirac no longer fit to lead the nation after the French rejected the European Constitution. The southerner knows it is ironic to love such a man who has the stink of Hitler on his breath, but like all demagogues,

Le Pen touched a nerve in the common psyche, and spoke a familiar language when he promised to protect the nation's heritage from bankers and free traders.

The southern peasants married the land and it was a good spouse; why ask Paris, or worse yet, Brussels, the seat of the European Union, to dictate the rules when the weather alone was a good authority? Besides, the true pagan thrust of the Mediterranean gave out beyond Lyon. Paris was the seat of another philosophy different from the passionate temperament and sunshine of the coast. So, Fréderick Mistral was inevitable, an Orc rising to defend his stretch of hills from dilution; as a writer he knew he must save the local tongue: in its faded words lay the soul-work of the ages.

His efforts did not get the Provençal language into the French curriculum, as he wished, but a museum, the Museo Arlaten, was founded in Arles on money from his Nobel Prize in literature in 1896, and is still one of the best collections of folk art in Europe. It preserves everything from combs to painted carriages, to dummy heads with the hair styles of all the villages, whose peculiar waves and plaits told a woman's age, family, marital status, and village origins. He compiled a Provençal dictionary and liberally salted it with invented words where there were gaps in the diction. Mistral was his own wind, blowing against time. Little remains of the *Félibrige* cultural push, though nowadays local city markers bear the Provençal name below the French. Apt is Ate en Prouvencao, Manosque to the east is also Manosco. Never mind that some of these Provençal names are of dubious origin; tourists love them, and the locals take a certain pride in having them.

The wind we call the mistral is sired by a westerly from the North Atlantic, and roars across the roofs of Lyon, which lies at the junction of the Rhone and Saone rivers. That is always a wind's cradle, some river bed where cooler air follows the water. The Rhone valley is a corridor of cold air drifting under the westerly, and when a depression forms out in the Mediterranean below Marseille, the cold Rhone air begins to chug forward like an invisible freight train, powered by down drafts of the westerly flying overhead. When the two connect, they become a thundering canon ball that sweeps everything before it out to sea. At some point the mistral hooks to the left and blows back into the land again, over the Esterels, a ridge of porphyry hills worn down like a nag's teeth along the coast, and as far inland as our own Luberon.

They say the mistral blows for three, six, sometimes even nine days. When it comes, the booms and cracks and tinkle of breaking window glass are unnerving. After two days, arguments break out; animals become testy, things stop working around the house. By day three, nerves are raw and it is best to avoid conflicts. Crime rates go up; drivers fight over parking spaces in the towns, children turn moody and sullen, disagreeable to elders. If it is a long blow, going the full limit of nine days, it is best to take your jug of whiskey to bed and hide out from your neighbors. Don't undertake any tasks, or burden yourself unduly – wisdom cautions. Take it easy, weather the storm. Your heart will race, your nerves stand up along your arms, your spleen will douse you with bolts of rage. You will want to gnaw through the bedroom wall to get at the great howling monsters striking the house.

But you sit, as we did, and let the battle rage and then subside, with faint rolls of a kettle drum, until the first dove cries in the olive tree – a single reassuring cheep. With that knowledge, you appreciate why all Provençal houses have their backs up against the north, with few or no windows. And why the region is rich in mistral legends, customs, and minor deities. It is called Jean D'Arles in the city where it blows the hardest. Only a mistral can stop a train of donkeys, goes one old saw; another claims a mistral can break off a bull's horns. Some guidebooks claim it can sweep a herd of sheep from a cliff. Finally, when all rage is spent, you see a neighbor emerge from a house, pick up a rake and begin scraping up the debris of the yard, setting potted plants aright, pulling open shutters and locking them in place. Peace returns; the great wind gods are once more in harmony with the world.

Driving down to Apt in the afternoon on the little *départmentale* roads criss-crossing the landscape, I fell into a peculiar mood. Perhaps it was the wind that did it; it has an odd effect upon the solid rock of the world; it blows it around like a curtain, lifting it up as if it were no more than silk or dreams. The great ageless earth becomes a kind of dancing wraith with the wind in its arms. It brought to mind a poem by the Texas poet William Barney, who heard the wind blow over the wild prairies of Fort Worth:

> In the middles
> of still nights I have come out here, middles
> with the white moon lowered down like someone set to read
> the print of earth with a single candle, I have come
> out here on these limestone slabs, these galls, these slant
> thick scabs that cap some hidden sore . . .

I know what I hear.
The blunt hills beat like smitten tines. What I hear
is long before, an echo of a primitive strain.
But echo is too quick a meaning. This is force cast back
on us from olden time, a sound that struck the farthest star
and now returns to shudder us.

If water has a soul, it must be the light that shimmers on it and remains long after the desert has claimed the ground. That light comes back to haunt the images in Georgia O'Keefe's desert paintings, which ache with a spiritual hunger for the missing ocean. There it lay through the hollow socket of a cow's skull bleaching on the sand, or in the vague luster of the dunes. The wind carries off the great seas and leaves behind these parched laps of rock. Perhaps that is the mystery of the mistral: it is the raging soul of an ocean that has lost its place in the world, and howls against the dry rock, dragging itself from cliff to cliff looking for its missing shores. Vassar Miller, another Texas poet, called loneliness a vanished sea in the prairies:

. . . the silence, the hush,
the quiet, the stillness, the not speaking,
the never hearing a word
are only the surge of its innumerable waters.

It was loneliness I felt coming down the little black-top roads, solitude that made me look for some glint of water in the hills, some token of the missing sea. It wasn't water I longed for, exactly, but some way to relate all this eternal rock and *garrigue* to my ephemeral life. I was a leaf blowing on a gust, drifting end over end against the endless sky.

The sea had been here; sandstone was its ancient bed; the hills were the strata of dry sea floors, imprinted with fossil shells, the ghostly outlines of fish and ferns and the vanished currents. The wind breathed back the memory of it all, and we crept along the valley floor like a mollusc full of staring eyes. The children were quiet, alone in their thoughts gazing at the faded hills.

Apt (derived from its ancient name Hath given by its founders, the Vulgientes) lies within a winding valley that skirts the blue slopes of the Luberon. One river with two names, the Calavon and the Coulon, the latter a mis-transcription of Calavon on an early Michelin map that is still posted on the road to Cereste and at St. Andiol, where it ends.

Coulon is perhaps the better name, an old word for pigeon roost, the stone towers that dot the Provençal landscape. But Calavon is good, too. It means stone river; *cal* from *calcaire*, and *caìllon* stone, and *avon* from the Celtic word for river, as in the redundant Avon River of Shakespeare. The muddy little river threads its way down from a spring near Banon, where the famous goat cheese is made, follows the valley into Apt and trickles west, carrying off the sulfur from the fruit factories, to the flood plains planted with cherry orchards, melon fields, and vineyards. A few Roman bridges cross over it where it fumes like the River Styx. After Les Baumettes, the Calavon wanders out to St. Andiol, near Avignon, to disappear into the Durance river. It is little more than a creek these days, feeble and reptilian, its silky dark water full of human abuses. It has a long memory and many secrets, and feels its way along the crooked bed like a blind man. Once, many years ago, it was a respectable watercourse full of seasonal torrents only the heftiest earthworks could divert. Now, it fed too many faucets and the rains no longer fell as hard on the Alps, where the small rivers are recharged.

Apt is old, going back to neolithic times; other towns along the "Domitian Way" are even older. Gargas, one guidebook tells you, has been continuously inhabited for 60,000 years; the ancient middens around it suggest it was once Eden for paleolithic settlers, an unending fruitfulness. Gargas fits into a little notch of the hills; you pass through its gaudy new center without a thought of its great longevity. The mayor had a dream one night of a pastel city bright as lime and oranges and cherry and set about modernizing his humble town. The result is a landscape Dorothy might have wandered into, a Munchkin town of edible cottages amid other confectionery shapes. This was the town you passed before you hit the N-100, the national highway, to join the traffic nosing into Apt.

I have driven into this little river town a thousand times and still can't explain the thrill I feel coming into it. The road is out of the dawn of time. It was once an animal track long before the first human being set foot on the riverbanks or the humped mountain behind it. It was one of the principal roads of southwestern Europe for centuries, since it traced the only passes through both the southern Alps and the Pyrenees. The Celtic migrations came down this way from Germany in 300 BC, on their drive into southern Europe. Hannibal led his elephants along the Calavon on the way to the Alps to sack Rome, the same path Caesar used on his Gallic campaigns in 45 BC coming the other way. Domitius Aheno-barbus, a Roman proconsul whose engineers built the Domitian Way, led *his* elephants into Provence to set up the first Roman colony in what the

Romans called the *val clausa*, or closed valley. They had discovered a box canyon from which the Sorgue River poured out from springs deep in the bedrock below the Alps, which over time became the Vaucluse.

From early Roman days, this leg of the N-100 was a major thoroughfare for travelers from Rome to Cadiz. Later, it became the pilgrims' road to the shrines dotting the hillsides all the way down to Compostela, Spain. Medieval armies marched through the passes into Apt to plunder the villages, lay seige to the forts at Castillon and Buoux, or to raze the castles perched on neighboring hills. Now the tourists have it and jam up its two lanes going into town each summer.

The houses on both sides of the road entering Apt are built of stone with little window boxes brimming with geraniums, some with courtyards behind an iron fence. They are shuttered fast against the sun. There is nothing particularly charming about such houses; I've seen better driving the back country of Hungary. Apt's houses are solid, private, smugly contained behind their dour fronts. They belong to shopkeepers and fruit workers – those patient cleaners, dyers, and packers of fruit in the local candy factories. Apt is a working town, sturdy and a bit colorless, *triste* as a friend of mine put it – a sad little place with a good heart, and a long long history of wars and religion.

If you are stranded in traffic some bright spring day, as we were then, a vision of their interiors begins to form. The rooms are dark, cool, redolent of mint and rosemary. Garlic and green pepper sizzle in olive oil in preparation for lunch, the main meal of the day. A *panier* stands in the corner crammed with baguettes and *gros pains* and one of those twisted, salty loaves called an *épis*. A beam runs across the ceiling hung with sprigs of thyme and bay leaf, bunches of dried flowers, a *tresse* of garlic bulbs. A bowl of *tapenade*, a paste of minced olives and *armagnac*, sits on the sill, bathed in sunlight. The dining room is dark, with gray light filtering through embroidered shades, hovering like mist over the long table, the sideboard, the large, high-backed chairs. A grandfather clock, gaudily painted, made in some long-deceased clock factory in Lyon or Manosque, ticks drily in the corner. The stairs wind up into an upper story, to cool, darkened bedrooms, the quilts and counterpanes slung over window sills to air.

To this wandering American, these houses possess the mysterious sanctity of age, inheritance, tradition passed down. The walnut and cherry cabinets hold faience bowls and tureens, a good set of china from Limoge, silverware from an Aix silversmith, damask and ancient linen, all folded away neatly on deep shelves, ready for some important occasion like a wedding, a birth, a returning veteran, a feast day, the New Year's dinner. Nothing much changes; a few gadgets in the kitchen, perhaps an electric radiator bolted to the wall, a new car in the garage, the rest unchanging, a slow descent of possessions from mother to daughter, father to son.

The road into Apt takes a slight curve to the left that traces the island boundaries of the original town of Hath, which once stood between branches of the Calavon. The southern fork is gone, the other winds along the north side in a walled trench with scattered bridges crossing it. The *lycée* Charles de Gaulle stands on the far side, with its dusty playing fields and gray buildings, where all three of my children would later attend. The water crawls over marsh grass and sandbars, the riverbed littered with tires and rubbish from the spring floods; a blackened tunnel arches where the river still takes in tributaries from the hills.

The first time we entered Apt, we gawked and chattered and pointed at everything at once. Traffic was heavy; people were going off to eat at other people's houses, tourists were streaming in to start their vacations. Some were just reaching their destination with back seats piled high with summer clothes and beach toys. We crept slowly into the city and parked at the Place Carnot, a shady square where a café had put out umbrella-covered tables in the parking lot. The municipal library and tax offices took up one side of the square. The streets ran off into the city in two directions, past the Church of St. Anne, honoring the bones of Christ's grandmother, the other curving round the ghost of a Roman building, called the *rue de l'Amphithéâtre*. The remains of a Roman theater stood across town on the grounds of the old vegetable market, with a few columns and steps partially exposed in the plaza. A small alley meandered to the left, the *rue des Anciennes Prisons*, where a medieval jail once stood.

It was after twelve, and everything was closed. We were among the last strollers before the solemn rites of eating and resting began. Somewhere in all this somnolent stupor gleamed a little bakery, its door open for stragglers. We sauntered in to buy bread for supper. A fussy, middle-aged woman was attending to her only other customer, a well-dressed woman smelling pleasantly of lavender oil, whose requests were met with scrupulous attention. The *gros pain* she ordered, just one, had to be chosen with care; one was too brown, the other too dry. A good one was drawn from a cord of upstanding *gros pains* in the bin and rolled into paper, taped, set aside. Some little cookies in the tray below were mulled over, fingered in a plastic glove, several pulled out of the row and laid nicely on a paper napkin, prodded into a bag that was smartly crimped, taped, etc. There was a square of anchovy pizza, the last in a long tray, that might do for someone at home . . . eh? Perhaps. A finger nudged it, an odor rose of burnt thyme and wet, dark pulp sour with olives and salty fish. Hmmm.

What did it matter that five anxious Americans were gawking at these two conducting their business? Five Americans from the land of instant gratification, used to eating a whole meal standing up in this languorous time frame. A bank loan could have been procured with less fuss. A car bought. A divorce granted. A murder committed, the murderer apprehended, made famous on the network newscast, tried, sentenced, sent up, the case appealed, good time awarded, the convict let out to a halfway house, a book written about his crime, with enough time to see the movie before these women would draw their transactions to their reluctant close.

Finally, without a nod of thanks to us for waiting, they ended their affairs and parted with the usual compliments. We were next. But the woman busily cleaned up her shelf, sorted her change into the cash drawer, rubbed her hands on a damp cloth, and ducked behind a curtain to attend to some other little business.

She came out a minute or two later and seemed pained to find us still standing there. We ordered two baguettes; our French was Chinese to her. We ordered again, and a third time, with wide open mouths and clearly enunciated syllables. *Doo baggh-ettes!* She took another beat, knitted her brows. "Ah*! Deux baguettes, oui!"* Big smile. We had come through. But there was something in her smile that chilled me, a barely-concealed indifference. She hastily took two baguettes from the bin, rolled them in paper and taped the flap shut. It was the same precision, but something was missing. There wasn't the intimacy, the glances, the private language of town folk; we were strangers, and suddenly we all felt it.

She rang up the register, just as I was making my next request. My finger was pointing, my syllables were forming in my mouth, but she had rushed ahead. Ah, something else? *Avec ceci,* she asked. She hit another button on the register, the subtotal, I think, and made a little face. She looked around for some consolation, but we were the only people in the shop. "*Oui?*" she asked, with a haggard little smile. In her defense, it was late in the noon hour, lunch was waiting in some aromatic nook of an apartment, and she was hungry.

Her small, down-turned face with its polite condescension suddenly recalled a parochial school nun who once gave me piano lessons with the same coolness. Our lessons began with a sigh expressing all her doubts about me. She would sit next to me as I thumbed the pages of my

Thompson workbook, her lips pursed in a stoic smile that soon drooped to a frown as I hit the wrong notes. She would play the tune herself then, which rose like dust and rose petals from the book, faded and remote as a muttered rosary.

I studied the little droop of the bakery woman's lips, its discontent aimed at the worn counter and its scoop for catching coins, which could easily have been the keyboard over which I stumbled. They were alike, these two, sisters of a secret order, who brooked no falling of standards in their brittle world; to be loved by them, one must know purely and fully all the knowledge they hoarded in their tundra-covered hearts.

She blew a strand of hair off her brow. In barbarous French I communicated my desire for three *cornets* of vanilla ice cream, *pour les enfants*. My hand patting heads to indicate the fact. She dug her scoop into the drum and peeled off a thick skin of rich yellow ice cream, and slid it onto a cone. The small hand that rose to take it was rebuffed; she propped all three loaded cones into a plastic holder, then punched the total. I reached over and gave them out, my smile fixed to my face like a Halloween mask.

The total came to twenty-seven francs. I gave her a bill for fifty. She laid it on the cash drawer and fished around for coin. She dropped a weight of coins into my palm, and I saw she had given me ten francs too many. I waited until she had finished, to see if she would catch her own mistake. She didn't. She was turning to go back behind her curtain, something she did with a quick twist of her waist. But I stopped her with a hand to her arm, and opened my palm with the coins. "Madame," I enunciated carefully, "*vous m'avez donné trop de monnaie. Pas trente-trois, vingt-trois est juste.*" Not great French, but the meaning was clear.

Why did I think she would suddenly drop all detachment and open up to me? I was giving back money she would miss at the end of the day. She would trouble over the loss, wondering how it happened. Here was a mistake, and I was helping to catch it. I was doing her a favor, but it didn't matter. Like Shylock, she would take my money, but she wouldn't dine with me at my table. I was from another world, and she would serve me, but never quite befriend me. She was walled in like an old village, the parapets set higher than a tourist could peek over. She grimaced at the coin in her hand, threw it in the till and vanished. Years later, I would come to understand that desire not to give in, but not now. I wanted love, even a little of it, to assure me I was doing the right thing, that I was in a possible home in this unfamiliar terrain.

But it was Apt, and the day was sunny and infinite. We poked along staring into everything. The aroma of good food seeped out of shutters and draped windows; we heard the echoing laughter of people eating overhead. We saw kids playing in an alley, looking up at us with smiles and stares that had slipped out of a medieval fresco. A door fell open in a stone wall, and there lay a green paradise of ivy, great vases of flowers, and a stair climbing to a balcony. The door shut and the vision was gone.

Street corners met in blackened stone, worn gutters, the air stale with crumbling plaster and rotting beams. A fountain burbled into a mossy basin, the iron bars over the water worn thin where buckets had slid along to be filled under the dripping spigot. Half the face of a gargoyle still stared out with blind eyes, its mouth puckering where the rusty water pipe jutted out. Echoes, footsteps clicking toward us from other alleys, the tinkle of glasses and spoons in the wash tub – all this music in the same scale, as if I were still plunking the piano in my ghostly youth.

Transparent history. That phrase ran through my head as we walked along, peering into a living, open air museum. We circled back into the *rue de l'Amphithéâtre* and followed its looping bend into the square. Was it here the coliseum stood? Transparent time, invisible presences. They were in the street. The *rue des l'anciennes prisons* ended in a row of dusty, shuttered windows. But the coughs, the sighs, the scrape of chain were mutely present in the shadows. Apt was razed so many times after Rome fell, the villagers gave up rebuilding it and moved in under the coliseum's arches, to live there in make-shift hovels for two centuries! Caesar's Apta Julia lasted barely three hundred years before the Franks invaded and leveled the place, leaving a smoking ruin. It was the beginning of a tedious history of destruction and rebuilding, time winnowing the dust.

A few gnarled plane trees shade the Place Carnot, and a fountain trickles water from the bills of four swans, one headless but for the water pipe, into a large basin where pigeons flap down from the church to drink. There used to be more plane trees here; this is an old square, perhaps the oldest in the city. The church sits off to the side, in a pocket of time. The river is down the block, past the *quincaillerie*, a word for hardware with the pots and pans still clanking in it.

I sat at a café table having coffee with my wife, while the kids played around the fountain. I had the view of the church, which lists a bit like the churches of Venice. It is the anchor of the city, dominating the main shopping street, the *rue des Marchands*, with its arches and wrought iron belfry, its blackened side entry. Its stones go back to pagan days, but the first basilica was erected sometime in the fourth century for the region's first bishop, Saint Auspice. Originally designated a cathedral, it was downgraded to a church during the French Revolution.

Like everything else in Apt, it has endured numerous razings. I once read where Charlemagne was present to consecrate its rebuilding in the 9th century. A local baron's son, a deaf mute, began clawing at the rubble with bare hands. He uncovered the roof of a buried crypt, possibly holding the remains of St. Auspice. When he touched the stones, he gained speech and hearing. As the story goes, he stood up and declared that a second, lower crypt held the bones of St. Anne. She had come to Gaul to escape Roman persecution after the crucifixion, and died here in Provence. The second crypt was dug up and became the foundation of the new church, making it one of the earliest Christian shrines in France. Pilgrims poured in from all over and brought Apt to life again.

In the middle ages, barren women came to the crypt to pray for pregnancy. There used to be a cradle there with a figure of the infant Jesus, which they rocked. It became the custom for girls to "rock the cradle" prior to marriage, to ready their wombs. Such rites brought the old paganism into the new religion; all around these hills fertility cults honored Venus for the same reason; now St. Anne joined the pantheon.

The figure of Mary stands on the central dome looking over the city, with the smaller roofs raying out under her feet like the hills of Provence, her domain. A man enters the church door more humbly than a woman; he comes upon things older than his own beliefs. Up and down the street on which the church stands are shops that cater lovingly to the health and beauty of the female body: quaint pharmacies, chic beauty bars and hair salons, little dress shops with three or four bright dresses in the window, busy flower shops. In this quarter of Apt you are reminded continuously, if subtly, that you are in the precincts of the Great Mother. Even the bakers honor her: their wares are a running calendar of saints' days and holy feasts, most to do with female deities.

After coffee, we found the door open and tiptoed into the church. In front of the altar is a stair leading down to both crypts. The first is large and dry, ringed with small sarcophagi; the lower is barrel-vaulted and cool, with a Roman altar stone designating the burial site of a devout pagan in "Julius' colony of Apt." As we went out, I peered into a niche covered with iron grating, where someone had pushed a wad of franc notes to the back. Perhaps a prayer was folded inside. This was supposedly the place where St. Anne's bones were found. The cradle is gone; its spirit lingers.

The lower vault reached a kind of bedrock under Apt's streets; the mind reached no further into earth. You could tell something pushed onward beyond the walls; the passage had been sealed up. Usually in such villages church crypts were part of a maze of tunnels connecting houses and public buildings. If a surprise invasion should sweep over the town, one could always rush down to the *caves* below the house, tear up a few stones in the wall and hurry along the tunnels to safety. Many of the streets bore tunnels under them, criss-crossing from house to house. Even the kitchenware store opposite St. Anne's has a showroom in an ancient *cave*, its back wall sealed up where it goes on.

Death and beauty merged in this city, embracing one another like figures on a Greek vase. Even our first stroll through Apt told me the city stood for some irresolvable paradox, a vision of dying and eternal youth. The city's Latin motto, loosely translated, is "the triumph of joy." Over what? Suffering? Disaster? Violence? The city was no architectural chorus to Schiller's "Ode to Joy." It had the haggard look of its ancient turmoil. These streets, squeezed together by town walls long gone but for a few gates and towers, still held the memory of its deaths and rebirths, which time had distilled into an essence, the ghostly odor of flowers blooming in stone.

When you drive into Apt, you pass a small road sign declaring this the candied fruit capital of the world. It's a small boast compared to the slogans of American cities – "Workshop of the World," "Gateway to the West," but a notch above the banner I saw draped over the entrance to Szeged, in southern Hungary, which read, "World Capital of Paprika." Well, so it was, and the stores offered four or five varieties of paprika, from sweet to mild, to stingingly hot, coarse to fine ground. In Apt's case, *confiture*, the making of candied fruits from the harvests of local orchards, and the mode of their transformation from plums and cherries into pale globes of confection in a range of muted colors – spoke to the mystery of time, the merging of life and death.

Considering all the products one finds in Apt, from olives to wine, lavender oil, and *calissons*, the almond meal candies that come in oval tins with lavish script and shields emblazoned on them, to the sedate, funereal remoteness of jeweled fruit laid out in fans and decorative niches of a candy box, you perceive the city's fascination with time. How long such candied fruit lasts, I have no idea. But their pale, muted souls in the window told me they could last for years in a widow's closet, among the *Belle Epoque* hat boxes and tatted linens. The candy might be taken down once for the dessert tray after a long dinner, to be nibbled with a dram of *calvados* and a *demi-tasse* of strong coffee.

The bright sun splashed drops of gold on the ancient square, as bees hummed over the fountain, landing on puffs of moss to sip the moisture.

Small boys watched us from their patch of shade, a battered soccer ball at their feet, their faces clear, dark, etched by the work of countless ancestors. They were the eyes and mouths of the *Albici* people, who farmed these hills from the beginning of cultivation. My children stared into this maze of time and rootedness, and wondered at it. We had seen other places as strange, but never this transparent or candid – where time glowed like moonlight over the old myths and spirits. The frailest sign of life, a daffodil nodding in a window box, found itself molded and duplicated in stone under the eave and along the sun dial of an ancient wall.

The pure dram of essence that bled from the cherry, or the grape, the beehive, the almond, the silk worm's cocoon, and the clay seam were caught in the cups of Apt and raised to everlastingness. Wind was in each of their transubstantiations, the cold, beating wind of spirit that blew immortality into humble life. The wind bore down on us in great rolling gusts that shimmied the car as we climbed the foothills to St. Saturnin and headed west to Croagnes, following the first threads of sunset.

Chapter Three

Of Work and Dreams

A *coup de mistral,* a blow from the master, drives out pollution, bad odors, spores, insects, mold, stale gossip, whatever hangs around as soiled air. All is blown away out to sea; the days that follow, the first dawn especially, are a thing to behold. You awake to the purest radiance. You are a child again and breathe the dawn of Creation, and look with fresh eyes into the cobalt deeps of the sky. You feel a holiness in the air – the lustrous perfection of the present.

After breakfast, we straightened things up and shook out bed covers, threw open windows, swept ashes from the hearth. Momentary winter had passed; late spring returned warm and placid to our hill. The bees swarmed over the ivy and roses, and floated against the windows, drifted over the beaded curtain of the doorway. They seemed curious, almost thoughtful creatures. They brushed your skin sometimes, and went over your ear with a moist buzzing noise, and touched the ends of your hair, rarely stinging anyone. My son Cedric was the first to be stung – being the most agile and likely to upset some little bee staggering home with a load of pollen. The rest of us were wary of the liberties good country bees took with us, but soon got used to having them flit across our eyes or hover at our shirt sleeves. They were attracted to our colors, perhaps, and our odors. A simple brush of the hand drove them away.

Then there were flies; these came in several sorts, none very bright. Most were small, black darters who hung around our bread, or found things to eat on the floor and window sills. They came down our chimney, or passed through the beads when a breeze fanned them out. They were a nuisance, but not quite the bother of the larger, black beasts that came in with a drone of wings and a stupid, aimless searching of our faces. They had a knack for hanging down in your eyes as you cut up onions or scraped plates in the sink. They made a kind of farting noise as they dove down from the ceiling at one's raised glass or piece of cheese.

Cedric was expert at holding his palms over a fly resting on the table, and of clapping an inch or two overhead where the fly inevitably got mashed. Others could be swatted with a dish towel or a roll of newspaper.

Or dashed flat by the swatters we bought to combat our little pests. It was diverting at times, when nothing else seemed worthy of note after a good meal, to sit in the tiny living room, before the hearth and the long shadows of afternoon, and swat the little devils as they landed. They made you vaguely nervous about sitting, as if they were sent to rouse you out for a walk. Finally, when their numbers became daunting, you got up, dusted off bread crumbs from your lap, surveyed the messy look of the place, carted glasses and cups back to the kitchen, and felt compelled to act. At least to go out and stand in front of the doorway, exposed once more to the radiant immensity of day. And off you went on your unstated errand, another stroll up the hill you had climbed dozens of times already, with a purposeful stride.

It felt strange being idle all of a sudden after years of competitive work. I felt a lot of guilt as I let things go. My little station at the window was getting cold; it got harder to shuffle papers, or open files that had a coat of dust on them. It bothered me so few lines of type were on the sheets of paper, especially this longer European paper which made writing laborious. Sheets didn't fill up when they should; there was always space for two or three more lines, but by then I was scanning the olive-gray hills for diversion. Too often I found it: a jackrabbit chased by a dog, a peregrine falcon roaming the air, a tractor hauling dung from the stalls with the magpies wheeling overhead. There sat the limp sheet with my words looking pale and flimsy on it.

I was learning, and shouldn't have made myself hang around the keyboard when there was nothing to say. I was so used to working I didn't recognize fallowness when it came. There lies a moral for Americans: thinking it's always harvest time makes us dullards. Work and no play, business as usual, success without failure – these are our vices and illusions. "If you're not growing, you're dying." Hmmm, not nature's law at all. Such false rules rob life of its seasons. I was a good example of that. Even when failures came, I could puff them up into partial successes, or call them trial runs, when in fact they were failures, impasses, dead ends. I should have known when to quit, and use the time to renew myself. I should have allowed myself to drift into silence, and to become used to the twilight of a room, the ticking of wood in the walls, the far away rustle of a tree in a wind I would not hear or feel. That bliss of nothingness is part of winter and late fall, and the earliest, numbing aspects of spring in this old earth. The letting go, to let some other will take over, is a kind of ecstasy when you are down. It will heal you to be carried a little while.

Here the earth is always resting and replenishing itself; winter is slow to end, and after a long sleep the earth comes to with a shrug of its hills and a great ablution of wind and rain to get it going again. Earth is in no hurry; the seasons are ancient and turn on a slow wheel. The farmers know not to prod the sleeping ground awake, but to lie down with it when it sleeps. The lesson lay before me in these fields, in the slumbering tempo of the farms. The old ways prevailed; the men and women who owned these sunny lands knew work must be leavened with idleness, that waiting was part of the process. It gave nature the upper hand. Work and rest, effort and surrender, these were the covenants of rural life.

Provençal farmers still plant and harvest by the ancient calendar of moon phases and feast days; they plow early in morning, take long mid-day rests, come out again when shadows lengthen and plow or cultivate in the cool of afternoon, sometimes working into evening by the light of their tractors. Rest surrounds each phase of work. The typical farm is made up of small fields scattered like patches of a quilt among other farms. Stone walls run down the hills marking their boundaries, with rutted tractor paths winding among them like a basting stitch. A farmer hangs a map of his land in the house, colored in with the crops he is growing. Squares of pink and blue and green scatter among the blank patches of his neighbors; his own little "quilt" may take up a hillside and constitute the glacial movement of inheritance across the centuries.

He must work with a variety of crops simultaneously, each with its own needs. Instinct tells him when to do things, but then, everyone else is out doing the same task on a given day. If he should happen to forget, a glance at a neighbor tells him what to do. If he gets too far behind, a jury of his peers meets at the bar each morning, whose judgments are subtle, wordless, and unbearably truthful.

Because the land rises and falls abruptly from one microclimate to another, farm life varies by a few days or weeks from village to village. You can follow the planting and harvests by driving across the Luberon valley and going up or down the slopes of the Vaucluse Plateau. Some farmers are out tying up the leafy runners of grape vines, while others plow around the cherry trees to loosen winter earth. An arc of time spans the little valley, with spring rising at one end, and winter sleeping at the other.

The man who bears the brunt of field work is typically short, stocky, weathered by sun and wind, with leathery face and faded blue eyes, a floppy jacket hanging from round shoulders, his dark blue trousers roped up under his belly. He has abandoned the beret and pipe of his father; he chews his cheek or sucks a tooth, and is always kneading his stubby, callused fingers. His nose and ears are bushy with black hairs, and he has more warts and galls than an oak tree. He suffers a touch of gout in his joints, which gives his walk a tilt. His gut is a furnace caked with wine dregs and bread crusts, and the fat of *daubes* and *civets*.

Though a creature of self-indulgence, and no stranger to *boules* or the pleasures of mouth and nose, he can be generous. He shares a portion of his bounty with deer, boars and magpies, and the gypsies who gather in his crops. These latter enjoy a dispensation earned over many summers; they return to the farms as the fruit ripens and the olives and nuts are ready for picking. They drive down in long caravans and pitch camp in his fields and orchards. The boys, sinewy with dark red tans, slink along in tattered field clothes after work; the girls are in loose dresses that sway with the wind. Good looking people, even the men whose days of picking are short, carry a weight of blunt, sometimes brutal authority in their weathered look. The women are wise and come into the supermarket smelling of raw earth and the sour odors of fruit pulp in their unwashed claws. They buy the raw produce, the cheap pasta and jug wine, and the crowds of tourists politely remove a foot or two from their aura. They laugh and shove and go through the world as if they were the real heirs of nature, and they are.

The farmer knows their worth and pays them fairly, but holds back friendship from an ancient distrust of their ways, their religion and lore. No matter how long relations have endured, they are gypsies still, and he is Christian. Everyone locks his door when the harvest begins; the camps are full, cook fires smoke, and there is drinking and card games after work. And tales of stealing begin to circulate among the villages.

The earth is so used to human meddling even the weeds seem polite; they cluster under unattended trees, and sprinkle the fields with wild flowers that shift their color month to month. In early May, wild broom brightens the hills with yellow stalks, and wheat fields are splashed all through with the red blooms of *coquelicot*. Berry vines keep to the ditches or roam along toppled boundary walls, helping separate the fields. Farmers rarely deal with them, though fires are sometimes set to burn back the briars. Even the kitchen gardens left unworked a few weeks bear a friendly wildness: the offending weeds are mainly wild onion and carrot or clumps of choke weed. Lawns are rare; they skirt the newer houses, where nut grass and thistles writhe under the herbicide spray.

The farmer is patriarch, husband, mule-headed father, artisan, mechanic, and wizard combined. He has learned a wise tolerance of nature, which doesn't always translate into patience with neighbors or his own children. His best friend and confidant is a short, high-fendered Massey-Ferguson tractor, with a squat differential hung with hoses, couplings, and a drive shaft for turning all his implements and contraptions. With it, he can pump water from his tank down to the fields, drive a hay baler, pull disks, cultivators and plows, drag the family car out of a ditch, grade his driveway, douse crops with manure and pesticides, and tow wagons of grapes, lavender, olives, almonds, and wheat. He knows every bolt and hum in the thing, and has a wall full of tools for repairing it. A tractor stands in front of every barn in Provence, or is down in the narrowest vineyard chugging along after dark, its warning light turning, headlights bleaching the ground ahead.

Such farmers, most of them married, a few single and lonely, start their day at the local bar with a shot of *pastis*, a liquor made from anise that clouds up when mixed with water, and tastes of licorice. They may drink wine some days, but no other breakfast. Fortifed thus, after a few cigarettes and a chat about weather, they trudge off to their tractors for the day's work. They'll meet back at the bar for a lunch drink, have a long meal at the house, perhaps a nap, and be back in the fields by three or four. When plowing is done, melon seeds are planted and covered with sheets of plastic to hold ground moisture. A thin hose is laid under the sheeting to dribble water in the dry months. There are wheels of hose in yards, and piles of water pipe to lay each spring.

With chores done, there is time for walking the fields to mull things over. And to indulge in the national sport of *boules*, which the *maçons* and farmers play in groups of three and four, some with berets pulled down over their crinkled eyes, others newly showered wearing shorts and sandals, turning the tarnished steel balls in their hands, waiting to strike an opponent's ball away from the *cochonnet*, the little wooden target ball where points are scored. Right into dusk, the men play at this inexhaustible game, with its roots in magic and the riddles of planetary orbits.

A farmer's wife is the repository of folk wisdom in the village; she remembers everyone living and dead. She is a walking almanac of custom and advice, with a complicated repertoire of skills in her head. She is herb doctor, gardener, canner, cook, seamstress, oral historian, and counselor – to her family, and to all who come to her. Her youth is gone; her aging has distilled the glow of foxfire through her skin. They are the carriers of the past, and embody its traditions, its morality, its caution and bitterness. They remember long after the men have forgotten; their cares are all rooted in the great mill wheel of life, the deaths and births that govern their village world. Their stature rests upon the dignity of the past itself, which they interpret for others; they often begin their counsel with "When I was a girl . . . ," or "My mother did things differently back then." They are the weight and seriousness of tradition. Marriages are not blessed without their input, their guidance of the rituals. They possess the great chests full of embroidered heirlooms to be passed on; they remember the procedures, the marriage customs, and make suggestions, which are usually heeded. They bear the gravity of being village elders. But not always. When I asked once where the post office was in a village, I was told there were two. One for letters, the other for gossip, where a crone kept all informed of local scandals. These sages stroll the roads arm in arm, gray, round, substantial as boulders, escorted by children or a dog. They outlast their husbands by a score of years, and are the ones who climb the hill alone to tend the graves.

Every farmer's god-given and inalienable right is to hunt each spring and fall. Though many woods are posted with "No Hunting" signs, others are open to anyone with a license. Unwritten law allows hunters to cross fields and enter properties that are not clearly posted, and for shooting to occur within fifty meters of a dwelling. In spring, after a long wait, the beginning of hunting season is posted in bars and rifle shops, and farmers gather on the back roads at crack of dawn, wearing plaid jackets and Wellingtons, their dogs running pell-mell over the fields. They walk in small groups up through the *garrigue*, along gullies and sandy slopes – looking for wild boar, grouse, pheasant, hare, anything with meat on its haunches. The shots ring out all day from the hills and fields. The dogs run amok, and are occasionally mistaken for game. It's common to see a hound with a perforated ear or a bald spot on its rump, dragging after its master.

Boars are now bred in captivity and turned out for hunting season; hence, the stiff license fees. The men have an instinct for where they run, and go up the same paths they have walked for generations. When a boar is killed, it is laid up in a garage or work shed, and the men who joined the hunt receive their portions. An ax does the sharing up, as the men stand around in a cloud of wine musk, puffing cigarettes, eyeing the meat falling from blows of the ax. At one farm where I went to buy a turkey, boar tails were nailed along a beam running across the work room, with dates scrawled above to mark the years in which they were shot. Under 1982 alone, eight scraggly tails hung down.

As I gazed out over the fields on my long stroll, a farmer passes with his dog, and serenity reigns over the landscape. I have begun to separate life from the strident tempo I have known. Here there is no progress; land is handed down, the work limited, bounded by other men's property. The fields are memorized, their beauty and conduct known by heart; the moods of the earth are a private language between land and human tenants. Change comes slowly, if at all; a farmer must accept the fact that he will do nothing new in his life, but will carry on the work of the ancestors while others invent the future. His own children will chafe at such rectitude and sameness, and leave him for a more changing life in the city. With nothing to alter, he is given the gift of time to fill with leisure and wandering, and rest. Under him the earth turns as always, unwinding the seasons from its great spool.

The farmers remind me of the Druids Caesar described in *The Gallic Wars* two thousand years ago:

> The Druids believe that their religion forbids them to commit their teachings to writing, although for most other purposes, such as public and private accounts, the Gauls use the Greek alphabet. But I imagine that this rule was originally established for other reasons – because they did not want their doctrine to become public property, and in order to prevent their pupils from relying on the written word and neglecting to train their memories; for it is usually found that when people have the help of texts, they are less diligent in learning by heart, and let their memories rust.

There are no rusty memories on farms. A farmer works from the heart, where memory lies, as the Celts believed. You find few books on farming in a *mas* or farmhouse; perhaps a shelf of reference books for children, some magazines, one or two novels or a tattered book of poems. But no evidence a farmer might read to keep up with the art of cultivation.

The ground rules, so to speak, were laid down by Celto-Ligurians, who roamed the land for centuries before anything was planted. And it was slow work inventing the Provençal menu. At Côte Rôtie, north of Avignon, the first vineyards were laid in early Roman days. There had been wine before, among Greeks, but never on the scale introduced by Romans, who also grew the first wheat for bread, the two essentials of good eating. Our word companion derives from the Latin *vino cum pane*, wine with bread. The Phoceans, founders of *Massilia* (Marseille), planted the first olive trees along the coast. Lemons, the wild sort, grew in abundance to the east, and were domesticated by early settlers.

"At Menton they will tell you," wrote Archibald Lyall in *The Companion Guide to the South of France,*

> how, when Adam and Eve were expelled from the Garden of Eden, Eve furtively plucked a lemon from a tree as they passed and hid it in her bosom. The Angel of the Flaming Sword was filled with pity for her, pretended not to notice and let her take it with her through the Gates of Paradise. For many years our first fathers wandered over an unfriendly earth, cold, hungry, weary and in want. Adam was bitter and despairing but Eve's heart was still buoyed up by the hope of better things. At last they came to a well-wooded, well-watered place where the high hills came down to a warm blue sea and where it was always spring, and they realized this was the nearest thing to the Earthly Paradise they would ever see. The lemon was yet unwithered, for it was the immortal fruit of Paradise. Eve took it from her bosom, kissed its golden skin and planted it in the earth. Soon all the slopes and valleys were covered with scented lemon trees; and from the lemon brought from Eden stem the myriads of trees which blossom and fruit all the year round in the place which we now call Menton.

But in our first summer in Provence, I merely stared and gulped, knowing little or nothing about farmers and their ways. I only knew I admired their lives, and liked the look of their fields and the slow, languorous rhythm of the farms. I often went to the cafés in Apt where they gathered just to savor the worn French that clanged in their mouths like goat bells. There was a raw, clean smell of sweat on their clothes. The wine they drank was dank as a cistern, and their cigarettes reeked of horse dung, earth and ashes – the bouquet of rural life.

On the road leading up to Croagnes, where it bends round in a half-curve, stands a large *colombier* or pigeon tower. This elaborate building, too broad to be a shelter for pigeons only, was simply that – a honeycomb of niches within a large brick column, topped with a tiled roof and vented for access within a border of brightly colored tiles. Guidebooks claim these multicolored openings, situated under the roof, were paved smooth with tile to prevent rodents from getting in. But their patterns vary from roost to roost and may also have served to imprint the roost on squabs as they left the nest. The towers loom up in the center of fields, or crown the hills, in tribute to the faithful pigeon, who vanished from over-hunting, and who now edges back into the villages today.

Nowadays, pigeon houses are bought by foreigners, who turn them into vacation houses and plant a few trees, build a garage or pool beside them, and put out the inevitable white table and folding chairs in the garden. The sudden lawn furniture beside the roosts tells you the past is fading. The new residents see no irony in their lives – as wingless pigeons roosting in tiny cages of stone, taking their summer pleasures while the few remaining pigeons eye them from a neighboring tree.

I walked alone up the hill above the manor, looking down on not one but two *colombiers*, one tucked behind the manor house among out-buildings, the other further down, below the hamlet. As you look out from this perch, you see the farmhouses scattered on the hills. Some are small and modest dwellings, others are huge with great walls around them. But all evolved from simple cottage origins, growing other rooms as needed. A *mas* usually started out as a *cabanon*, a square house with a kitchen and sitting room, several bedrooms behind, perhaps a lean-to for goats. As a family grew, new rooms were added on at the ends of the *cabanon* and angled to form a courtyard. The design was not accidental; one walled in the family and possessions against predators and thieves, just like the towns.

You couldn't quite see it from where I stood in the lane below the long sloping hill, but these houses were made entirely from the local materials. Nothing was brought in from beyond, unless it were an heir-loom brought down from the city or a newfangled tool for the farm. Otherwise, field stone and oak tree were the essentials of all houses here. Take for example the wooden beams of the house: the large unsplit beams or *poutres* tied the walls together. Over them ran the *chevrons*, which were logs quartered up; one side of a *chevron* was laid against the *poutre* with the other sides forming the banks of little valleys to be filled with plaster. Onto the *chevrons* were laid tile or brick to form the floor of the upper story. Earth, tree, and stone were the elements of Druid religion; the trees came down from the sacred forest, the stones from the living earth. They were the gift of the gods to mankind, who sheltered in them.

But I had lingered long enough on this long stroll over the country-side. It was time for coffee and a another try at work. My desk awaited me. When I climbed the narrow steps to sit once more at my window, I found a spider had woven strands of web across the typewriter. The coffee steamed and charmed the air, but the paper was cold and unworkable when I rolled it in. I was making motions; I was pretending. I was thinking of other things. There, on a canvas chair in front of a rickety table, sat Pip, my landlady, reading a book. Her legs spraddled out lazily over the edge of the path. A vineyard ran below, and off to one side lay the walls of a cemetery where Croagnes' departed lay together.

She was a private woman, keeping her considerable knowledge of the region to herself; she wouldn't open up, or treat us as anything but renters for the month. She seemed to wall off her role of landlady from the rest of her life, which belonged to her art – where she explored an austere vision of the world through skeletal clothing, the mere ribs and stays of jackets and shirts made from bits of stiff ribbon sewn together and hung delicately on hangers and other frames. It spoke to some sense of the vanity of style and fashion, which she stripped down to its basic, paltry architecture. When a call came for me one afternoon, she muttered the fact and let me find my own way through her house. She was gone when I came out of the pantry, where the phone, seldom used, lay shelved among catalogs and musty papers. I fumbled my way back through the vaulted rooms, sparely furnished with good tables and comfortable chairs, and some few artifacts found along the roads – shells, rusty objects from a landfill, whatever caught the eye and spoke to some fleeting moment of enthusiasm reduced to this relic.

Her husband, Bill, a sculptor and photographer, was a pack rat who scavenged the local dumps for things to weld or assemble. He taught sculpture in England and kept a studio in London, where he labored over instalations of florescent tubing that ran crazily over ceilings or up walls and over filing cases, had shows occasionally in Apt or in the local gallery at St. Saturnin. It was all Beckett-ish statements in wood and neon tubing that gave a dry laugh at bureaucracy and the dull life of cities. He too was a critic of the 20th century's passions and illusions; like his wife, he was a dark prophet of the office where so many languish doing things that will not make sense to the future.

What brought them to Provence, I wondered? New Zealand was another sunny paradise, even if the human culture that planted itself there is curiously stale, a version of England from the 1930s when I saw it in 1990. They had come over in an earlier migration, part of a generation that fled city life in the 1960s for brighter worlds. Their own dream was to have a stone house on a look out, and make a living from a rental or two while they pursued the art of living simply, gardening, working out a complicated and endlessly entangled view of what made them leave behind an indoor, claustrophic world of glass and florescent light. And now we came along eager to talk about Provence and art, or gave the impression we did, since we hadn't actually talked. We were perhaps a reminder of themselves at some earlier time. Even so, I liked them; they were dreamers, satirists, idealists in middle age, taking apart something as vague and subtle as the average person's work life, foot by foot of its file cabinets, suits, pale ceilings, desks and chairs.

I sat with them one evening over wine and candles, a belated invitation toward the end of our stay. Some Brits were in for a quick nightover from London. One was the publisher Simon Cutts, who had put out a book of photographs of my landlord's sculptures. The talk roved for a while and came back to Provence. I mentioned Beckett; he seemed to fit this company. The publisher beamed and told me his theory of the title, *Waiting for Godot*. It had to do with a Tour de France bicycle race at about the time Beckett was hiding out from the German occupation force. He was holed up in a barn at the Bonnelly farm near Roussillon, just off the N-100. I knew the sign for his farm; his widow sold wine there still.

"Well, if you know races," Simon Cutts said, "you wait all the time for the leader or your own hero to come along. It takes hours, sometimes the whole day to see your lone straggling pedaler come along looking for a drink or a bucket of water to be tossed over him. The rest of the time the road is empty or clotted with late comers trailing hours behind the pace setter. Godot was a racer in that Tour de France," Cutts said. Someone had seen the listing in an old newspaper for a rider named Godot. "One waited, don't you see, for that man to come along the empty road. Like waiting for the German police van or for a god or fate to deal with you finally."

We slurped up the plonk in thick-stemmed goblets, and poured more from a plastic jug. There were *bidons* of wine on a cupboard and along the floor; a *bonbonne*, a bottle wrapped in a flat-bottomed basket, stood in the corner. I bought a new one and would leave it for them as a gift when we went up to Paris in a few days. We would never run out of wine in this house; there was enough for a whole summer of drink and talking.

Lawrence Wylie lamented the fact that he had not asked his friend Bonnelly for information about Beckett. That was in his new edition of *A Village in Vaucluse*, one of the little classics on life in modern Provence. It's a study of Roussillon's families and folkways, the decaying past, the vestiges of tradition in the modern town. He knew everyone, and yet this one story had eluded him. Beckett up in the loft of a barn watching through the chinks in the roof for Germans, informers, anything along those roads and fields that looked suspicious. Waiting patiently in the heat while the radio droned on about the race. Interesting thought.

The play carries that monotonous tension through from these red hills, the impending fate that moves leisurely through life. Pozzo, Lucky, Estragon – tarragon, the sour herb used in spicing vinegar. A sprig of tarragon floats in the vinegar bottles sold by the jam merchant in the Apt market. What else lingers of place in that strange play? The tree whose singular leaf or two appears out of nothing along the empty crossing. I've seen the plane trees pruned back to a few leaf nodes that produce one forlorn leaf by mid-summer; the mulberry trees are sawed back to their fat stumps and look like elephant legs with knobby toes and a leaf here and there. Hope? Perhaps it comes down to a man staring at a landscape, dreaming into it some other reality while he waits for death.

Afterward, we walked in the little circular path around our house, out to the front, to look over the hills at Gordes and St. Sat and down to the faded luster of Apt. The breeze was rattling the spindly rose bushes below the wall. We could make out the rooftops of another hamlet below, *La Tuilière,* "the tile maker," where smoke dribbled out of chimneys and dissolved into the night sky. It was quiet now; only the slight creaking of limbs in the woods, the silent flapping of bats hunting insects in the cool air. The fields were thinking. An ache rose through me from the ground I stood on, a dull ache of desire for this landscape, a longing to be part of it.

Toward the end of our stay, with a week or so remaining, I screwed up the courage to visit someone whose address I had been given before leaving Texas. It was Gustaf Sobin, an American poet who had been living in Provence for the past twenty-five years. I'm not gregarious by nature, and have rarely called on strangers, even on the recommendation of my friends. I was given a list of names from Clayton Eshleman, another poet of Sobin's generation, to look up when I had gone to Paris the year before and made my excuses when I got home. I had seen none of them. Now, I was calling on Pip's phone in the pantry, with her gloomy permission, and heard a reasonably friendly voice inform me he had been waiting for my call.

I drove over to Lacoste and up a steep winding car path to a vineyard, then over a lumpy, pot-holed dent in the grass that led to a clump of walls and tiled roofs. I parked and greeted my host, who loomed over me in a friendly, stooping sort of way. Sobin was large boned, a Russian Jew by descent, the son of a dye maker in New York who had gone to

Choate, the same school James Laughlin had attended, who would later become his publisher. He went on to graduate from Brown University. He had the manner. Brown taught him nothing, he told me quietly on the terrace, under a trellis sprawling with grape vines. It was the prep school that had properly encouraged his writing and given him a direction in life. They now display his books proudly in the school library, among the books of other past luminaries. He was the second son, the first had received his father's love and encouragement. The second son sold his father's dye chemicals for a while, then saved his money for a trip to Paris. He seemed fated to become famous himself. As he told me, each summer he was packed off to Hollywood to stay at the Beverly Hills Hotel with his mother and brother. One day a woman was swimming gracefully in the hotel pool and his admiration drew her over to him. He told her he couldn't swim and she proceeded to instruct him in the basics. It was Esther Williams. On another occasion at the same hotel, he lost his autograph book and was crying in frustration. A tall well dressed man ordered hotel staff to pull up all the cushions until it was discovered. Gustaf then asked the man for his autograph. He smiled and said he wasn't important enough but granted his wish. His name was Richard Rogers. At Key West, Florida, Gustaf met Ernest Hemingway and had a life long impression of him as the American writer who had bridged the Atlantic for other writers.

We had moved into the house by now, to sit at the thick wooden table in his kitchen, my back to the hump-backed fireplace with its long neglected mound of ash in the grate. The kitchen was in disarray, with heaps of vegetable peel on a cutting board, some jars filled with nuts, raisins, rice and lentils. The sink was stained with iron rust from the well water. The doors of cabinets were loose, darkened under the iron handles from long use. The floor, made of a porous sandstone cut in slabs, was covered in the usual kitchen grime. Wild flowers of all colors peeped in at the door, and the smell of thyme wafted in on the breeze. He poured me the rich, dark local wine from the Lumières *vinicole*, and we drank in long, leisurely swallows, draining one bottle, opening another. A clump of home-corked bottles stood along the wall beside a cupboard. His hand would fall down to the side of the chair and grab one by the neck without looking down. He did that twice or three times while we chatted away, fully absorbed in our words.

He discovered writing early, he told me. After college, he wasn't sure what to do with his ambition. He would simply come to Paris and look, wait, listen, try to discover the next step. He met the poet René Char, who told him to come down and look at Provence. Char had lived much of his life in the Vaucluse. During the war, he had become a hero of the French Resistance, organizing the local farmers into a guerilla force from his headquarters at Cereste, a few kilometers east of Apt. He lived much of his later years in the hills above the little canal-ringed town of Isle-sur-la-Sorgue. So my friend packed his grip and took a train south, came down to look around at Apt, Lacoste, Bonnieux, Goult, the towns perched on the blue folds of the Luberon.

I listened carefully. He was telling me a guarded secret about his life. He seemed to know it mattered greatly to me how he had made his life veer down to this precise hillside in the thinning sunlight. I needed to know. Did I even swallow as he spoke, tapping the rim of my wine glass to his words? Was there a key to his story, a principle others could apply, and thus root themselves here as well? He took a look around at the landscape, walked to the parapet of the café at Lacoste and looked out at Bonnieux, down to the valley and across to Gordes, up into the shadowy recesses of the castle once belonging to the Marquis de Sade. The cobbled streets angled up steeply into the byways of the village, lined with houses crumbling away under the wind.

"I decided in that moment to live here," he said.

Wonderful, strange words. More wine poured between us. The bottle empty; a mild headache forming just behind my eyes. I had had enough for one afternoon. We got up, looking each other in the eye, knowing we had reached down into each other's heart. There was the interest in words we held in common, and the tradition of writing that we both traced to Ezra Pound, whose work had lured him here. But more, he was my countryman, and he was here, successfully. His hopes had not faded into wry humor; he was not waiting for something to come into his life. Instead, he bore the relaxed and affable look of someone who has found himself and looks for nothing else. He was the first stranger in paradise; now I was the second.

He gave me his book of poems that afternoon, *The Earth as Air*, and I began reading it by the fire. It had turned cool again and I gathered up the last bit of kindling and sticks and lit a fire. There were candles in the room, a bowl of olives, a cruet of wine. It was the proper setting for reading poems about Provence. I don't know what I expected from him, perhaps a deliberate music, a skillful lyricism that gushed a bit about beauty and mystery. I was unprepared for the limpid, steady music that formed. It was precise language, factual and accurate, and if it longed for anything that wasn't already there, he hardly mentioned it. It was poetry that had found its subject alive and manifest, in the ground before him. His words celebrated things, their living reality under the first light of dawn, the time when things glow with substance and are no loner dreams.

That cut to the heart of America's sorrows, I thought. We too had found a paradise but did not recognize it, did not understand it. It had to be torn down and remade in the image of some memory of other home-lands. There is no home in the world but the one under our feet, and yet it wasn't enough. The religions we brought taught us to believe our real home lay elsewhere in the vaporous heavens of afterlife. We refused to draw succor and encouragement from the world we found. We placed a veil over our eyes and imagined new worlds – artificial ones, heavenly ones, imperial ones, every kind of world but the one before us. Our liter-ature pined for such dreams and visions, as we wasted the resources of the world we lived in. And all along Native Americans showed us how to accept what was there before us, but we ignored them.

The small corners of America where the land is enough are guarded by ardent writers who cannot rest from defending their odd and singular stance to life. Robinson Jeffers wrote long and hard on the belief that the Pacific coast of America and the wild things in the back country were sacred and should not be changed. He stands out as a lone eccentric voice in America, someone who insisted to the point of shrillness that we were here already in the Promised Land. Few agreed, though Whitman and Emerson were behind him, Scott Momaday and Gary Snyder would soon follow. Pound was another celebrant of the real world which lay before us in all its splendor and perfection, which we destroyed through blindness and religious ignorance. The Provençal troubadours, he argued, were the last poets to behold the gods of nature before they perished in the Enlightenment.

If I have learned something about America from all my scholarly endeavors, it is that we are of two minds about the world: either life is a vale of suffering and tears from which we long to escape, or it is the Paradise of pagan dreams, the green temple of the gods on whose margins we are permitted to worship and live extraordinary lives. There seems no middle ground in this duality – heaven is either elsewhere or it is here and now. With either view rests everything else you think and believe. If heaven is elsewhere, nothing will suit you completely; you will work continuously toward your dreamed-for destination, or languish in faded hopes and unanswered desires. You will hang up the flimsy neon tubes of memory and continue to expect the shattering of dull reality by some bolt of heavenly magic. If heaven is around you, you have no need of fantasy; you may rest in your labors, and sleep in the lap of the good Earth. It comes to that; the complexities of American art, in all their convolutions of argument, grow out of these simple opposites.

Such thoughts before the fire, with the book closed on my lap, gave me a perspective in which to understand my landlord and this American poet. Somehow the one seemed trapped in the Protestant despair that runs all through the Anglo-American world; he lived here in the sensuous glow of Provence, scavenging the pieces of an unassembled utopia from dumps and memories. In so doing, however trivial his art, he articulated the brooding and the longing and the synthetic dreams of the Western world. He rejected the splendor that surrounded him, through which he walked each day to hunt up the rusty bits of junk, the discarded symbols of the long human attempt to build a bridge to heaven. His work would never be done because the mission to escape would never be accomplished in one life or in all lives. It would occupy human imagination for ever, this scramble to leave, to find an artificial haven at the end of the universe.

Gustaf had broken through; it took him ten years, he says in his poems, to break free of the prejudices of his culture, but he got there, and embraced the visual as sacred sight. He could stop thinking the Earth was a half-way house of the soul. When he did, he knew he could rest, could sleep with the sleeping Earth. He worked in spring, he said, and rarely wrote in the fall, when things dropped back into their slumbers once more, and the fields lay fallow and dreamless.

Is that what poetry was really about? Loving the earth for what it is, loving reality and not asking for more than it was? If so, neglecting poetry in our time is a symptom of a larger malaise of the human spirit, which now prefers to imbibe the make-believe malice of TV and the sham violence of film over the simple virtues of humanness, peace with the way things are and always will be. Our rage to clone, to alter sex and identity, to transplant organs, to adulterate food, to swap credits to pollute, to deny the obvious destruction we wreak upon the landscape, to grovel for money and power in a shrinking world of human affairs, the waiting cataclysm of an injured nature – all this lies about us as we walk away and enter Provence, and discover what our philosophy has tried to obscure: *le paradis n'est pas artificiel.*

Chapter Four

Jack Rabbit

Our first dish of *ratatouille* came out of a butcher shop in Apt. The butcher, equipped with great moustaches and a thunderous laugh, ladled several rounded scoops of the southern stew into a plastic box, then piled up a mountain of pink sausages on the scale and sprinkled rosemary needles over them like a priest at a ritual. His wife looked on with beaming satisfaction. We carted our lunch home and sat down in the white dining room, in the warmth of the casement window, and dined on the treasures of the earth. The rosemary had withered up and bled all its potent resin into the sausages; the oven was full of pungent fumes, and the kitchen, dining room, even the little beaded archway smelled like leaves burning in fall.

I opened a bottle of Gigondas and filled two glasses; we cut up the *gros pain*, sliced up a ball of sharp *mimolette*, peeled the sweet chestnut leaves from a *banon*, a melting, buttery cake of goat cheese that stung our noses when we bit into it. The *ratatouille* was a dark, pithy stew of green pepper, tomatoes, zucchini, melted garlic, the loose, earthy flesh of eggplant, and pools of olive oil speckled with herbs. The sausage crunched in our mouths; our tongues were a rapture of spices and fragrant meat. We ate and swallowed, reached for more, chewing in enchanted silence.

The wine had absorbed the wild mint and onions from the hills around Gigondas, a town settled by Romans whose stone wine vats are still in use there. Its name derives from the Latin *jocundus*, meaning delight, for the good wine produced there. The bees mix the wild seed of the *garrigue* into the pollen of the grape flowers, whose earthy scent passes down into the fruit to double the soul of the wine. The fields come back in the wine's finish; they fill the tongue with vanished summer breezes.

We walked the road up into the cherry orchards afterward, and then I sat in the living room like a stuffed goose, working the crossword puzzle from a *Herald-Tribune*. My appointment at Lacoste was not until five. Gustaf kept his mornings free to write in the little stone shed he had built out on the edge of his property. I had passed it coming up the rough track to his house the day before. After we finished talking, he took me down to see it. It was like a monk's cell, a spare little room with a cot, an electric heater, a writing table below a small window looking out toward Gordes and the tip of Mt. Ventoux. The table had the look of old parchment, dotted with the bleached scrawls from years of writing.

The way he worked, he told me, was to stay with the phrase underhand; he wouldn't, or couldn't, go on to some other paragraph or line until things got settled. There was no going back once the thing had been done correctly. He was like a farmer who couldn't simply cut across to the next furrow when a boulder popped up. The farmer dug out the rock and plowed straight, or suffered the jibes of his neighbors. It was slow work; poems could take years to finish, and some failed to see the daylight. Sometimes he'd bolt from his chair and go stalking the goat paths that ran along the slope behind his property. It might be hours before he'd find his word or phrase; and the debate that raged under his scalp would have made the boars cower from his look. He was a powerful, willful sort of man, with great long arms and a broad span of shoulders. That he should take this large frame into an office little bigger than a phone booth to wrestle his poor muse is an image to ponder on sleepless nights. He would proceed no further until the problem was solved and he had the word that would tenon to his mortise. The room bore the heaviness of the struggle; it was close inside, full of the fever of that perfectionism he imposed on himself.

I had faced scruffy writing tables in my own career, and had dug into my chaotic life with a poet's interest, but not with the heightened quest, the steady passion of my friend. He had set out to prove that as an American he could survive in the remote hills of Provence and produce good work. I thought of Paul Bowles living in Morocco all those years, writing desert stories and puzzling over the Arab psyche. Provence was hardly a desert; but it was an odd, secretive, multilayered thing that would take long study to master and put into words.

There were relatively few American writers living abroad these days; the profession of writing, alas, has spawned its own bureaucracy and now demands office hours and high visibility among one's peers. Sad to say, few would heed the call of the wide world, or the lure of small voices singing from the crannies of Provence or Casablanca.

Of course, expatriate life among artists and the social fringe has a rich history. Bryan Morton's guide book, *Americans in Paris*, lists 61 writers who lived in Paris over the last two centuries. Their sojourns in the City of Light were important, if not for the quality of work the city got from them then for the freedom it gave many hidebound North Americans, who proclaimed their delight with café society, music, dance, the female in her liberated and deified aspects to sitters at home. All this joyful expansion came back to America's readers, who may have been tempted to close their bibles and open their *Baedekers*. One hopes so, anyway. The dour, guilt-ridden American mind was due for a mote of sunlight, and the seductive airs of a satyr's flute.

Of the writers who seemed to make the most of their experience abroad, I think of Gertrude Stein toying with the logic of prose and reconstructing the sentence into a piece of verbal magic. She went to the heart of American gravity, its prose, which bullied all of reality into humorless diction. She liberated prose, wrested it from deacons, lawyers, and Comstocks and showed how it could be rearranged to say fresh, new things about the mind, the eye, the world seen through imagination. God bless her for it; poetry could live again, even in prose wrapping. There was a new there there, beyond Oakland where the rose is no longer a flowery Victorian cliché but once again a rose to such modernist lights as Matisse and Cezanne, and to the poets reinventing their medium to "make it new." It's amusing to think that the feminizing of American prose should have come from a woman whom Picasso painted to look a lot like Spencer Tracy. No one else could have been so bold, so capricious and lasting on a deep subject. Paris was her nutriment, her spiritual fountain each morning at No. 27 *Rue de Fleurus,* a block away from the glorious Jardin du Luxembourg, Marie de Medici's palace grounds, the grand woman of Paris who introduced not only opera to France but her collection of Renaissance paintings created Paris' reputation as an arts center. The busts of France's notable queens are all arranged in that garden to pay just tribute to the women who rose to power and enriched the French mind.

Stein had been William James' brightest student, as he said later. Interesting, because William's brother Henry was the other great liberator of American prose, also an expatriate and finally a British citizen. Henry James understood the Italians better than any other American since Nathaniel Hawthorne, which conferred on him the notoriety of a man of eros and contradiction. He perceived the wildness of Italy under the gaudy cover of baroque marble. He turned up his nose at seductive Paris, and called London home, but we surmise this was safe cover for a man tuned perfectly to the nature of women. His Daisy Miller will forever enshrine the youth and greenness of American girls, their pure instinctual grace before the stodgiest obstacles of society. He is credited with having given us the first fully-fleshed, healthy females in American fiction, beginning with Isabel Archer. Shall we say, he was the first to depict the innocent pleasures of women without judgment? It took Europe to guide his pen along such unfamiliar routes of imagination.

The expatriation of American writers and artists marked the greening of parched souls. Everyone thought so who went over and saw for him or herself the cultural bounty that still poured from the wells of pagan life. The Romans and Greeks gave the West many things, but we are not here to celebrate the ones school children yawn over: great buildings, civil laws, democratic institutions. They gave us the female in her richness, wholeness, and power, and from it the arts took sustenance for millennia. Woman is Europe's coherence, as Henry Adams was to say, but American education lost sight of this pearl of the ancients in its glass eye. A slow walk through Paris is a trek through stone and timber and gardens that translate the female psyche into civil splendor. She is everywhere looking down, gracing water spouts, adorning lintels and showering the domes and porches of great buildings with her love. Paris is the Great Mother spread over a ten-thousand meter wide radius of activity, the spread of her granite skirts.

When Ezra Pound and T.S. Eliot got to London early in the century, they sought for poetry what Stein and James had won for prose. They faced the enormous task of weaning America from its daily pill of moral stricture. But for all its piety, poetry was religiously empty. It had little to do with the sacred way, or with visions of any kind. It preached the gospel of the school masters: behave thyself. It wasn't too surprising, therefore, that Eliot and Pound should turn back to the roots of Western faith to invigorate modern poetry. Eliot embraced the erotic Christianity of 17th century verse, where God and sex mingled freely on the same page. There stood the balanced and healthy psyche, the "undissociated sensibility" he praised in John Donne.

But more to our purpose was Pound's discovery of Provençal poetry, whose pagan beliefs he scrupulously analyzed in *The Spirit of Romance*. There our sunny landscape reemerges and graces the prose of an American writer sure of his steps: he praised the love songs, and saw the Greek gods returning to 12th century France after a long exile from the mind. The refined and beautiful women of the love courts of southern France were the avatars of Artemis, patron goddess of Provence, Aphrodite, Circe, Calypso, and Persephone. The women of *Les Baux* hardly complained if they were mistaken for the immortals; so much the better. But beneath these verse conceits lay serious issues on the relation of nature to the human psyche. The troubadours reworked the Greek link between desire and the forces of nature; under all things human and natural ran the principle of love, the fuel of the cosmos. Nothing endured without the force of attraction, the passionate centrifuge that whirled from Diana's lap to the great vineyards of Bordeaux outward to the stars. Men knelt once more before the gardens of the Earth, waxing lyrical and sexual over the muses who guarded soil, rivers, and the weather. If modern ecology has a father, it is Pound, who set out to repair the broken links in Western nature religion and called it modernism.

These were the tribal roots of white men, this devotion to sacred earth, the transfiguration of nature into gods and goddesses. Eliot's first book of essays was called *The Sacred Wood*, which refers to the grove where the priest of Nemi guarded the sanctuary of Diana, the Roman version of Artemis and goddess of nature. The image of such a priest, who lived until another could slay him and take his place, consecrated the male's role as husband of the earth, a theme that runs throughout Eliot and fills *The Waste Land*. The Priest of Nemi was Adam in the pagan book of genesis, Eden's first farmer.

The rerooting of poetry in pagan worship failed to interest ordinary writers, but the pagan revival was implicit in all the arts of the Modernist era. Matisse painted sacred nature in his luminous flowers under a Provençal sun; Frank Lloyd Wright built the house where Taliesin and Merlin would preside over Emersonian nature. Pound's importance lies in his discovery of a positive ethic for Western life, lately maligned as the cause of environmental contamination and decay. Pound's dreamers and poets of the pagan era were sensitive, sublime lovers, Druids of natural beauty and coherence. And their late and final flowering in the medieval era occurred in the most beautiful countryside of Europe, along the Mediterranean coast from Tuscany to Provence.

Gustaf was a party to these things and came to Provence to explore Pound's ideas, and to work from the residue of female religion still visible here. After our chat in his little *cabanon*, I understood better what he had been living for all these twenty-five years. He was a man of intense religious longings whose faith had no precise focus, except to celebrate nature as some divinely coherent force. He wasn't sure where the force concentrated, only that it worked itself out as order and relation among the objects of the landscape. His way of perceiving this divine beauty was through a lush imagery of fountains and lapidary metaphors, limpid descriptions of the light oozing out of dawn over fields and orchards. The poems were musically incantatory, like Gregorian chants and litany. He seemed to have skimmed off the best of the sacred music of Christianity and grafted it to Jewish and pagan roots. That happened here; it was the work of Provence to bring us all back to the gods, one way or another, and to leave us wondering what to form out of our knowledge of them.

And if there is anything new to add to Pound's argument it must be Bruce Chatwin's wonderful study of Australian aborigine culture, *The Songlines*. It records his journey to the Outback where he discovers the power of the native "songlines" chanted by men on walkabout, who bring to life once more the sleeping gods of the continent. The songlines, Chatwin argues, are both pathways and songs that invoke the deities along the way; they go from one end of Australia to the other, and may pass down into the sea and come up at the severed edges of Asia and go on, running through the Earth in all directions. The songlines are the routes one takes to encounter the gods, to refresh the spirit and slough off mere selfhood. A life lived too long "in town" dries up the soul, and one must lay down tools and walk away from ordinary life to commune with the gods. For Chatwin, this is cause to renounce the Anglo civilization that clings to the coasts and renounces such behavior as primitive nonsense.

There were twenty-six chapels, convents, monasteries and churches inside the cramped walls of medieval Apt. Hardly a street existed without some form of temple or religious house on it. Most are boarded up now, or renovated for some other use. A few harbor elderly tenants who hang on rather than give up their cloistered gardens and high walls. But the spiritual depth of the town was unique; its richness lingers, even if the people do not publicly worship any longer. On Sundays, the old folks come to services while the young are asleep, or at the cafés. But as some-one said to me recently, the spiritual life goes back too far to be lost by one or two generations of modern Apt. It will survive in some other form, as singing, festivals, ritual dinners.

The middle ages were a continuous songline of religious chanting throughout the length and breadth of the city, and along the pilgrim route from Rome to Campostela. Once I stood in a narrow street beside a boarded- up church and heard what sounded like a choir singing in its blackened ruins. It wasn't ghosts, just reverberations of movie speakers from the cinema occupying the other end of this de-consecrated sanctuary. But the timbers remembered and echoed with the sound of chanting.

A song heard in the streets still gives that quiver in the spine, as if the voice of one person could suddenly throw spells over the whole city. The guitarists playing for coins often set up under the archway of the church, where the echoes resonate and expand their voices. It is a lovely sound, the mild strumming, the rise and fall of words in a song. One feels a twinge of embarrassment at so much personal freedom, someone filling the street with his voice; passersby look down, quickly toss coins in the guitar case and move on, their spines tingling for no apparent reason.

But to hear the whole night turn on the rising notes of a choir four or five hundred years ago, voices flowing together like a tumbling waterfall, would have stopped a listener's breath, made his knees tremble. Song was perfected here; the song as we know it, fluid, tempestuous, erotic, owes everything to the poets who once sang of love in these empty castles. When the troubadours were no more, the convents rang with the thin, high music of nuns' voices, the abbeys floated through the night sky on the monks' tenors and baritones; the gods were still served.

Perhaps it was the heavy lunch that put me into such reveries over the past, and of my friend's long reach for it. The wine made me sleepy. I wanted to go on reading my newspaper, but the stories were tedious: money problems around the globe, the failing fortunes of America, the struggles of a crowded planet to make room and feed all. The news seemed to relish all this chaos and hopelessness. *Plus ça change.* It was more interesting to peer out the door at the cobbled wall of my neighbor's house. There the sun spread out in a tangle of light and shadows, tracing the crevices of stone like a mind lost in its memories.

At five o'clock I drove down the steep hill over the valley to Lacoste, which I could glimpse between leisurely dips in the road. Gustaf had come out to his gravel drive to welcome me. His tall frame was diminished by his stance, the stooping over, ankles crossed with one shoe toed down over the other. Deep voice, large, soft hands shaking mine, a thick brown sweater draped over his shoulders by the sleeves. He had the nonchalance of someone raised on money. All that was behind him now; he scraped by with what he earned from teaching at a local arts school, and what a small trust fund paid him.

We sat out under the grape arbor on the terrace. A little later he led me down to the *borie* on the edge of his property, a strange little building that rose up out of dry stone to form a dome, with a smoke hole and low, doorless entry. Inside was dry ground littered with yard tools and a few bricks. Hardly ever used. A shed. Could have been a garage moldering away under the elms of a little New England house.

"When I drove Char up here once," he said, tilting his head to tell a story about his beloved René Char, "the road used to cut straight up where the vineyard is now. He saw the *borie* on one side, the square house on the right. 'Feminine and masculine,' he said, pointing to them."

Round, yes. The French call a woman's curves *les rondeurs*. But the *borie* was not sensuous, it was massive, unconscious, shaped out of the silence. Inside, it was taller than I expected. There were no chinks in the closely laid stone. It was dark and echoey inside, cooler than the sunshine. One entered such a shape of stones with an odd feeling; the self evaporated and reduced you to whispers. I had heard of whole villages wintering over in such buildings to escape the plague. What would become of them after all those months together in such leveling darkness as this? Nowadays, only stray dogs and vagabonds used them. They were solemn, almost crypt-like buildings that had sprung from the dawn of the mind. And yet one felt their kinship to cathedrals, and all vaulted, silent, humbling places.

We went back to the terrace and sat again. But we had covered the big subjects already. There was time now for looking off into the fields, for studying the lay of the land from this edge of vineyard. The vines came up within a few feet of our shoes, and sprawled out in leafy rows along the yellow earth. What vines thrived in always surprised me: rocky earth glinting with shards of quartz, loose sand, parched and aching earth where the roots roamed looking for beads of moisture. Across the way stood the long, bleached valley with its squares of gray and green ranging off into the vague hills.

I hadn't spent a quarter century staring into these hills and ravines; I couldn't see what he saw. I didn't know how to begin to ask what was there. But I felt it; I sensed that we were present before some slow unfolding of miracles, a pageant of light and pattern coming toward the human eye in the grand language of nature. Was it all the rags and flutters of Aphrodite rising out of the moted sunlight into our minds? Pound would have said that paradise lay in the intricate sublimity of all these details, how they met and formed a vast tapestry of relation passing beyond our grasp. Indeed, there lay the *borie* as a poem in stone, its edges meeting and voicing the living nature of rock, its powers to change into any form and remain itself.

But there we sat, silent and meditative, staring out into an olive and sand-colored world trembling with light. How could it have been otherwise but a soul fleshed in green leaves and earth? How could we have turned our backs on such a world and claimed ourselves the only thinking reed? To grasp nature one must leave the self; it can not be seen with the eye of one's ego. It is when the self drops away that one begins to share the breathless wonder a potter feels who knows the curve rising under his fingers is the shape running through all animals. It is the wonder of the monk whose brush stroke gathers all variations of the wave into a single curve at the moment of his self-annihilation. The wonder an aborigine must feel when he throws down his hoe at planting time and sallies forth into the desert, with the foreman screaming after him from the ranch house, and the heavens opening before him as he sings the first note of his songline.

I sipped wine and listened, and looked out from my place at the table, thinking of something that had happened a few days earlier. Cathy and I had stopped to admire a creek and the bridge crossing it. Behind lay a path that went up into the cliffs. We decided to follow it and came upon a house with a gate falling from its hinges. The roof of the house had collapsed, and kids had scratched graffiti onto the plaster walls. The hearth stood, but the mantle was pried off. Some gnome had lived out its days here, looking at the woods from the square window. We went to the back and climbed down a short wall, continuing up the path where it disappeared among channels of a reservoir. Gardens had been kept here long ago, and there were catchments for the rain that poured down from the cliffs. Weeds still thrived on moisture trapped inside the rocks. How lush, deep, and strange it all was. I began to claw my way up a cliff pocked with niches and small footholds. I'm no climber, but I sensed the path had some other logic to it and wanted to know where it led. Dogs or squirrels or a fox still tramped down the wild flowers and kept the path open.

There, on a high shelf, buried deep in the riven stone, lay the noble hem and flowing blue robes of the Virgin Mary. A pillar stood beside the niche, carved with the words "I am the Immaculate Conception." It had been the work of pilgrims long ago; a sprig of wilted flowers lay at her foot.

She looked out from her shelf all these many years, hardly touched by the weather. A shrine, a statue; I felt disappointed by it. It had no more mystery than a chapel. But sitting here now, looking off into the vineyards, I felt the slow weight of an idea forming in my head. The statue served a purpose I hardly ever thought about before; it was the metaphor of higher vision. It brought down to ordinary minds what others had experienced at the heights of understanding, the holy chill that tenses every nerve and leaves the body breathless, suspended. But what had come from nature as dizzying sublimity and coherence hardly translated into speech. It required these elemental metaphors of beauty, the divine woman, who must stand for the radiant convergence of energy, the momentary understanding of a god. All across the ancient world, the epiphany of Earth's spirit took this form of the divine woman. Even Aphrodite is only a crude shorthand for the perfect order and processes of reality; she is the reductive equivalent of some higher metaphysical Eden of forms, a creative unfolding glimpsed by the early Greeks and by numerous peoples before them. She was coined to represent the beauty and fertility of cosmic events; no doubt she existed somewhere for the first poet to conceive of her as this remarkable equivalent of patterns which cannot be described without losing their beauty of design. Aphrodite is linked in the mind with mere chalk statues and crude figurines, and is part of the simplistic shorthand by which the most difficult philosophical epiphanies are translated. And her importance lies not only in her beauty but as the final calculus of nature: she is the perfect metaphor of order's fertility, perhaps the imagination's greatest achievement.

The statue of Mary had the lowly and efficient function of communicating this sublime metaphysical relation, albeit shorn of the sexual dimension. The human mind, with its simple logic and narrow apertures of sense, was made to perceive practical things. The shrugs and murmurs of the world itself were too fine and lofty for the brain to bear. When they were heard, or felt, the simple column of marble would do – for in producing a figure out of stone the sculptor reproduced this divinest of all mysteries: the incoming of the spirit of earth to human sense. A statue counterfeited vision, yes, but it served its purpose. I had hung by my fingers staring up at Mary emanating from a cleft of fertile rock. I was the Priest of Nemi for a moment and didn't know it.

Come to think of it, all shrines, crosses, leaded windows, statues, choir voices are a poor man's handbook for higher visions, the rudimentary diagrams of untranslatable ecstasy. I have no better way to explain my thoughts; I must put them bluntly, guilelessly. What I saw in the woods gave me the thrill of vision itself; I felt the ground gathering before me in this chalk figure of a woman. She had been molded by the faith of ordinary hands who had fashioned her shape out of an ageless longing to know the world.

If I couldn't actually see, I could feel awe and wonder. I was not dead to the world, merely sleeping. The hills that drew Celts and Romans still called out, as if the land were the other half of our souls and continued on across a wide river as the unconscious side. There lay the silent twin, the Other, in repose along the darkening hills, as we sat, he and I, partially stirred, partially woken to its voice. I know he felt a deeper happiness; it was written on him. All the years spent coaxing that blurred, elusive spirit up into words had paid off finally; he had gotten closer to the boundary, the river where the hidden life begins. When he looked out over the hills, was this the poem he was laboring to compose: the words fleshed in trees and stone, descending the slopes toward his waiting pen?

I don't think fifty words passed between us in the hour we sat together. But we had been thinking furiously, and our minds shared some of this frenzy at another wave length. I was exhausted and hungry. I was thankful I felt these animal desires to eat, to crawl off to bed to sleep. I needed steady ground under my shoes. I was tired of shuttling all these shapeless possibilities across my mind. The land had resumed its stillness below us, and now the sun bleached the color out of the fields. Evening had come on.

I got up and took my glass to the kitchen. He followed behind with a heavy step. He was not finished yet; there were still things to be sorted out. I wondered if he would go back to the table after I left, to continue his meditation. It would be a pure, velvet night again, with stars piercing all through it. It would envelope the land and dissolve all the human boundaries erected on it. It would wash away the whole history of consciousness and bathe the earth in moonlight.

On the drive back, the yellow headlights groped forward like insect feelers. A jack rabbit scampered ahead of me and leapt into the woods in a single, graceful arc, plunging into darkness without fear. Something on the other side would catch it, and it leapt with an innocent trust of the dark. Perhaps it was no more than the cover of night, or a tangled slope, or a dry creek bed full of watching eyes. But there lay the whole secret of life in that one bound. I envied its ability to plunge into this other side, this unknown, as the car passed with its droning pistons and blinding glare, the whole equipage of being human. It had slipped over the edge of one kind of knowledge and now pawed its way through the stark branches, the tangle of undergrowth, nosing forward like a dreamer. It moved with only its eyes above the conscious line, roaming the elemental world. This was the darkness the arts groped toward, and often missed – the place where rabbits slipped from their bodies to become the night, whose belly the potter touched when he formed clay into vision.

When I got back to Croagnes, a lamp was on in the living room. Everyone had gone up to bed. I found a plate of food in the oven and nibbled at it for a while. I came in to the fire and sat down with the book I had been reading the night before, Walter Benjamin's *Illuminations*. Benjamin was the last mystic to come out of modern Germany, who believed there was a pure language, a divine tongue, under all the debris of modern literature. When he left occupied France for the U.S., he was stopped at the Spanish border and refused entry, whereupon he took his life. Brecht declared his death the first great loss of the war. His work dwelled on the meaning of borders and boundaries in art, and finally he died on one.

In "The Storyteller," he makes the startling observation (in 1936) that we were losing "the ability to exchange experiences."

> One reason for this phenomenon is obvious: experience has fallen in value. And it looks as if it is continuing to fall into bottomlessness. Every glance at a newspaper demonstrates that it has reached a new low, that our picture, not only of the external world but of the moral world as well, overnight has undergone changes which were never thought possible. With the [First] World War a process began to become apparent which has not halted since then. Was it not noticeable at the end of the war that men returned from the battlefield grown silent – not richer, but poorer in communicable experience? What ten years later was poured out in the flood of war books was anything but experience that goes from mouth to mouth. And there was nothing remarkable about that. For never has experience been contradicted more thoroughly than strategic experience by tactical warfare, economic experience by inflation, bodily experience by mechanical warfare, moral experience by those in power. A generation that had gone to school on a horse-drawn streetcar now stood under the open sky in a countryside in which nothing remained unchanged but the clouds and beneath these clouds, in a field of force of destructive torrents and explosions, was the tiny, fragile human body.

I turned out the light and felt the woods creep closer to me in the dark. This was the murmuring darkness, the magic place of dreams and changes, and it seemed wholly alive at this late hour. The stones whispered; the trees moved without wind; the ruins of altars remembered the ancient sacrifice. The hills were rising like waves far out at sea, covered with starlight. Somewhere upon them solitary human beings walked the paths, looking for some empty *borie* to sleep in for the night, or passing through woods that were hushed with listening. There lay the groves where stories are made, and where human beings change back into their animal forms again, carrying lanterns and banners from one sleeping village to another. It was easy to believe the soul was not inward anymore but outside and around me, the whole of nature. The rabbit who leapt free of me in the dark had crawled to a corner of my mind.

Chapter Five

Pagan Dust

L eavving the Latin world behind is like dropping lemons from your diet. The tanginess is gone; the sun drops behind a cloud. The green hills lowered behind us, and our regrets were keen. But there were pleasures ahead and I drove the empty auto routes north, with the southbound lanes jammed with vacationers. After the long hours of rolling wheat fields, the stately towers of Paris rose up and we cheered; over its grainy outline bloomed a halo of northern light, a curious stone-colored light Paris breathed out of its human landscape.

I maneuvered through the maze of ramps and squeezed onto the Periphérique's long, snaking lines of traffic. Our notes on the apartment we had rented directed us to the neighborhood of Les Halles, in the center of the city. Twice I was swept down into the racing traffic of a tunnel and flung out into a spaghetti of intersecting avenues as taxis and airport limos blasted me out of their way. I crept through streets that led back to the edge of Les Halles again, carefully tracing my steps to avoid the tunnel, only to find the numbers halting one digit from our supposed address. Then nothing. Or rather, a wall of glass soared up where we should have found our door.

We were late for our meeting with the landlord; the traffic gave me no chance to comb the cluttered block of signs and windows and scaffold and construction crane and dump truck and moving van and crowds and pigeons and noise and . . . . Finally, I pulled into a side street below the new glass mall at Les Halles, the great fantasy of domes and jutting roofs covering the ancient marketplace of Paris. Fish restaurants still ringed the area from long association with the stalls. But already the glass and steel confection had faded into a desolate arcade, with a few teenagers leaning on railings under a twilit sky. I raced along to all the phone booths trying to find one that still took coins. They had all been converted to cards. I finally found one in a nearby bar, called the landlord, who curtly informed me I had the address wrong. It was the *Rue* Halle, not Les Halles! The agent had scrawled the address on a card, and I had miscopied it. I was to thread my way down one side of Paris and up another (across the Seine) to the 14th, to the great circle at Denfert-Rocherau, take *Avenue Genéral LeClerc,* turn onto *Rue Alésia,* then creep along until . . . until I found the number on the door. I would be greeted there, however late the hour.

When we arrived at the door, the landlord was in the Egyptian restaurant down the street, having his dinner. I peeped in and found a lanky, alcoholic looking Brit dabbing bread into the sauce on his dinner plate. He looked up, brightened a bit, wiped his mouth on a napkin and came away after nodding to the waiter about the bill. He took his meals there routinely, I learned. We parked the car in the musty little garage and trooped up the steps to the apartment – a suite of crooked rooms with a broken sofa, some cheap dining furniture, a small kitchen that led out to a patio covered in roofing tar. We were the eyesore of the block, towered over by plush condominiums. The last surviving two-story structure from an earlier Paris – now only canyons of high-rises lining empty streets.

It was Paris, but the sun and lemons were behind us now. The house was a heap of loose brick waiting to be razed for another apartment tower. Leaning out over the wall of our patio, we felt a bit like the sailors of a rusty freighter tied up among the new ships in port.

The landlord had my money in advance, a ferocious rent for what we actually got, and did little more than grouse about our tardiness. Even so, I dreaded having further contact with him. He seemed a bit slippery and sinister, like Fagin, and I'd just as soon unpack, flop into the needling springs of the sofa and contemplate my next move – perhaps a corner bistro for dinner. As I puttered around, I found the bathroom, or rather the stall, situated midway up the stairs. It was so small you barely had room to unbuckle, crook your knees, and sit there, ludicrously suspended over the passage where others sighed and clomped up and down.

As I was hauling suitcases up the stairs, adding a few scrapes of my own to the battered walls, my son ran to inform me the landlord was waiting in his little corner shop below. There were instructions, keys, details to go over. I threw my things into our bedroom, onto a wobbly mattress that sagged mysteriously under its cover, put my toilet kit on the scruffy dresser, cracked the window, which looked out over a moonscape of chimney pots and antennas, and came away thinking I had seen all this before – when I had run off to New York after high school and languished all one summer in a tenement on 15th Street.

Mr. Albritton was somewhere behind the peeling door of his corner shop, once a *tabac* with a "*mazout*" sign still swinging on its hinge. In former days, *mazout* or kerosene for the furnace, was dispensed from neighborhood bars; a husband could grab his fuel can and saunter down the block to have a drink or two while filling up. The landlord came around finally, fished for keys, patted his pockets, looked hopeless, found them in a jumble of papers and junk on a work table behind him, and motioned me into his chaos. A chair was pulled out of the clutter and I sat down. This promised to be an inquisition of some sort. I didn't care; it was dusk now and I was tired.

But he had been rummaging in all his cabinets trying to find something, and with a sigh of pleasure, plunked down a new bottle of Famous Grouse whiskey and two smudged water glasses. The cork was pulled, and he poured off two hefty portions of booze and we toasted with a clink.

"Now," he said, getting down to business. "I thought we should get to know one another. I'm British, as you can see," eyeing me closely for any hint of prejudice. We pulled on our whiskey to prepare for any difficulties lying ahead. "You're American, is that right?"

"Yes," I replied, beginning to find the room less cluttered than I thought. It was merely broken up, as if in the first stages of being packed up. A life of accumulation, of indifferent existence, scattered across the dusty ledges. A dusty fan, a broken table lamp, some chairs roped together, a pile of phone books stained and damp, magazines that had slid from a table to the floor years ago. Bits of plaster, a bucket of dried blue paint, some posters rolled up and shoved into a coffee can. A dinner plate full of cigarette butts and an empty lighter. Twenty years ago this was a thriving corner business; it had come down in the world to this humble calling, the landlord's cubbyhole. A kitchen went off to the side, obscured by a tattered velvet curtain; a bed, unmade, hid behind some sacking he had rigged up on a wire stretched to another door.

"My mother's building," he said, interrupting my survey of the room. "I help her rent it out, but I don't really live in Paris anymore. I live down south, near Vence. It's the end of an era with us, you see," waving his hand around. "We're selling off the place, getting out."

He was perhaps fifty-five, maybe older; whiskey had loosened his eyes and mouth a bit past his years. He was thin, sinewy, still quite agile and hard. He lived as simply as he could, doing the minimal work required to keep an income. The ground he was selling was worth millions; a mother living in London would get most of it, but his own portion seemed enough to make him look off with a vague smile.

He poured more whiskey and settled back in his chair. He had nothing to discuss regarding our accommodations; I had no particular questions to ask. The keys were on a string in front of me. But there was no indication we should do anything but sit.

"You like the south," he asked, casting for a subject. "Frankly, I don't think much of it. I've been down there for sixteen years now, in a little place, a hamlet, that doesn't even get mail service. We bought cheap and did the work ourselves; you know, brought in power lines, dug a well, that sort of thing. In those days, you could pick up a house for a few hundred quid. People sold off buildings that would fall down anyway. They laughed when we came along to buy up their ruins. Brits came in droves, looking for the sun. That's always at the bottom of British roving, you know: the sun."

I was feeling light-headed. We were drawing on warm whiskey, and it was coming regularly. If I took a sip, the bottle passed over my glass before I could blink.

"You know the difference between Yanks and Brits," he said, leaning forward, wetting his lips. "You had a wilderness, and we lost ours before we were ever a country." He sat back to watch the effect of this insight.

"The wilderness was important," I ventured, reluctant to get into a seminar on the subject. "I don't think it meant much to us, though. It was something to overcome, to prove our manliness."

"Gave you your unconscious, I'd say. Ever think of England that way – that it lacks one? See what I mean," he said, refreshing our glasses, "we packed all our gnomes and Druids off to Ireland. The only thing left on the island was a bit of common sense, and we made too much of it. That's why Brits always come looking for the sun; where there's sun, there's passion. We're a people without any, no place to go to get away from all the bickering that goes on."

"I've always found your gardens suspect," I said, feeling my liquor. "They're a bit Freudian."

"Ah, well . . . it's a rainy culture. You get that much rain, you're bound to have enthusiasts growing giant zinnias. But look here, there's no wild-ness in an English garden. The only thing we got out of rain was the notion of individuality. And for good reason: when you're cooped up too long, you get on each other's nerves. You have to have your own space, your own rights. Pity the States took our example so much to heart.

"Ever see an Italian garden? It's like some hairy monster, all thorns and mangy shoots, bunches of unmowed grass, yet something's right about it, something beautiful and deep about such chaos. It goes back to other times; the Italians haven't lost their old ways. They still think the ground's got some sort of spirit in it. We prune everything back, make sure it has a purpose if it grows. You know, a human use. That's why," he said, suppressing a sneeze, "we were such good empire builders. We'd find some primitive tribe lolling about enjoying life, build 'em a few chapels – are you religious? good – preach a lot of sin to them, and before long we'd have them acting just like us. It's our peculiar talent, but it doesn't give us much to think about. We have to invent our darkness; Agatha Christie and all that."

We both took long tugs on the whiskey and looked around the room, avoiding each other's eyes. We were like two men who had just had a good wrestle and were catching our breath. He had been brooding on these matters for some time, I suspect, and took this chance to air himself. The agent had told him I was a professor, and so was his previous tenant, who left behind invitations to his lecture on the history of Paris bakers. Perhaps Albritton had collared him as well.

"Is that why the moors are always popping up in English novels," I asked? "I've noticed when a writer can't find anything murky in his characters he sends them off to the moors to have a mystical experience."

"It was a mistake to give in to all those revolutions and let the middle class come to power," he said, looking mournful. "As long as there were kings around, you could expect a bit of vision from on high, a bit of attention to higher things. Once the royals got shoved aside, the middle class came on. They'd been waiting a long time for their turn to rule. All that paperwork, and now a chance to pull the levers. Trouble is, they don't believe in anything. Never have. There's no outside to them; they just count things, and hoard the surplus. I've never seen a more tedious bit of history than the one we're plodding through."

"After the war of independence," I said, "George Washington was given the choice of being king or president. He thought it over for an hour, and settled on becoming president. The republic hung in the balance while he went over the advantages on both sides. In the end he opted for the middle class, and power suddenly became like money: anyone could have it if you worked for it. That meant everyone would be born on the starting block, and you had only yourself to blame if you lost. It gave everyone a fair chance to win, and the whole of life became a series of overlapping contests. It meant you had to be hard, ruthless if you were going to get ahead. Our culture sees everything in terms of competition; we battle the odds at every level, from love to aging and death. There is no rest or calm in us; we win one thing and see another prize pop up behind it, and go after it. Supposedly this is reality; Darwin had characterized all of life as a struggle of the fittest. But there are plenty of situations in nature where there is no fight at all, only a set of balances and exchanges. But we ignore that side and go on competing in the name of life."

For that lengthy harangue I was rewarded with a topping up, and I sipped off the rim the part that would have dribbled onto my shirt front. It was now past nine o'clock. I idly wondered what my wife might be doing for dinner at this moment. I had the uncomfortable feeling everyone was sitting on the broken couch waiting for my footsteps. More likely, they had gone out alone to find something to eat, and above me was a dark, empty apartment.

"Don't you see," my landlord said, scushing up to the edge of his chair, "the French are the only ones who accept monotony in their lives. They know part of the day must be given to the mechanical tyrannies of life; at work they sort and pin together little scraps of paper this thin," he held up his fingers, "and check the smallest details in leases and deeds and disgusting things like that. They actually *like* doing it, you know. They educate their kids by making them scratch away at some boring tract or other, hour after hour, copying like monks in some scriptorium. They learn to abide the tedium of life that way; they don't put everything in terms of winners and losers. They know they'll get up from work, go home to a warm bath, put on fresh clothes, sit about talking brightly, have a big splash at the restaurant, stay up till two in the morning chatting away over cake and coffee, and get up the next day to dull work again. You can do that if you mix the dull part with the rest. The French enjoy life, they aren't always fighting over a bone. The Brits and the Yanks can't be idle for a minute, or they might lose ground. Don't you see?"

"I know a man at the local bank in Apt who has worked the same job for years, and will continue pinning together ten one-hundred franc notes and laying them in a compartment of his desk drawer, recording them in a ledger, cashing my checks or exchanging currency for the rest of his working life. Day in and day out. But when the bank closes, he puts on his tweed jacket and sporting cap, takes the arm of his attractive wife, and is now a man of the town. The change that comes over him is wonderful. He's no longer a drudge, but in charge of the evening, his own man. Everyone nods to him as he saunters along with his leather bag strung over his shoulder, smiling and socializing all the way to the café, where he will chat over drinks for an hour with his cronies. If he were American, he'd rush straight home to dinner, watch TV and go to bed. There's nothing left after work but the dregs of the night. That was my father's life, and the life of all the fathers I have ever known. I didn't know it was a British disease as well."

"We don't have it as bad as you Yanks, not by half. A chap I know worked in one of your banks and quit after two years. The money was good, but he wouldn't die for it. He told me no one took off in America; everyone worked to the limit. If you went for a long lunch, you got stern looks coming back, as if you had a couple of tarts on your arm. All his friends had cellular phones and left messages everywhere they went; they got little beeps sitting in the barber chair; they'd stop at a traffic light and get into a deal on the car phone. He threw it up and came back home. 'We're a bit old fashioned,' he said, 'no match for the Americans. But they work themselves to death and I don't intend to do that. There's more to life than money.' Maybe he's an exception. But he stands for something British – even Crusoe liked to romp a bit on his little island. You know what they say about the English, don't you?"

"What?" I asked, seeing double now. I was reeling rather merrily on my chair, with the junk flying in orbits around my head. I felt myself occasionally sliding off the chair and righted myself with the merest pressure of my finger tips on the edge of the desk.

"A Brit who doesn't have a little French in him isn't civilized! The French part softens up our little adding machine hearts. We invented the individual, which is just a molecule with legs on it. You put a country together with only individuals and you get an ant hill! Now, pour a bit of French blood into an Englishman and you get a human being keen for family, friends, a few nights out. Suddenly life isn't so dreary; there's a few pleasures to pursue. Something to laugh about or gush over. There's a nice bit of pagan dust in gallic men."

All this mixing and stirring made him grab the bottle and pour fresh scotch into our glasses. It didn't matter any more; I was numb from the waist up. I could have gone the rest of the evening receiving his mild harangues, clearing out my host's brain while we drifted on the river of scotch in us.

"The further north you go, the colder the mind becomes. I've seen Swedes come down out of their ice and look as if they didn't believe they were alive. They were staring into the mirror at a pub as they drank ale. They were white as ghosts, and wouldn't get within a yard of anyone else for fear of being touched by an elbow. Imagine trying to spread that kind of gospel around in southern latitudes! And yet that about sums up what we did for the last four hundred years."

The sound of someone's high heels clicked along outside and interrupted us. We listened to the tapping, two tones, one higher than the other. Perhaps the heel had worn down on one shoe. I never understood the power of high heels, why they should be so alluring, especially at night. But the clicking was such a clean little noise on the ear, and filled us both with longing. We sat like two dogs at the hearth heeding a sound in the woods. Two sharp little notes struck the pavement and brought to our minds all the shapeliness of legs and floating skirt, the fluid shimmers of a body passing under street lights. I wished I were out there now and could see what sort of woman made such music. Our hush was suddenly awkward. We were not meant to lapse into soggy silence. He was clearing his throat again to speak. I slouched and gave him my soberest face.

"The French hung on to their pagan links. The Provençals kept the earth in their heads; they live in some sort of myth world, nodding at ghosts and talking to themselves. You feel strange things pass over you in that part of the world. . . . Churchill was inordinately fond of the French. I'm not, I can tell you, bloody bastards, not an ounce of civic spirit among them. But they're like the Greeks, at times; they call the spirits out and dance with them, if you get my expression."

Alas, we were fumbling now. I detected a slur in his speech; the topping off had missed the rim a few times and puddles stood to the right of our glasses, soaking into the wad of receipts that lay there wrapped in string. He dabbed the drips away with his handkerchief, but didn't rescue the receipts. "Bah," he said, "they must be ten years old, but mum likes to keep records."

"I think my generation may be the last of its kind in the world, I mean with the whites on top of the heap. I don't care what the academics say about mixing things up, making a stew of culture, we're at the end of our road. We've drawn the thread off the spool, and there's no more slack to it. We have mucked up the world with our ideas and they don't pay off like they once did. Never thought it would become so grim, and yet I feel a quiet pity for our kind. I think we were a handsome and noble race at one time, when we had some mission in us. We taught the world how to think without feeling, and there's something to be gained from it. But we thought you could make a world out of such peeled logic, and it ruined us. We forgot how to feel, or show compassion or tolerate differences. That's the tragedy of our race. We needed whiskey to be passionate. We forgot to be human, especially when there was business to conduct. I feel all our achievements will be forgotten and the vines will cover our monuments, as they've done every other great tradition. I hate being part of its lingering, if you know what I mean.

"You know," he said, his eyes swimming around. "The whole thing went down when the Catholics lost out. They were corrupt, tyrannous bastards, but they gave people something no one else has – beautiful visions. Gods, saints, a fable about the soul. Such magic, such spells could be cast by those cathedrals. Life was holy; nothing stood beyond the reach of God. You can't have it back; there's only the empty buildings now, but sometimes even they're enough, just to poke around in and feel that power to turn glass and stone into something mystical. I'm a windbag, aren't I," he said, half muttering his words. "You've been patient hearing me out; I suppose I'm lonely gabbing on like this. But I don't have all that much to do these days; when this place goes, I'll retire altogether to my patio. You must come down sometime and see my place; you'd like it."

He fell silent, though I hardly think I noticed. The time passed slowly. I heard a gentle thud behind me and saw my son peering through the glass door. He motioned for me to come. I got up and took the keys, and backed up slowly to the door. Albritton looked up, waved his finger in the air a moment, and looked away again, smiling. I closed the door and saw him get up to lock himself in for the night.

Upstairs, in the apartment, the table was set and candles were flickering. A meal had been cooked and laid on the table: chicken, baked potatoes, a salad, a bottle of wine opened and poured. I sat and had a cheerful dinner, sobering up slowly as I ate and listened to the children chatter away about Paris. When it was over and we had carted all the dishes to the kitchen, I suggested we take a walk before bed. We headed down the steps with our keys and an umbrella and stepped into the cool night air.

It was a soft evening. Signs splashed greens and reds on the pavement; the cloudy sky had turned amber. The street lights splashed on the cars, the metal shutters, railings, stoops, the metro's hooded entry. A church stood bleak and closed against the faded sky, behind its iron gate. It had the appearance of something abandoned, like a house without windows or doors. Along the opposite side glowed little shops sparkling with mannequins wearing the latest styles, the hottest colors, bright, well-made shoes and hats and scarves.

The figures in one window hovered over the red maple leaves tumbling from a basket; a new rake and broom leaned against the wall. A woman crooked her finger and appeared to be chatting; a man smiled and reached for the rake. A child wore stiff trousers and white shoes, and held a leaf in his paraffin-coated hand. Price tags hung from everything. The lights gave off a brittle glare that forced odd shadows to creep under the folds of their chins. Someone had forgot to aim another spot up from the lower corner, to smooth away the fierce theatrical tension of the scene.

The window hinted at something mysterious, withheld. I suddenly realized the figures were posed like saints in a stained glass window, with all their holiness drained out of them. The figures seemed baffled and hysterical that there was nothing more to life than clothes and tools. The child especially looked contemptuous, with the shadow growing under its chin like a tuft of beard. You could feel its hands itching for the rake to destroy the glass window holding them back. I don't know what they would have done had they freed themselves and gone into the city. But their hearts seemed full of malevolence for the world that had lied them into existence.

"Paris is dying," Albritton had said, interrupting a lull in our conversation. "It's no longer a place of spirit; that's why it strikes you as mere bustle and business. It's living on its past; it doesn't take a genius to see that some essential force has gone out it."

"But what gave it life? What was the force?" He looked at me as if to say, why ask me? We both inherited this century. Or did he simply look away again, concentrating on the blister on his wall paper, a mysterious swelling where loose earth and drainage wanted to burst through. Only the paper held back the decay, the desire of the wall to simply collapse at our feet and for all the empty dark rooms above us to come down in a heap of lath and dust and broken water pipes.

"If the temples are no longer used, the gods go away. Like any great city, Paris has its cycles. The young are not here creating visions, inventing new names for the gods. They're off somewhere else, maybe in Lima, or some corner of Bombay, in Trinidad. I don't know. But the brilliance, the juice, the imagination is gone. There's only the merchants to cash in on the memory."

"I remember reading that Robert Rauschenberg, the painter, came to Paris to study in 1948," I told him. He said that to become a painter one had to go to Paris. Later he wrote that he was perhaps fifteen years too late. He must have seen what you see, that things had changed."

"Exactly," he said. "There are times when Paris springs to life, and the artists set up and create as if voices had come out of the ground and inspired everyone. The city is young again, ageless and perfect. But now it is pretentious, filled with nostalgia for its youth, like an old woman sitting alone at the bar."

"I thought New York was all that."

"It is, but so is every city. One always wanted Paris to be the capital of love and dreams. Now, it's a mess of banks and tourist shops, and hamburger stands."

A café brightened a corner, with tables and chairs set out for the late night crowd. A few couples were sipping drinks. An American was bent over his calculator figuring out the price of two cups of coffee. His wife yawned and looked around with an air of disappointment. She was cold, and pulled her jacket around her. Her husband couldn't quite make the calculation and gave up. He leaned back, whispered a complaint to her, and she took out a large bill. They waited for the waiter, who stood under the awning rocking on his heels. Romance was souring, eroded further by the hum of a pump pulling foul water from a sewer nearby.

My children scoured the scene for an ice cream bar. I had promised them ice cream cones as a reward for walking. They were tired, sleepy, but clung to the hope of finding a stand open. Finally, a *tabac* appeared, that haven on deserted streets, with a chart showing all the flavors stocked in the big freezer behind the door. I paid and we strolled along, lingering as if to press the city to enchant us, to give us something.

When would it reveal itself as the Paris of my childhood? Surely its soul lingered in the gleaming cobbles, or hid in the shadows, moving into street light with the face of a beautiful woman, the eyes serious, the mouth parting as if to smile before stepping back into the shadows again with a click of her heels. Perhaps Paris was only visible to the young. Maybe my tired children beheld its charms, its vitality. Now that I was middle aged, I was blind to it. It all seemed mere blackened granite and iron, privacy and withdrawal. I could not bring myself to admit such feelings to the family; I continued pointing out the beauties of each street – the tall windows hung with brocade drapes, the grand piano with its vase of roses, a railing topped with brass points, the door inching open onto the dazzling glimmers of a party.

It was a borrowed luster, as if Paris imitated itself. It had ceased to be a royal seat; the Louvre sprawled out with its vast bureaucracy of art in the old palace grounds. Business hummed, and the middle class ran things from a computer screen. You could feel the heavy tempo of practicality driving things. The dreamers had departed, leaving behind the sturdy, causal world of clerks and bankers. But the madness still poured from the gargoyles and caryatids, the foaming light of the fountains, the great park swards going off under the trees. Who could say it had died, rolled over for good? Impossible. It was too much a part of the mind's expectations not to exist in some form or other forever.

The Seine rises from a spring near Dijon and is named after the Celtic goddess Sequanna. Its source had been a Celtic shrine; when it was drained in 1963 workers found hundreds of votive offerings in it. The river runs through the city like a sine curve, arched, majestical, a figure as old as the universe with its crest and descent to the southwest. Whatever it has become, it called my father back to go hunting for his own Paris when I was a child. I remember following him around to all his war-time haunts. He pointed out the rooms, the windows even, where he had stayed as a young intelligence officer. Already he had been assigned the job of stalking, questioning, hunting down war criminals. But he had known a kind of raw, delicious freedom here, and he wanted to relive it, even with my feet echoing behind him. I smiled, I listened, I drifted off to the sound of his voice remembering the nights, the days of a winter in Paris. It was pure joy, and pure sorrow – he was older.

Now it was my turn. And there she lay, the great trenches of granite rippling with windows and iron balconies and flower pots, and the dripping of rain gutters. It was here, it was perfume, it was the mesh of light seeping into the ivy walls, the moist, rotting fences of back gardens, the secret gray rooms with their soft beds and the sleepers within them, tucked down, buried under the pagan dust of their Gallic blood.

"The real France," the historian Jules Michelet remarked, "is northern France." I suppose it is, since the *langue d'oil*, the language of yes, dominates the country, and is the official dialect of the nation. There are two French cultures, the one centered in Paris, the other anchored by Marseille. "Africa begins at Lyon," Charles de Gaulle is supposed to have said. The south belongs to the other way of saying yes, the *langue d'oc*. The two have never got along. But then Milan has always distrusted southern Rome, and New York never had much love for southern Washington D.C. Two Frances, polarized, at odds with how to live the good life. But something even more persistently French flows under the two halves of the country. Albritton had put it well.

"A lingering magic, perhaps. Habits go deep in France. They eat well and drink deep because they still believe spirits are in their food. They associate taste and pleasure with communion," he said, lifting his own glass. "That much is redemptive. The Protestants are never good cooks, have you noticed? America is a heathen nation, to judge by its food. England is a disgraceful backslider as well. Don't go near a Dutch kitchen, it's full of Luther's admonitions. But I don't encourage you to think of the city as a capital of good food any longer. The gods are gone; the food is like an echo out of time."

Perhaps it was there, crossing the cool, abandoned streets on the way home, I suddenly knew my trek across Europe to all the literary haunts would be a waste of time. The Paris that was, that had been imagined, hungered for by my own countrymen of sixty years ago, had turned to stone.

Chapter Six

"J'ai Un Crayon"

o too my students on a tour of Europe through the eyes of American writers. One rainy morning I stood alone in a Zurich cemetery, under my umbrella, staring at the jaunty figure of James Joyce sculpted in white stone, seated before his grave smoking a cigarette, musing behind thick lenses on the ineluctable modality of the visual. Another foreigner who had beat out his exile. No one came with me on this last little journey before the trip ended. They were weary of travel, broke, homesick, indifferent to surroundings; they wanted to go home and forget about Americans trying to find themselves in foreign countries.

But something had broken through during our plodding trek across the continent. There was more to America than inventors and business-men. This much they glimpsed through their glazed expressions and occasional hangovers. The thought that someone as elemental as Hemingway might labor over his own identity, and seriously struggle to articulate it, and lavish on himself and his sex some treatment of myths – well, it raised the thin, penciled eyebrows of a young Texas woman loaded with purchases, who pursed her lips briefly and thought of her tough father. Perhaps, she told me nervously, perhaps he was more complicated than she thought.

But for the majority of students, Europe was a bore. It hadn't moved fast enough; it was dragging its past behind like a ball and chain. The sooty monuments were all right, but none of them addressed the era that opened before them. Had Europe been napping all this century? Had it missed the occasion of so much violence and social drift? Were there no marble statues of punks, or teenagers hunched over their Gameboys? All these sober faces in museums gave no glimmer of the road ahead. They all stared out from their small window of time and gave no sign of prophecy. Or so my students believed.

They went through all these symbolic landscapes with the same literal-mindedness they brought to a page of writing. They read granite as stone, and parks as grass and pathways, and the vast domes of churches as mounds of hammered copper. The figurative universe behind such things lay hidden, inaccessible. They were the refined product of an America that had successfully rid itself of Europe's imagination. The symbolic world of memory and desire evaporated from their gaze and let stand in all its forlorn nudity a chipped block of stone covered in webs and soot, which they passed without a second look. Though on its meager platform stood the body of Winged Victory, the muscular wings struggling to lift the whole edifice of flesh above Samothrace into visionary air. But we dawdled less than a moment on the stairs and passed her by.

These young countrymen had simplified the world into their personal needs; nothing else existed, or if it did, belonged to that marginal second tier of things that recalled the past. This was their only acknowledgment of the impersonal universe, the infinity that lay beyond their immediate cares. I found their attitude menacing and powerful, a stunning refinement of ego and its strict radius of desires. Their brisk minds took in vast quantities of life and unerringly chose the few things that mattered personally to them: food, clothes, expensive cars, their own kind. The rest was detritus and hardly mattered. There was always the racing pulse of the sexual in their movements, thoughts, their quick chatter, their jerkiness and blunt emotions. Nothing rested in them; the lectures went slow and they squirmed over the dull stretches; the journeys were long and they played cards with frantic interest. They were shiny creatures from the New World who found the past painful to contemplate. It refused them a place, and seemed a rusty gate that had swung shut behind them. We had raised them out of a handful of premises that cut all connection to this other world, in whose ruins and dirt lay secrets of the body, the vast testament of love that should have struck awe in them.

They raced through life grabbing at possibilities, using them up as if the earth were on fire and wouldn't last. The past confused their knowledge; it should have withered and disappeared long ago, and yet lights burned in ancient windows and music poured out of old gardens, and robed lawyers climbed the worn steps of darkened law courts with their clients. What kept such past alive when all else in their lives perished the moment it was consumed? If they could have answered such a question, it might have led to larger thoughts – the timeless rhythms of nature, its eternal renewal.

On my soggy evening with Albritton, he had waxed eloquent on the subject of British pride: "They paint good portraits of themselves," he said, "to celebrate their individuality. They don't paint countryside much;

too vague. They like to see their own gobs in the foreground, with house and garden sprawled out behind like parts of their bodies. They worship at their own shrines, you might say. British mugs hang in all the musems and country houses, but you don't see much painting of things that aren't property. An Englishman is a hard-boiled egg whom you have to mash down before he'll mix with anything. Two hundred years of the Raj and we brought back snooker, a few spices and words from the oldest culture in the world. I call that being difficult, don't you?"

In Raleigh Travelyan's painting, *The Golden Oriole*, the only touch of India are the servants holding litters and waiting attendance, or the lush foliage climbing the hill to an English country house. Croquet wickets and mallets claim the soil for England. They had brought their own world with them and did not want another race to penetrate their psyche. They sit in fabulous attire staring out of the eyes of a sceptered island, aloof and water-bound. That same hermetic seal kept my students in check, and permitted them to walk through their own history with polite indifference. Somehow Anglo-Saxon solitude had stolen across the Atlantic with the migrations; we were all gathered behind its pale.

When I got back to Paris an invitation came to teach in Kuala Lumpur, and I promptly accepted. We packed up hastily and rushed home, rented out our Bryan house and flew off to the equator for a year. The children were put into the international school, and we both went out to the nearby jungle fringe to teach Malays our language and literature. There I could witness the disappearance of empire down to the empty plinth on which a statue of Queen Victoria once rested. Apparently Malaysia was now a laboratory for socio-linguists; I met one over dinner in Singapore, Lester Faigley, who told me English was disappearing here faster than anywhere else in the world. He had come to observe the phenomenon, as if people were being struck dumb in the streets. They were speaking Bahasa Malayu instead, and dabbling at English in college. The white world was withdrawing, its borders shrinking back from global hegemony. The Malays danced out on the campus basketball court at night, a willowy ballet composed of thin, agile men weaving and stepping in unison, with the jungle rising up under the twilit sky behind them.

When our year was almost over, we went up to one of the hill stations to escape the heat. There were bungalows scattered around a retreat once used by British officers recovering from war. It was going to seed and the bungalows were big, gloomy buildings without much charm, but a few days of cool mountain weather usually revived us.

Cathy and I sat out on a wall overlooking the rain forest one evening, chatting about Provence. We missed it. It had formed into a kind of opium dream during our year away, a lush, vague place full of blossoms and cool winds, a place of seasons and change. It popped into my mind that she should stay on in Provence with the kids while I went back alone to teach for a semester. I would return in spring for a sabbatical. Why not? We would put the children into French schools and start taking down our own borders with the world. We went in to supper giddy with new plans.

I had thought a lot about Provence during my year away. I was glad to be going back, to pin down all my impressions to something definite, concrete again. My journal was full of recollections, snippets of dialog, sketches of the landscape, everything loose and disorganized. No central impression or idea of the place. But I was haunted by it; it had an importance that ran beyond my thoughts. I would while away the hours in my little cement closet on the campus at Shah Alam, looking out into the gray shaggy jungle wondering what it was about Provence that gripped me.

Perhaps it was just coincidence in 1988, but everything I read seemed an angry indictment of my race and sex. The press bristled with accusations; the white male seemed to be the source of every malady and curse on the planet. Not a day passed without some new disclosure of corruption, deceit, mismanagement laid at his feet. The white male was cold, scheming, angry at nature, bent on his own exclusive power over others, a tyrant over women, a bad parent, a racist and persecutor, with monsters like Hitler, Mussolini, Stalin and Franco as models of the tribe. Hardly a point on the map of white civilization survived without its scandals, ravages, and misery as the hands of this contaminated sex.

And there was little Provence eking out its natural life under the boughs of the olive trees. It was hardly innocent of violence and treachery over its long evolution, but there remained the evidence of some overwhelming goodness in men that couldn't be dismissed. They remained lovers of the earth, good guardians and patient priests of the land. My heart ached for such a place, because it stood for something blameless and right about men. The developers were coming, the ruinous expansion of commerce was tearing up fields and farms, and a parade of limousines was heading down from Paris to take control of the new cash cow of France. But the swarthy men still chugged along on their tractors, and the monks sang in the abbeys, and the husbands, thin, brown, wearing shorts, smiled serenely at their naked wives sprawled on the beaches at Hyères.

The white vision had not separated from death or mystery there; its fullness and joy could be felt on first contact. Marseille brought in all the good things of earth to supply the Provençal table – all sat down in gardens and dining rooms to feast on Indian eggplant, American red pepper, Greek olives and Roman bread, South American beans, the wild grasses of the local hills, a celebration of the sun's path around the world. The spoken word is a patois of Spanish, Italian, Latin and old French, the slurs and stammers of Provençal, bits of Greek, the great sluice of the mouth from all the coasts of the Mediterranean.

Perhaps we conferred more innocence and pleasure on the farmers of the region, on the festivals and the old ways than is there; but we did so in honor of this haven of sensual good health. It was a psychological cleansing to step into one of its villages and know your small indulgences formed part of a great embrace. The pressures of urban life relaxed, and one awoke long dormant emotions by walking, eating, stretching out in the sun.

The arts that sprang from Provence celebrated this surviving wholeness in Western life. The Post-Impressionists burst upon a dingy, pre-war Europe with these images of sensuous youth, the pagan garden of the race. It had not been lost. If one wanted racial forgiveness, a sense of grace or innocence, it came through the pores of the skin while standing in the full sun of a vineyard. The vines grew out of a fertile relation between man and world that has survived the turmoil of millennia.

One could forgive the poor tourists who came there from all parts of the soiled, polluted continent, and from points beyond. They were no different from the pilgrims who had marched through on the way to the holy shrines. They were coming from large cities where nature had been ruined, and were there to be cleansed, to renew their faith in the organic world. They brought their artificiality and greed with them; they partly despoiled the thing they had come to enjoy; they displaced the native life and customs by their presence, but they came as sinners to repent, to be reborn in the old covenant, and go home again tanned, healthy, reinvigorated. Who could blame them for seeking such relief? Who would grouse against the California towns that had borrowed Provence's style, as if to say, here too we may be washed in the blood of the sun, even if we've chased the gods away?

I had had enough of preaching democracy in the shadow of Vietnam, of staring into the eyes of pious Moslems and reading their distrust. I came back to Provence with the gravity of one returning from exile who is chastened and forgiven.

It was evening when we arrived and were driven up to Goult by my friend Gustaf. He left us there with our suitcases in a dark living room, our children numbly climbing up to bed after the long journey from Malaysia. I hauled up luggage and stumbled about in the unfamiliar rooms, and came down again to sit in the small, warm living room with a glass of wine, our first in a long while. It tasted of prune and rusty chains and leather, the hard, sour barn smells of an August day – followed by a wave of thin, ghostly sweetness that mingled in the breath and cooled our noses. We drank the ground and sky and it welcomed us.

I got up to explore the kitchen before retiring; it was cozy and efficient, with long rows of spice jars, a good stove, all the essentials for making French meals. A window was dark behind a shutter; I flipped a light switch on the wall and dragged the side door open. There was a small, crowded garden outside, guarded by long, spindly hollyhocks, a walk way that passed down into the obscurity of the yard below. The odor was of warm weeds and stone, the heavy scent of roses bunched on a trellis on the far wall. I shut the door, and we trudged heavily to bed to sleep long and motionless through the first night.

It was already ten when we awoke; the sill of our window was bathed in a milky sunlight, and there were bees droning on the window panes. Below stood the small street that wound around through shadows to the road passing down to Roussillon. The house was bright and cheerful, and smelled good. Someone had made coffee in a neighboring house, and its pungent aroma was almost like music. We went down, pulled open the garden door, threw back shutters, drifted around in the radiance making coffee and breakfast while the children slept. It was August, the hot month, and there were no breezes to speak of.

We sat down under the tangle of vines along the house and drank our coffee at a small table. Women passed by slowly, looking in at us as they uttered a soft, musical *"bonjour, madame et monsieur."* It was like a benediction to us. A child came down rubbing his eyes and sat without talking; there were gray little bags under his eyes. He was disoriented, trying to wake up with the wrong body clock. Another came in and sat down, slit-eyed against the brilliance. A third was in the kitchen looking for cereal. Their world went on seamlessly, over borders and continents, with a wild innocence that ignored all our human distinctions. It was another morning under the same old sun, and it was time to eat.

Goult has a fine castle that once belonged to the Agoult family, powerful barons of the region who married into the Simianes east of here, and tied up most of the farms and villages of the Vaucluse. They fought occasionally with the bishops of Apt and with other barons, but for the most part collected their tithes and rents and lived well. The Revolution ended the old political structure, but the memory of the separate towns and their relations to one another survives in subtle ways. Goult is remote and not much given to tourism. The people here are still pleasantly provincial and follow the quaint customs. The bar has a few chairs outside where teenagers like to flirt; the square is empty most of the time, though a circus came through and set up its little tent in a corner. A man with a dog-and-pony show performed for a handful of kids and one or two moms, while his wife ran the stereo for each act.

Another time tents were put up and a few artisans displayed furniture and pottery, and the wine makers came to sell a few bottles and give free tastes. The town turned out, but it was a small affair and after a day it was gone again. The *épicerie* was well-stocked and run by a cheerful woman and her daughter. It was fun to shop there, though prices were steep. A church on the square had a side room used by artists to exhibit paintings. One sultry day we strolled around with a few villagers to look at the work. There were no geniuses around, only a few shy attempts to paint one's gratitude for the light or the wild flowers.

We took all our meals in the garden, around the little white table piled up with baguettes, olives, crusty little cakes of goat cheese, the spicy sausage called *merguez*, sliced peppers, and couscous. We ate ravenously; we lingered and talked. We were outdoing each other with praise for some garden or mountain view or stroll around the village. Everyone took off and found something new to report back at dinner. Night walks especially were a pleasure – to go drifting around through narrow streets, under the arched passage of the castle and up to the brow of a steep hill, where some ruins were scattered around and a few crookedly standing houses looked out over the valley.

Goult seemed to have several personalities, as villages often do. Along one side were small, shady little dwellings where young families and pensioners lived in cluttered rooms. The food always smelled rich and spicy coming from their windows. The TV blasted away in a back room and there were occasional cries of a baby followed by the low, rough-edged voice of a mother. Another side, going up the hill to the top of the town, took the full sun and view of the hills. These houses were larger, the windows hung with lace-work that blew back on polished chairs. There were touches of Parisian taste, good sofas, a set of framed prints of wild flowers and fruit, smooth, silvery-white walls bathed in shadows.

Much of the town lay within a grid of tiny streets where the oldest families lived. These were the quietest, with hardly a whimper from their rooms, and only the soft, sweet smell of roses from the garden. A few summer residents had infiltrated the quarter, but they were obvious with their smart brown shutters and trim stonework. One foreigner's house had taken over several smaller dwellings and connected them with courtyards and passageways. I toured it one afternoon when the German owner was away, a man high up in the management of Volkswagen, or was it Coca-Cola? The place had a forced gaiety about it; rooms were strung out over a maze of hallways, many of them dark and gloomy, serving as foyers or vestibules to other rooms. It had been designed for summer parties and long week-ends, and had lost whatever practicality the rooms had in earlier days.

At the gate to our own little place stood a fine house with an iron trellis. Its long windows were shuttered fast, but the green of the slats had faded into pale ochre. It was for sale; a hand-painted sign hung on the door with a telephone number underneath. The larger rooms looked out to the road; the north wall was stark and windowless; to the east lay a scrubby garden close, rife with weeds and thorn bushes. A ragged broom had spread its wicker shoots all through a rose arbor. But there were echoes in the garden, behind the iron palings, where children had once played and adults fallen in love. You could almost hear their voices whispering in the lost paths. It was a dry house full of memories, with a hushed and formal sadness about it.

It stood there waiting for a buyer all the month we lived behind it. Only once did someone go in to look it over with an agent, but came out soon after and went away. The sign stayed; it was a house too much in town, too large for ordinary use, too expensive for the average buyer. It would weather out its limbo; it had solid walls and a sturdy roof. But its life now spoke darkly of things to come – it was another sign the past was closing, slipping away from the living world.

That is what made Goult fascinating to us, its links to another era: the elderly and the middle aged sauntered along with straw hats and shopping bags going about their errands, carting up wine from Lumières, having small dinner parties on the long, vacant Sundays we idled in our garden. They had no need of strangers or summer visitors. Their lives were balanced and content; you could hear their clear, honest laughter over the stone walls. They were asleep in time, going by the habits passed down to them. There were times they came out wearing their formal best, the men careful and slow as they walked along, a cane or umbrella to steady them, followed by their wives and married daughters, who wore all the colors of the rainbow and smelled like a morning rain scented with lilacs.

They were here as the final flowering, the last bloom of the past. Behind them would come agents to sell their houses, and the eras would give way to one another. We were seeing traditions that might be ending with our own lives, whose origins lay deep in the cemeteries down the road. Sometimes a house would be filled with guests, music playing softly on the radio, with the tinkle of wine glasses and the raucous laughter of relatives. Smells of roast lamb wafted through the iron grills and a flutter of pink and white dresses floated behind the lifted curtain. Someone had come of age, perhaps, or was engaged; some turning of the axis of the world had occasioned this gathering, closed to the general public and the prying eyes of tourists like me.

How I loved this brittle, spun-glass world, with all its privacy and custom. I did not want to break in on it. It was best savored from this distance, out on the sidewalk, where I could hear and imagine all the intricacy of its rites. At night, the houses bloomed with lamp light, and there were short, echoing resonances in the words spoken in stone rooms. The ceilings were strung with varnished, blackened beams, and the white walls were hung with paintings of the fields and hills. The money had filtered down from farms and other businesses, accumulated through wills and marriages, and pooled in the accounts of these living links of the chain.

Along the back slopes were small farm houses with a placid, unstirred air about them, as if nothing could disturb the roofs and polished tables and worn tiles and nonchalance, not even war. I liked strolling down that way, with the dogs coming out to look me over, deciding I could pass without trouble. I would run my eyes over the little vineyards, the barn with its Massey-Ferguson parked outside, the water hoses coiled up on a spigot, dripping into the green scum of a gutter. It was life as it should be, somnolent, dreamy, silent and unhurried. Mosses grew along the back wall of the house, its old cement gleaming like onyx from the oil and tires that had moldered there. Timeless and still, everything tucked into its accustomed place.

There were tufts of lavender and great showy bushes of rosemary along the drives; sills bloomed with geraniums, hydrangeas, violets, and pansies. A kitchen garden was crammed with mint, chamomile bushes loaded with white blossoms, basil and artichoke plants, tomato vines, fennel, sprigs of woodbine, a scraggly sorrel tree. Its variety came from compost and dropped or blown seeds, the gifts of neighbors, the original plan long since forgotten. A dog slept under the branches of an almond tree, among the fallen green nuts.

In the evening, after supper and dishes, we would sit in the garden and repeat the French lessons I made up. None of the children spoke any French yet; they had picked up a few words from our stay in Croagnes, but almost everyone they met that summer spoke English. Now it was time to knuckle under; they were going to attend school in another month. So, repeat after me, but carry a tune please:

> *J'ai un crayon*! (DAH dum de-dum)
> *Tu as un crayon*! (Ta-DAH um de-dum)
> *Il a, elle a un crayon*!

Again,

> *Nous avons un crayon* (Da-dah DUM dah de-dum)
> *Vous avez un crayon*! (Da-da DEE dum de-dah)
> *Ils ont, elles ont un crayon*!

Voila! Your first verb. We sang our conjugations for a few minutes and I would say a few more words. It was slow work, but no one was really trying to learn just yet. It was fun, and the songs were something they would hum around the house. My running joke with them was no breakfast if they couldn't sing the tune. We ate heartily afterward.

There were moments when I worried about the outcome of our plans. I didn't like going back alone, staying in our big house by myself, trying to run the whole operation and keep money flowing across the Atlantic. But it was only for the semester. The other worry was whether the kids would pick up French quickly enough. This was their window for learning a new language; if they got it now, their tongues would learn how to curl into those rolled r's and arch up for diphthongs. If not, they would have soggy tongues that would never get to the music of true French.

After a year of listening to highly-inflected Chinese and the click-clong of Bahasa, it was evident we English speakers hardly used our mouths at all in speech. Everything slid off the lips and hissed through partly clenched teeth; you could say almost anything in English without moving your lower jaw. Marlon Brando certainly could; Clint Eastwood was adept at talking without facial motions. George Bush made political hay with "Read my lips," but his mouth had few moving parts. It was more of a challenge than he thought.

To speak French or Italian requires the use of the whole mouth and lips, and a tongue that can coil, hoop itself, spring, flutter, go flat, swell, bat the air, and whip the teeth at dizzying speeds. A good talker, a Parisian, can rev up his chatter to the speed of a whirring lawn mower, and make perfect, lovely sense to his listener. An Italian can go even faster, but the music seems a bit worn, the syllables rutted and grooved in the mouth like a cobbled street. It was lovely to listen to good French in the streets below our bedroom window; the music rose and fell in such voices, the melodic patter reaching toward singing and easing back again to talk.

But there was never mere talk: the mouth is all in France. It must kiss, and suck, and purse, and smile, and laugh and eat, and drink, and devour with all the force of its hundred tiny muscles. Speech from such mouths made you realize that in the body's geography certain nerves converged to form a rich delta of sensation that longs for arousal. To speak is the parallel of good eating: the vowels must be chewed forth into the listener's ear, and savored on the tongue for every morsel of their flavor and meaning before being generously scattered to the air.

Good speech tenses up the rest of the body; a woman preparing to talk rises slightly on her feet, pulls in her arms for better leverage to gesture, fills her chest with air, tightens her stomach, uses all the powers of her neck to swivel and nod the head. When talk begins, her eyes roam like search lights for body language and facial approval, and her voice covers the full register of its larynx, stretching every nerve of its ganglia to produce glorious, musical words. And not just words, but a vast oral tradition rich in figures and tropes, a wide range of colors and humors, and a complete system of tones and body rhythms. A good, intimate conversation on the street between three strong women is a concert, an orchestral suite, whose responses will have stirred every hollow and bundle of muscle in their bodies. If information passes between them, it is incidental to the elaborate music of their encounter.

When morning talk began within earshot, I would hike up on my elbow in bed to drink in the whole thing. I would catch half of it; sometimes a voice would lower and fall into a river of gliding syllables, then rise again on a laugh, and soar up into the shrillest reaches to punctuate some wildly funny ending. Then another voice would start sober and low, in full agreement with the ironies now established. But the second voice, entering somberly like a cello, would rephrase the leading theme in its own artful variation, inviting the viola to counterpoint the fugue with its own tale of woe or humor, as all three reached a crescendo of laughter and began again.

Sometimes a man's blurry, staccato voice would break the silence, followed by the screeches of a child arguing back, concluded by the full, rich tonalities of a clarinet-voiced woman who would put the matter to rest. Dinner resumed with the thin scrape of forks, the long pauses of silence as glasses were drained. I listened intently for these lonely, provocative noises in the dark of a Goult evening, as the little village smoldered in tawny gleams of moonlight and the slivers of street lamps, moving through the ritual of dinner like a ship drifting on the endless sea.

Gustaf had arranged for us to rent a small vacation house at Les Martins, one of the hamlets below Gordes, which meant we could enroll our children in the local school of this wealthy commune. We were delighted. The house itself was of an odd shape, long and narrow, and had once been the hamlet's laundry shed. It belonged to a distinguished family, the Ignatieffs. George, the patriarch, had been the Canadian ambassador to Moscow in his prime; he was long retired, and his wife, a pale and delicate woman, was already in the first stages of Alzheimers. They had the refined and effacing manners of the well to do, and their son, Michael, was a familiar face on the BBC as an anchorman to a daily show of commentary and interviews, who later became known in the U.S. as a writer for the *New York Times* and as an advocate for war in Iraq. He was a good friend of Gustaf's. Portraits of St. George, the dragon slayer, were hung here and there, along with Russian icons and other stuff of a long and leisurely vacation life in France. The long open front where clothes would be beaten and hung to dry was now filled in with a line of double doors opening onto a terrace. The wash basins lay hidden under a wooden stage where we put up beds for the children. The other end of the long central hall formed a dining room, with a brazier built against the wall beside the dining table.

The kitchen was at one end of the house, and the rest of the bed-rooms at the other. We spent a good deal of time walking the length of the building to get from our small apartment to the kitchen fifty feet away. Cathy and I took the little apartment with its own door to the terrace, and a mezzanine bedroom under the roof beams. Below was a small fireplace that belched smoke all winter, and a tiny bathroom with a sitz bath. We were snug and happy in our new lodgings, with the long terrace beckoning to us each sunny morning.

Outisde lay a sloping lawn that dropped down to an ancient pond full of goldfish. A spring burbled into the dark water. Beyond lay a tilting lavender field that ran off into a wide plain, with the Luberon stretched out beyond. To the left was a creek nourishing the wild poplars that soared into a shaggy archway full of whispering leaves.

Back when properties were cheap in Provence, some families got together and bought up the farms in this hamlet, shared out the properties and each rebuilt a dwelling for their vacations. They would meet in summer and have parties and bring in other cronies from their foreign service days; the kids grew up playing in the back yards and swimming in the neighbor's pool. There were good times here in the 1960s. The elders were now frail and didn't come as often; some had died off and left their houses to the children. The parties dwindled down to a Fourth of July bash at Peggy Ferguson's house down the path. The place had the atmosphere of one of those New England lakes where the well-to-do once spent old-fashioned summer holidays. You expected to find a wooden canoe hung up in the rafters of a shed, but there were no lakes here.

Gustaf and I filled in the papers for getting the kids into school and went up to the mayor's office in Gordes to have them stamped. A meeting had been set for nine and we arrived early to the mayor's ornate office, with its fine windows looking out over the streets of Gordes. Everyone was hard at work poring over ledgers and *cadastres*, the town plats, which had been scrawled over many times with elaborate notes. The great volumes opened with a puff of dust and a ghostly sigh. Here was the legendary French clerk hard at her discipline, ferreting out the elusive facts and figures within the great wickerwork of words and figures filling each page. My soul itched at the sight of so much dullness and inertia, but these young, attractive women seemed almost giddy with excitement as they sped around and guided their pencils into crevices of print to change some digit or add a character. Their eyes were bright, their faces clean and open, mouths humorous and poised to laugh.

Two of the women were very pretty and small built. One stood finally to her full height of five feet and brought the room to a halt with her beautiful body. Large breasts swelled under a soft, pink sweater, and her every movement danced with voluptuous shadows. She was aware of herself and caught us both staring at her with American wonder, but a generous smile bloomed and vanished as she strutted off for more ledgers. No one minded this brief distraction, or lost a second in the work each did. A large man with a round head leaned intently over his calculator as the stub of one puffy finger flew like a ballet dancer over the keys. He was expert and magical, adding with one hand and recording with the other. It made all this drudgery seem attractive to see it done with confidence.

When the mayor arrived, the air crackled with his entrance. He was short, crisp, thickly set, wearing a well-tailored suit and a fine raincoat.

He slid from his coat while one of his staff caught it deftly in his fingers and swung it up on the coat rack. The two women stood up to be kissed, and he held each by the shoulders and kissed them on the cheeks three times. They sat down promptly as he conferred with associates and turned briskly to greet us with handshakes.

We sat down to business with the mayor and his subordinate, a tall man with a soft, haggard expression who did all the talking. The mayor studied his manicured fingernails and rubbed his hands luxuriously while it was explained that we had chosen the wrong school for the children. They must attend the larger school in Gordes, not the hamlet school just down our road. My friend objected, and the talk rose higher by a note and sped up. I lost the French. Tensions grew and chairs got pushed closer as my friend and the mayor's man leaned into each other and fired off volleys of rapid, popping French at each other. My friend's voice dipped low, then rose and cracked like a whip, and the mayor responded with a single, high-pitched syllable at which the associate paused, veered round and changed his attitude. Something had snapped, and now everything fell into place, as if the mistral had just blown itself out.

It seems, as I learned over coffee afterward, they had a plan to centralize schooling at Gordes and to close all the surrounding hamlet schools. It was a cost-saving measure, one of the mayor's projects for trimming redundancy in the system. But the little schools offered more teacher contact and smaller classes, better meals at lunch, and more activities. The hamlet schools were good and couldn't be closed so long as attendance stayed high. My children might be saving the little school at Les Imberts, hence the fight.

But the mayor didn't like having two Americans argue with him; it didn't look good. The secretaries had made a face when the voices got hot. Now things were cooling down. We were home free, I thought, but it was a good long while before all the ceremony of the occasion could end. Talk flourished with great verbal arpeggios and long solo digressions on both sides, and finally, like wind murmuring after a storm, the talking died down to a haunting, barely audible lament. The differences were resolved, the sky was calm and clear again, and besides, it was well past the hour one should have his mid-morning coffee.

Our honorable mayor stood up to his full five and half feet of Napole-onic bearing, shook our hands smartly, papers were signed and initialed and copies made, and off we went. The kids were in at Les Imberts and the mayor was satisfied we would be gone after a year. After which, if one can interpret things by the lift of eyebrows, the school would be home to sparrows and straying vines.

I marveled at my friend's pluck and told him so. He looked pleased. He told me their game was all front and no back. They were trying out their scheme on us, and had no real power to keep the children out of the local school. Besides, why go to the wall over two American kids who would be out after a year? Once he knew that, he said, he could raise his voice and back them off. But there it was, the moment just at the beginning, where the Latin mind revealed itself – the quick fight, chest expanded, the mouth fully engaged, voice deep and large, the overpowering physical aggression that springs out of the human body like some wild spirit warding off challengers, scaring adversaries. I would have folded surely; all that noise would have ended it for me. But not for him. He knew the tactics, even loved their purpose, their showy ceremonial character. It was a cockfight full of spread wings and eyeball challenges, but no swords lashed to the ankle for a real kill. Just show. But good Latin show, operatic, superb, and above all a celebration of the mouth as the great organ of the human spirit.

How wonderful is the mouth that dominates the Latin face, and gives and takes so much. At the café afterward, I saw such beautiful and powerful mouths purse and draw coffee up sip by sip, and then savor, swallow, and speak with that luxurious fullness that wrings the soul dry.

I was treated to the sight of a woman nibbling a small tart with her coffee: those supple lips that were speaking one moment with pure rubbery ecstasy now firmed and clenched and ovaled to receive a morsel of singed pear. The teeth did the rest, then the tongue intellectualized over the contents, and the throat dispatched the results to another bureau. But the mouth was in love with itself, singing and nurturing and shuttling wind and words and flavors all at once, while a man watched and listened in a bewitched state.

We were packing up once more, regretfully, I think; we liked our little house and garden, our life in this village. Goult lived on apart from the coming roar of tourism and commercial development. It sat on its hilltop like an elegant dame, aloof, contemplative, well-dressed, decaying gracefully under the warm sun and the slow, silvery rain.

J'ai un crayon
Tu as un crayon
Il a, elle a un crayon!

Chapter Seven

Changelings

Now that the family was staying on for a year, I decided it was time to buy a car. There were dealers along the N-100 going into Apt, and after a bit of comparison shopping I decided on Renault. They kept a few used cars on the lot, parked among the large new models hung with astonishing price tags. Even the used cars weren't bargains. One green car, ten years old, sat behind the garages looking suitably passed over. It had the sad, unadoptable look of a dog at the pound. I rather liked it, but had no idea if it ran or was even for sale. The manager seemed a bit impatient when my eyes fell on the thing. He was still pointing off to some other prettier model going for a steep sum.

I kept edging closer, peeking inside at the odometer – which was right up to the limit of zeroes. Good tires, not a bad body. Hood looking a bit pale, half a shade lighter than the rest. I heard him begin a pitch about it, officer in the Foreign Legion. . . kept it up, single-owner car. I arranged for a mechanic to take it for a drive, and off we went down a little single-lane road at bolt-stripping speeds. He liked the car, he said, very solid. Nice buy.

Price was cheap, about two thousand dollars, I think. They would do all the paper work, a formidable task, as I would later discover with another car. I signed papers, gave them cash, and drove the car back to Goult. I came up through the backyard and parked it near the garden. It was a good car, light green, big brown seats, soft and comfortable. Large engine, a regular guzzler. Not too smart at four dollars the gallon for the premium it drank. But wheels finally. We hadn't had any. We were walkers, and occasionally cadged a ride into Apt from friends.

Now we had a sedan which purred and rolled out smoothly, and went along without complaints. Power windows, a quiet interior, no air conditioning. Down we rolled into the cool, shaded back roads to Rousillon so the children could play in the ochre pits. These lunar towers and crevasses were all made of a friable crust stained with iron ore that wore away under the weather into fantastic forms. It is like a miniature Grand Canyon with bruised-red mesas and deep fissures lined with yellow and rusty earth. The ochre was mined and sold to the textile industry for dying clothes. It once gave a cowboy's bandanna its red color, among other things.

During WWII, the U.S. stopped importing French ochre and used cochineal and artificial coloring, and the mines closed. They were used briefly as mushroom farms and then the tunnels were abandoned. Tourists like to clamber up the soft sandy paths, getting bright yellow and red from the dust, to explore all the nooks and crannies of the pits. They stand their wives and husbands up against the rims of these abysses and take their photos, with the wind pushing them back on their heels, like a scene out of a Hitchcock movie. Kids go sliding down some of the smaller cliffs, but below them hang dark openings that could send them sprawling another fifty or a hundred feet. No one seemed to worry, then. Years later, they built railings and hung warning signs about the dangers.

We hung on to ours as they went up the path and headed for the first tunnel, a round shaft plunging into the mountainside. It went back and ended in a blunt wall, as if the dye seam ran out at that point. Others roamed around deep inside the mountains where the mushroom farms were set up; the wooden boxes where they were grown were still scattered around in some of the passageways. Afterward, we dusted off all the powder from their clothes, washed off hands and faces under the little spring at the end of the path, and found a table at the village café. Our car sat out in the sun looking a bit more personal now.

When I mentioned cowboy bandannas to my friend in Lacoste one afternoon, he brightened.

"What about his pants?" Gustaf asked.

Pants?

"They were woven in Nimes, where you get the word denims, *de Nimes*. They were tailored in Genoa, hence jeans."

The boots were introduced by gauchos, who brought them from southern Spain. They also brought their sombreros from there as well, and took them into Texas through colonial Mexico. The cowboy came from the marshes of Provence, the Andalucian desert, and other regions of the Mediterranean. His closest relative now works the cattle ranches of the Camargue, south of Arles, where he rides the famous white ponies of the Rhône delta. There is a distinct resemblance between our Texas cowboys and the *gardiens* of the Camargue, who raise the black bulls for the arenas at Arles and Fontvieille.

We sat admiring the afternoon parade of tourists and locals going past the square up into the cork-screw streets of Roussillon. There is a clearing at the top of the village where a large round dial gives you the names of all the hills and the distances of cities north and east of Provence. Mt. Ventoux sits up above the smoky ridges, hard, bald, alone in its brooding prominence. It is said that this granite peak is the force that cools the mistral during winter, giving it an icy edge before it whips down on innocent little towns like Roussillon.

In the late 1300s, Petrarch, the inventor of the sonnet, climbed up to the top and told his friends he could make out the Atlantic and the Mediterranean from there. Some have seen the Mediterranean, and others the beginning of the Pyrenees, but not both seas. You can sometimes pick out Mont Blanc in the long, shimmering chain of alps going up to Switzerland. Petrarch was the first, so it is said, to climb a mountain for sport. And perhaps he told the first mountain-climbing story as well, cousin to the fish and the bear stories.

Facing the clearing and the stone dial are houses with powerful walls and small, fortified windows for taking the brunt of mistrals each spring. A few ragged gardens stand out on the edge of the cliff where the land drops into the valley running below Croagnes and Gordes. These gardens are windswept and bitter, like those along the Maine coast. There is something permanently wintry and defensive about the cliff houses here, which stare off into the formless depths behind Mt. Ventoux as if trying to read the future.

But in Provence nothing remains one way for long. On the road down stood a flower garden, all the blossoms trembling in some mysterious draft. A large green weed sprawled out in thorny coils among the pansies and violets, blown there from the wilds. It had crawled among the regal irises to fondle their roots, while large bees floated above like nuggets of amber. The earth was black through the lattice of green stems, where a worm arched its glittering folds and slid into a hole with a velvet shrug.

The ride home was soft, the air silky and cool over our arms and legs. We coasted down the hills and purred along the valley roads with the wind rattling the almond trees and turning up the gray-green nuts under the leaves. There was a smell, sour at first, then round and deep as cigar smoke, pouring off the hills. The fields were hot and a light mist played over them from the irrigation nozzles, which jerked and veered round like dancers trying to fly, their wings made of diaphanous vapor trailing behind them.

Apt was busy, and very brittle under the full sun. The buildings were peeling, and the streets rang like metal under the tramp of shoppers. I felt despondent, as I often do when the light bleaches everything to the color of white bread. It brought back memories of childhood in Philadelphia, when my mother took long naps in the afternoon while I stood at the screen door watching figures shuffle along in the colorless void of our street. So Apt languished in this late August afternoon, white and decaying, paralyzed with torpor.

We wandered back to Goult for our last few things and left the house smelling clean and new again. I lingered over the garden of spindly hollyhocks and roses, the walls glinting with ladybugs. A sharp tang of herbs rose when I parted the leaves to pick a primrose hidden below, my souvenir of soft blue mornings at the table.

We brought down our bundles and suitcases, our bags of shoes and toilet kits and food boxes, our books and typewriters, our chattels and moveables from a wandering life, and put them in a heap in the dining room of the new house. We had arrived. We were making another footprint in the sand. I threw open the wide double doors of the terrace and light rolled in on the somnolent air of the room. We undid the beaded curtains, dragged the table and chairs out of the hot sun to the mulberry tree, which threw out a cone of cool gray shade.

We made beds and shook out throw rugs; I thumbed the books along the wall of the living room and found some good reading for winter nights. The drawers were crammed with pencil stubs and worn out playing cards tied up in rubber bands; yellowing notes and invitations to long forgotten exhibits; letters bound up in string from ten or twenty years ago. There were faded newspaper cuttings and scraps with recipes jotted on them. A memo book listed local restaurants with a rating system of checks beside them, and notes like "Too expensive," "Good service." There were packets of typing paper and envelopes, even stamps left in the little drawers of the secretary. My children could hardly keep their aching fingers out of all this treasure, but this was no ordinary rental house. It was someone's private dwelling, a life went on here like knitting, the stitch half purled to the needle. We had come in on a play in progress, and now stood around with our suitcases wondering where to join the plot.

The settling in would go on in earnest after I left. It was unpleasant to think I would be leaving soon on the train to Paris, saying goodbye to a family I had never left before. Now came the first test, the first crisis – with all the nervous adjustment that would take place in the long evenings when only one of us would be there. I could sympathize with all those characters in movies and novels being written out of the story, going off bravely with a wave from the train window.

I was, in fact, making my children relive my own experience of long separations from my father, who traveled to India and Africa all the while I grew up in a mother-only house in Beirut. Did not all this travel make fathers mysterious, men who seemed to die and return to life again bearded and wrinkled, full of strange silences? Even so, his going off threw us more deeply into foreign life. I don't know why, but having only a mother around taught you to be bolder, braver, more resourceful – perhaps from some obscure motive to replace his power in the house. I recall vividly how Beirut sank into our pores during his long stays in Africa; even my mother went out on her own, emboldened by other women left at home. We tumbled into matriarchal law, where sons were given their liberty and women held sway with dazzling flexibility. Dinners were late, days long, nights open to vast new possibilities.

I was the instrument of fate, changing my children's lives for good and all. I knew they would never be the same after this, but acquire another tongue and make it as familiar as English. Their minds would one night dream in French, and they would laugh in French, and smell French, and walk and talk and act in a new cultural rhythm. Beside it would be their Americanness, like a suit of clothes hung in the closet. They would revert to their own identity the moment a rock song hit the radio, or a friend called from Texas, or comic books arrived in the mail. But the soul would divide and there would be two sides to reality, two rooms through which they could pass freely.

The kids had seen their schoolhouse by now and had mixed feelings about it. The teachers were energetic; the older one, Mme. Courtasse, lived in a stately *mas* with orchards and gardens. She ruled the school with a firm but forgiving hand, and once invited my wife to a true Provençal Sunday dinner, seven courses in all, with walks in the garden before dessert. She was the product of countless generations of southern living and would pour her soul into my children when I left.

The younger teacher, Domi, spoke Provençal among her various skills. She took the greatest pleasure looking into the eyes of the two girls and reading something there. Domi belonged to a new generation of southern women who went on to higher schooling, and now had jobs of their own. Their husbands were farmers still, or worked menial jobs in town. Domi's husband ran a small farm and drove the school bus at Goult. There were dangers lurking in such marriages where men kept to farming and women modernized themselves and started careers.

Madame Courtasse was tall and elegant; we found ourselves doing all the smiling while she looked on, saying little. She had seen a lot of youth grow up around her; she knew their limits, their needs better than we. She was sizing up our own as we spoke and walked around. The schoolhouse was small, built sometime in the 1920s with the cautious faith Provence would remain as it was. It was inadequate for the community that now crowded into Les Imberts. Two rooms went off a central doorway, one for toddlers, the other for first and second graders. A matronly plane tree shaded the playground, its branches wagging fingers at all the horseplay that went on beneath it. The dining room was cheerful and drank in eastern light. There, amid the low murmurs of children, would sit the two teachers over an elaborate lunch, raising glasses of cold Chablis to start the meal.

Our children would be trained by the same hand that cut the vines back to blackened stumps, and bent the limbs of peach trees to espaliers. The children would be formed to an ideal, and pain would guide them. Their nurture would be graphs and figures and dates, knowledge stripped bare of petty inducements and revealed in all its Cartesian lucidity to minds not yet awake. There would be a vast repertoire of songs and stories and poems to be memorized, whose monotonous enchantment would wear away the edges of their individuality.

The French did not altogether trust children; they had no patience for the wild spirit they brought into the world. This they valued in their dogs, whom they raised as if they *were* children. The wildness was driven out of kids the hard way, with sternness and punishment, until it whimpered and gave up the ghost. In its place came the manners of adults, and the strict path that others followed. But the harshness had its own buried pleasure principle, which took time to understand. The passion for order is a Roman heritage, which the French apply with the flat of the hand; they yank the wildness out by the roots of the hair, and dismiss the ground of childhood imagination as an outpost of the empire. In the meantime, the pagan seed is fed with all the rituals of daily life, and through the cultivation of sensuous pleasure. Colors abound in their work, and beauty is as important to teachers as are good sums and proper penmanship.

The products of such training bore the marks of their repression; French children moved a bit stiffly, sat with a shyness that came from being made to sit, and reacted coolly to elders. The Americans, as my children were soon to be called, stood for lawless merriment and passion, the kind that smoldered in the pit of every French heart. But it was removed from children so early they could only dream about it – or split a gut watching versions of it in American cartoons and Jerry Lewis movies. A southern French child sat quietly, ate all his or her food, even the string beans, cleaned the plate with a hunk of bread, and drank a bit of diluted wine alongside the fruit juice. The boys would grin guardedly and the girls would smirk. Though beaten down and pruned to the stump, they were cherished members of the family treated to good food, expensive clothes, a measure of serious respect from parents, and given a set of values that put life at the top. Their own minds were well-stocked with information, and their bedrooms were no different from many American ones: lots of books, a computer, record player, rock posters, the latest clothes and pump sneakers. The contradictions abounded: old-fashioned formality, American-style clothes and games. Urbanism had come to Provence, and the children were being raised in two traditions: the old ways, and the life of the city that beckoned to them.

The freedom my daughters knew was as foreign to their French friends as life on Mars. Indeed, later when there were guests to the house, Signe would pounce on the kitchen and make elaborate cookies or cakes, with her friends staring open-mouthed at such license. Nothing on earth could persuade a French mother to turn over her most cherished room to a child. And here was Signe throwing flour in the air, dousing table and floor with blizzards of it, smearing slabs of butter onto pans, lighting ovens, filling the sink with dishes, sitting around like a peasant chatting the day away with the kitchen looking like King Kong had raged through it. And the poor girls beside her would be thinking how her mom would kill them all when she found out. But mom would come in purring like a cat and find all this ruckus and chaos very sweet and would fill mugs with cold milk and lay out dishes for the chefs to dine on. Such gardens of pure and endless joy open their gates only in dreams, and here was the American garden open seven days a week including Christmas.

My children would enter the classroom and pass through a long, dark tunnel from American individuality to the collective soul of France. They would suffer mental pains they did not know existed. Their hearts would break at the scolding and withheld affection, and melt again when lunch came around with all its taste and fanfare. They would burn with rage and lose all hope, and struggle against a mountain of foreign gabble and confusion, and be lifted up again at the sight of their two tormentors leading them in song or unfolding the wonders of wild flowers on their walks.

Maxine was the more delicate and vulnerable of the two girls. Thin as a wraith and with a mind spun like crystal, how would she respond to the hard shake, the growling voice of an impatient adult glaring down at her? I worried about her. She lived in her own world much of the time, where things ran in a delicate, fantasy-rich slow motion, with talking voices behind the wall, and shadows that became furniture for a miniature house. She would idle her days away building theatrical sets for actors who might well be the mice we sometimes found in corners of our closets. She dawdled and could kill an hour trying on different skirts in the mirror. What would a teacher of Mme. Courtasse's lordly disposition do with her? Raze her to the ground to rebuild her? I hoped and prayed Maxine would find a way not to give in.

It was the part of our plan I hadn't thought about much. I didn't know if my love of French ways included the reshaping of my children's character. Did I want them to be turned more toward others, less toward themselves? Did I think it was better to have their instinctual energies pruned back to let some other fruit ripen in the mind? Did I want them to become lovers of sense more than of action? Was it worth it losing the rough edges where creativity takes root, just to make them part of the group's affairs? Don DeLillo remarked once that the future is crowds. Should a parent mold his children into individuals, or prepare them for life in the tribe?

And what would my open-faced, sunflower of a child, Cedric, do with hard grinding routines day in and day out? Already he had run afoul of adults with his perky talk, his observant eye for the weaknesses in my friends. Once I found my buddy Bill Hussey seething with quiet rage at being taunted, or so he thought, by the penetrating questions posed by my son. He had heard money being talked, and now he was facing poor Bill with barbed questions about his own worth, and the evidence of his clothes to suggest otherwise. Bill, like me, shopped at thrift stores to save a little money, and there was a slightly out-of-fashion look about his scuffed shoes, the pleated trousers he wore. My son would soon find deportment far outweighed cleverness in the scale of virtues of a French schoolroom.

I didn't face such questions directly; they simmered in my mind as the sun dropped behind the house and the lavender field lengthened and disappeared under a moonlit crust. The mulberry tree was my green cabinet, where I would try to sort out my worries. I felt like Abraham with three children to be sacrificed. Well, it wasn't quite that serious. My dread sprang from not knowing what die I cast in shaping their lives. Would they refuse to change? Was that better than lowering down into the French soul and rising again, tear-stained, weary, and transformed?

My son, I knew, would make it somehow in the lower level. Domi explained there would be no reading or writing there; they would march around in the sunny, dappled yard shouting all their songs, or line up for exercise, or go for walks through the village of Les Imberts, picking leaves off the privets and feeling very collective. Little by little, words would form and take meaning in his head, and his tongue would begin to use new muscles to speak. He would leave the known world of English behind; no longer would there be one language for everything, but two. The cosmos would grow large and ambiguous; he would discover the ambivalence of things, their duality in a world of parallel names. He would stand between them, with the apple and the *pomme* in his hand, facing the world, *le monde*, by himself. *Je t'adore*, I would tell him. I love you, *mon fils, mon cher*, my beloved son.

We lingered in the school yard on our first visit, uncertain what to look for among the windows and shadows. The somber building, set off in its dusty square of earth, seemed too much like a vise for squeezing out the feral traces of youth; the walls were pale with whimpered cries. The two women, young and middle-aged, passionate and wise, would now be my children's foster parents. I had given them up; my beloved offspring would return to me as changelings.

"Twice the mind, twice the spirit," our New Zealand friend said to me as I shared my doubts with him one afternoon. We had met him in Goult, a slight man with white hair and a pointed chin, more like an elf than a human being. "Call me Kiwi, I'm Ken the Kiwi," he said, coming out of the *épicerie* one afternoon. He had seen us in the streets, took a liking to strangers who wandered around like himself. He lived in the German's new house, with its passages leading everywhere through useless rooms. He was the house-sitter and paid no rent or bills. He simply lived there, sleeping in one large room on his cot, with his lamp and books and a bag full of fruit. He lived a mendicant's simple life, though he was too clever to have to beg. He had some sort of pension from his working days, he told me, but not enough to live on.

"If they'll learn French, they'll have twice the world to live in. You'll see. You know, like the two taps on your tub. Hot and cold. French and English. Now they can mix them up to their own taste. I'd call that a distinct advantage. I speak French, but it's poor man's French, what a bloke might say with a clothes pin on his nose. Like this," and he fixed his mouth in a gape, clamped his fingers on his nose: "Mersey beyang, mon syeur. Not bad, eh? I'm not college educated like you. I learn everything as I go. That way I don't have to load my brain with useless knowledge. Earn what you learn, I say."

He was popular at the village *fêtes*; he went around asking the women to dance, pulling them onto the dance floor under the eyes of their husbands. He would dance with his small arms outstretched, nothing intimate or cozy. He just wanted to show off his ballroom dancing, and he was good. A graceful, tiny figure whirling large women around to the music pounding from the DJ's flat-bed trailer, the loud-speakers piled up on either side and hung from trees. You could see his white hair flashing blue and black as the strobe lights flickered over the dancers. He would be turning a big woman with his arms stretched, his toes extended, a wistful smile on his pointed face.

Ken the Kiwi treated me to a glass of wine at the Lumières cafe, where we had our chat. It was four or five days till departure and I surprised myself getting into serious talk with him. He listened carefully, thinking over what I said. He was a vagabond, one of those creatures who wandered all the paths of the world and slept where he could. Eventually he would drift down to Lumières from Goult, and take a room at the pilgrims' hostel across the road.

"Don't worry about it; you're doing them a favor. Besides, do they need all this freedom you Americans love so much? I sometimes think all that talk of personal liberty is wasted words; how much of it goes to a purpose? Isn't it just a way of filling time when you're a kid?," he said, folding his arms and eyeing his empty glass. "This freedom bit is all a cover-up for having no particular use for kids. They all hang around the lamp post waiting to grow up. And then they come up with these notions of freedom, liberty, their glorious individual selves, as an excuse to have another Coke and burger while they wait."

I ordered him another wine.

"It's rather similar in my country, y'know. It's the disease of the English-speaking world, if you want an opinion. We are lonely types, cut off from each other. We don't have society in our countries. We've over-used the notion of self and all that lah-di-dah. We get so involved cultivating this here little thumb tack we call a soul we forget what it's pinned to: a social animal. Now that's where the French come in handy. They love the body, they pamper it, they think sex and eating and drink are part of God's plan. What's the good of a self if it won't join the world? You can't have a self without a body to stuff it in! But don't tell me about it; I'd be back in Dunedin if I disagreed with the French. Awk! Awk! OOh la la! Hey, thanks for the drink."

At home again, I puttered in the kitchen cleaning some shrimp for tonight's dinner. A white Bandol was chilling in the ice box. Cathy and the kids were swimming in Peggy's pool. Already friendships were forming, the year ahead was acquiring its domestic logic. I felt like a visitor in the house, someone who couldn't make attachments to anything because the time was short.

But here was the house with its long table, its walls flaking with lime wash, rafters strung across a wooden ceiling. The dark and the silence ruled here; it was a summer house, not a working dwelling. It stood on the edge of a farm and served brief visitors; it had a northern feeling about it. The world of English, the "cold" tap as Ken would say, was here in the muted colors, among the chairs and beds and the division of space into territories. Inner and outer worlds were bounded, with corners claimed where someone would sit long hours sifting his thoughts, drifting through the mental landscape. The room had spun out of long refinement of the self, and had lost contact with the world outside.

The house was like an English dictionary, specific and defined in its privacy, with the world around it bursting with color and motion, forcing speech back to nuance and dreamy generality, the genius of French. Inside lay the private soul refining its vision of inner life, while nature's lust and energy rolled on radiant wheels over the house, bearing Aphrodite through the world.

It was my job, the sun seemed to say, to rewind the fibers of the white dream in my children, to weave the cords of the spirit, a little earth, a little mind. They need expanding, said the wind, rising over the roof just then; they need a wand passed over the mouth and tongue, said the birds landing in the poplars as the day lengthened.

It was worth it, all my struggle and doubt. Let them be dragged from the room, the "room," into the world. I wanted them to be different, to be mixed with earth and have some wonderful trance laid over their tongues. I wanted their mouths to grow rich in speech and taste, to savor the world. If it meant giving up some of the uniqueness of self to get there, it was worth the sacrifice. The peach trees around Cavaillon, all spread out in the same way, drank the sunlight in great gouts and poured fruit from their limbs. That was the test of life, whether one bore fruit or not. The isolated soul seated in its introspective corner bore only thoughts, the ghosts of reason. I was doing the right thing, I concluded. I was opening them, pulling off the roof of the soul and letting sun pour in. I was Gertrude Stein and here were my three sentences.

I strolled along the little dirt path through the cane brake to the pool and saw my family floating around luxuriously in the emerald water. I felt my heart go clear again. I was smiling down at them; I couldn't be happier.

In the evening, when we had gathered at our table under the mulberry tree and dug into our shrimp and rice, and salad, and sat back from empty plates well satisfied, I could think of nothing to long for. It was here under the soft night stars and the creek's whispers. I had learned this much from Provence: all one desired could be summoned and embraced. It was a lesson to carry back with me, and remember each time Provence became an imaginary landscape. It was here, it was as real as the ant that crawled along the plate. It was transportable back to America as well: for Provence existed the moment one seized the joys of life. I would practice until it became second nature, this pleasure in what was knowledge to the hands and tongue.

I was being observed now, and when I looked up from these small promises I made, I saw that my long face was now the cause of laughter. I joined in; who should be left out of such heavens?

Chapter Eight

Of Faucets and Cock Crows

It is now three months from the day I left Provence, a cloudy November morning at the office. I have piled before me the lecture notes for today's class, the books I will discuss, some papers I have graded, and a postcard sent to me by the children. It shows a small village house with its sills loaded with amaryllis and gentian, and a sprig of passion flower curled around the rain gutter. The shutters and windows have been painted deep green. The door looks into the silence of the house; its window panes give back the silver lacquer of the sky.

They called a few minutes ago, just before sitting down to eat dinner. It was a promise Cathy had made. Now, as I looked at the post-card, they were passing the bread, cutting up chicken, drinking their apple juice and talking in the dining room over the candle light. The shutters would be drawn and the drapes pulled; it would be cool out, and already they were building fires in the hearth and the little brazier in the dining room. A fire would be crackling behind them while they ate. Someone dropped papers outside my office, and it sounded almost like a log popping.

Their voices were warm, excited on the phone. I was looking up into the overcast sky, the beginning of an autumn storm as they spoke to me. They had winter in their voices, a cheerful quickness. School was hard, one said; *very hard* another said. *I don't like it,* I heard Cedric mutter. One spoke and the other used the ear piece that hung on the back of French phones. Maybe two listened on the ear piece while the third took a turn talking to me. I heard the faucet running in the kitchen; I could see my wife bending over the sink, the overhead light on. Outside would be the sloping yard, the brown, naked mulberry limbs, the pond smoldering in sunset. It was all there; life was in progress while they spoke. I smelled supper on their breath, or wanted to. I heard the noises of the house go on long after they had hung up. I received kisses from all, including Cathy, who said things were going well. I was sorely missed, she added.

The image of a place strengthens in memory; its detail melts away and one is left with the simplest and deepest things: the light in the tree, the shadow falling over the terrace, the outline of black branches against the moon, voices in a house. One holds these things differently from other experience; they are the stuff of recognition, and represent far more than their literal signs. The ultimate meaning of place lies in childhood, what one saw once, briefly, in the moment some new emotion was born in the body, and the thing, the light bulb, becomes its symbol ever after. Provence, *my* Provence, was made up of such things; I knew this, that its map was emotional, perhaps purely so. I had spent my two ends of summer there going around finding its surface shimmering with clues to my childhood, which unlocked the more I looked.

But the more interesting thought is that others have come there as well and felt a similar response. Perhaps there are certain places in the world where the symbols are no longer personal or individual but tribal and give us back certain moments of our earliest life. They awaken in us the origins of emotion. Was this in fact the country of innocence which we all recognized the moment we saw it? Is that the discovery of Cezanne when he painted the fields around Aix, or of Van Gogh when he painted the child-like forms of his bedroom at Arles? Wasn't Mistral's museum, the Arlaten, a kind of attic of French childhood, with its bonnets in dusty glass cases, and its prams and carts, walking sticks, and pipes the accumulated nostalgia of a people? Was Provence memory itself?

Calling over made me feel I had plunged back into some strange yellowing world of eternal childhood, where the voices of my children were more like my own childhood voice. From this distance, sitting in the quiet, artificial world of the office, with its hollow walls and vibrating floors, I had called back into a hidden place where nothing was real and yet natural, pure, everlasting in its simplicity. Soon, the cool night sky would enclose this landscape with its lantern light and its blue roads, the black fields dotted with trees where the moon rose like an eye, the eye of reverie poring over the dreamers below, recognizing all the symbols of collective infancy that lay heaped in the rolling countryside. Provence was eternal childhood, and all its symbols converged to give this strange myth of return its poignant beauty. The elderly were always old, the young always children, and if you were lucky and came back to it in good health, you too could remain what you are, forever.

At lunch I ate alone at a table in the corner of an Italian restaurant; I was still thinking of the sound of the faucet in the kitchen, how clean and precise it was. The good faucet with its narrow hiss, barely a note in the clutter of background hums and squeaks, and yet steady as a line on a page. Now the rain poured down off the awning outside and hissed into the gutter; the faucet continued its slender theme from there to here. But no one else paid attention to it. Inside, among these tables sat many business couples, all involved in serious discussion. Food lay before them smoking or cool, hardly touched but for a fork that had been pushed around and set down again, as hands went up to gesture, fan out, roll, pinch, offer and retract below two intense faces keenly exploring some secret together.

There we were in a great adventure together, whatever the trek headed for. Waiters stood by patiently with pitchers of ice water looking for some momentary break in talk to refill glasses. Otherwise, a complex rhetoric of the human spirit filled the room with its murmurs and laughter and occasional pauses for a sip or a quick bite. A woman stretched out leisurely after some intense exchange had worn itself out. She was forty, and had dressed to a precise code that identified her as a businesswoman, not an academic. The academic women wore dark colors and clothes that diminished their femininity; they were more aggressive than business-women. Occasionally someone would sit with legs crossed, always a vulnerable posture in conversation. Invariably lies would be told, and in this moment, as I studied the woman's profile and her long legs, a question was posed to her. She smiled, and her foot jerked upward an inch, but the man she was with couldn't see it. This was the surest sign of lying, of covering up, of conscious deceit, and another weaker smile spread across the man's face, the look of concealed disappointment, or was it knowledge?

Food was unimportant to such people; it hardly mattered what was on the plate or in the glass, it was there to revert to during moments of crisis or tedium. One came to talk primarily, and to eat on the margins of their ritual. It was talk that muted expression and tone of voice; all the talk around me was the American talk of buzzing, which went up and down in volume according to some biological key hidden in the room. Everyone was aware of it and talked in unison with its force, which might have been the waiters zipping around or the role of some conversational leader whose ups and downs controlled everyone else.

I liked the sound of it, though it was dull and circular. You knew this was the latest form of confessional box, the table with its mild food and boring drinks, where one could bring up the bitterness of office life, the squabbles and rivalries and disappointments, and where it was always someone's turn to hear the other out. Later the roles would reverse and the talker would be the wise listener, sorting out the plot and putting in a word for justice.

This was America, with its displacement of sensuality, its emphases all converging on the tribulations of egos and careers. The mouth was important, but not as it was in Goult that splendid morning when the mouth of a woman became a garden of magic blossoms singing in all registers of the animal world.

This talk was strategic and political, and moved chess pieces up and down some invisible board between the talkers. Things were always following their causal paths and ending up as good or bad moves, sending the speaker to one or another position in relation to enemies and rivals and the obstacles of human order. The postures of such people, I noticed, seemed schooled to interiors; there were no signs that such bodies lounged on grass or spent the day strolling over fields. The outside lay there like an exotic aquarium, in which the strange sharks and porpoises turned out to be cars and trucks, and the odd crab or lobster walking sideways or backwards were people rushing along in the driving rain. Talk smothered the life of the outside and gave it no relation to our interior world. We were here as if we had landed in a space ship and this ground was no more than a backdrop of incidental events to what transpired over the coffee and mints on the bill tray.

I couldn't help but feel that the problem with such life was not that it might be emotionally tedious or repetitive, or that it was fraught with tensions that would eventually ruin our health. It seemed disconnected from the realms of memory, and occurred within a universe of mere incidence. It lacked myth or recurrence; it had nothing to do with the rain falling or the great gutters swirling with dirty foam, or the underworld that heaved and slid on great blocks of clay from the torrents that swamped it. We were out on some marginal orbit of details that had no gravitation or organic form; and thus nothing that occurred in the room was memorable or followed some ancient pattern. Business changed daily from one fortuitous event to another, never the same and never very different. And talk broke up like atomic particles to map this uninteresting shake of the kaleidoscope of reality, which explains why the range of emotions in the room was so narrow, so thin, so unlived.

A very young girl sat with dim eyes as a man sternly went over some issue with her; was he her professor by chance? Or her lover? It was difficult to tell. He had been going down his fingers ticking off items that upset him, and the girl was sinking into the victim's role. She swallowed each accusation; the man's voice, becoming more assured and tyrannical, lowered and slowed down and began reaching deeper and deeper into her psyche. She put down her fork and brushed her lips with the napkin, and seemed to be folding up inside. She was a frail and sensitive creature, with a fine nose and paper-thin lips. She looked as if she hardly ate a cracker in a day, and now, with the salad heaped in her bowl and a great mass of spaghetti lying in a cold lump on her plate, she had the forlorn look of a marble statue staring at nothing. The man had seized the full weight of his advantage and sat back with his final point, at which the girl rose, made for the bathroom, and the man looked around the room like a salesman who has sold his quota for the day.

Missing between the two was any trace of love or common desire; even if it were her professor, not once did Eros darken his gaze or smooth his words to her. It was pure business played out on a desolate plane, and the girl was all the more distressed for having no sensuous appeal to make to any of it. It was there, some grimly durable surface, like formica, on which life's game was played out.

The man, as I was to learn from the waiter a moment later, was her boss, and he was firing her. He would bolt from the table and leave her there to find her own way home, which made her stand by the empty table for some moments until she was shown to the door. That is when the waiter explained the situation to me. The girl went out into the storm and walked slowly away. She had no nakedness to protect her; no fruitful mind in which the great pleasures of the world are stored. She could not go somewhere and laugh into some young man's admiring face. She would not sing like a great song bird to her lover in the café. She was wholly involved in the life of work, whose rigid processes had now excluded her. Momentarily, she was dead. She had entered the wasteland of America, where the unemployed are the dead souls roaming without identity. She had nothing to give; the world refused her. She drifted, perhaps to a dark apartment where she would cry the day away. Perhaps she would spend her days phoning for new jobs, or go home again to parents in Oklahoma, and marry the mechanic's son, and live in a mobile home with her family for the rest of her dreary days. She was dying of grief when she left, and the diners hardly noticed, hardly turned, so concerned were they for their own desperate lives. There would be no Ken the Kiwi to dance with, and no young man to roar up on his mobilette to make her feel like Aphrodite again. She was going away, and no one seemed to care.

After work, I drove home through the dripping streets. Nature seemed tired and withdrawn; the fences obscured what little there was of it. Trees poked out above the palings of a cedar fence; someone had built a tree house in one of them. The houses were closed and protective; they invited no second looks. Curtains and blinds were drawn tight; I imagined a dim light left on in the kitchen, or the laundry room, with carpeted halls leading to silent rooms, all waiting for the return of a family. The houses were built close, crammed into small lots with abutting fences. There was no sign of life among them; all was quiet and empty and dripping.

In the black neighborhood which ran along the railroad tracks entering Bryan were shacks and huts, some of them so crooked they were ready to tip off their cinder blocks. Tires littered the dirt yards; a car stood in a driveway lacking a hood. Rain puddled in the engine and soaked the seats through the open windows. A cat slept on the back window ledge, its ear following the hiss of my tires. Inside were adults gathered around a card table; overhead lights were on. Children were crowded into the room and listened or watched TV. The windows were fogged. The culverts ran brown and gray with muck, the sewers gorged with storm water. Along the road were hacked and broken trees where the phone company cleared out the high branches with a steam shovel. Now the wires ran free through the gaunt, shattered core of many oaks.

That was poverty, in all its hues of brown and gray and black tar, broken brick, glints of glass in the mud. Even so rejected a world had its compensations – in summer, the chairs were arranged in a circle in the yard where the men sat watching football on TV, while the women cooked up a pot of crawdads in a peppery soup, and laid out platters of fried okra and boiled corn. The kids romped, the teenagers sulked or flirted in the shade of a hackberry tree, and something flourished in the yard as old as villages and rural ways.

I was home now; the phone will not ring again. The children are sleeping in their beds. Cathy is reading on the mezzanine, above the garden and the little orchard. The schoolhouse is dark; its desks are clean, the blackboards washed. The fountain pens are resting in the pencil bags of countless back packs. They will scrape all day tomorrow and there will be bumps on fingers where the pen has made a callous. The drone of teachers will be heard while I am sleeping. There will be coughs and creaking seats and foot shuffling, and a loud voice scolding some loafer in the back row, and the sky will brighten and go umber and purple again with the clouds blowing in. All will look out and think of the fathers and grandfathers who will be cutting vines or turning earth in the fields. Laundry will be gathered in; the last carrot crop will be pulled up hurriedly from the fields and taken to the wholesale market at Cavaillon. All this will happen after I have gone to bed. I stare into the twilit depths of the yard, sipping a scotch and watching the six o'clock news.

As an American, I understand things about this country no foreigner could ever penetrate. These are my people; if we do not embrace one another, it is for reasons buried deep in our common experience. If we separate these blacks from those whites, and the Latinos from everyone else, there are reasons – some of them beyond race or religion. They go to the heart of Americanness and cannot be rationally explained. There are different shapes of the human soul; some that need others to live, some that don't. We follow our needs and live accordingly. In the big wooden house where I live, there are no sounds of nearby human life.

America is that endless flight from our memories, invented or real, of an "old world" of manual labor and bottom dog life. We invented the car to escape from walking, the microwave to get away from stoves; our houses sprawl over lawns in imitation of the class above us. We air-condition to avoid the heat, and welcomed every form of artificiality until we were cut off from contact with anyone but our own family, and lost the children to TV and their own worlds. The picture we carry of our ancestral origins is of toothless women and cross-eyed children, of men pulling a boat up on the rocky shingle, or of fighting for a lord who sits his white horse safely above the battlefield while the peasants bled to death. America is built on the fear of that past returning; our architecture, our science, our food, and our culture are ramparts built high against the return of nature.

I'm forced out into the rain again to shop for supper; it is a dull chore and I regret having to go. The supermarket is lonely, a large room that makes everyone sheepish. Heads are tucked down, carts wheeze by loaded with bright boxes and cans. The produce section hisses with mist from the little nozzles buried in the lettuce and spinach. The air is cold, and the freezers are all humming away with boxes of frozen food. No one is buying; the place is almost empty and I roam around with benumbed curiosity. So much food, so many ways of selling it, all this glorious energy pouring out of a nation – it's intoxicating and overpowering. A hundred kinds of potato chips, aisles of cookies and snacks, and quick dinners. Everything tuned exactly to our ways of life, right down to the specific flavors and bite-sizes people prefer. There is no end to this cornucopia; it goes on row after row, and if there is one thing missing, one thing only, it is the semblance of living origins. The food, good as it is, enriched and beautifully made, comes from nowhere. It simply is. The meat is uniform, the fish is headless and filleted, the vegetables are immaculate and root-less. This is the food of symbolic people; they have cut their ties, and eat abstractly. They have moved into some rare sphere of life where the world is excluded. My countrymen are all wizards and dreamers and have renounced the soiled and smelly earth, which lies somewhere in our ethnic pasts.

The girl who weeps is nowhere to be found; I would have invited her home to dinner if she were here. Poor Niobe, she has lost the only world she knew. And its meanings are laid out here in a great profusion of packages painted with the colors of the flag. It is late, the floors are being cleaned with wide brooms and mops; a line of black boys comes down the aisle pushing the handles. It is hard to see what should be cleaned; the linoleum sparkles, the carpets are unstained. But the brooms come hissing forward over the waxed floor and catch gum wrappers and hair pins and a little dust. Otherwise, the white ceilings go off in long bands of florescent light, and the machinery hums quietly like the sound of a sea shell. The room is full of the earth's plenty but there is no earth; even the pictures of celery stalks are stylized and cartoon-like. The faces are pale under such brilliance, and the bodies loose and indifferent that go by, hips swinging languorously from side to side in the trance of shopping. Music lulls us and propels us forward at the same tempo, the feet catching up and drifting behind its tinny percussion.

I was lonely, not hungry. I bought a few eggs and a can of beans for a ranch supper. On the drive back to the house, the clouds begin to separate, and behind them lies the night sky speckled with stars. There is great beauty in the Texas sky. It is the pure, unreachable face of nature that hangs over us, close, shimmering with mystery. The river banks will be noisy with frogs; life will begin moving back to its niches in the dark. The dance halls will fill with men and women looking for partners for the night. Already the parking lots are full in front of the movie house, the Mexican bars, the barbecue joints. Main Street is quiet and empty; a man hurries to his car from the row of darkened pawn shops.

At home, I linger in the kitchen with my can of beans. I dump out the scrambled eggs on a plate and eat at the counter. I run the faucet over the dishes and hear that delicate echo again where all are sleeping. I go up to read in bed; as I turn pages, the cars go by below, their tires hissing over the last moisture on the streets. The sewers ring like muffled bells with their muddy torrents.

It is possible to live in America. The presence of the wild is only beyond the fingers. It lies there waiting to be opened, to be brought back to the mind. If there were some Orpheus who could talk to the country and tell it what it has lost, show it what is missing in all these narrow streets without companionship, perhaps ... someone would come out and shout from his porch, and others would raise their sashes and look to see who had gone mad from television and boredom. There would stand the little nobody who had done his chores for forty years wanting something more from life. He would want a picnic, and demand that all attend, and then pull down all the ugly signs that clutter his street. He would demand food stalls in the parking lot each Saturday, where farmers could truck in their produce and yard eggs, and show children how onions really grow. And there should be beer kegs and wine barrels for the adults, and a band to play old songs in the high school basketball court. And there would be movies shown in the alley where all could come with folding chairs and bring along snacks and cold beer and laugh the evening away. And small markets would grow up, he would say from his porch, yelling until his voice cracked. We should support them, pay a little more, make sure the farmers had some livelihood. Kids could take up farming who had no other future; we could help, we could bring ourselves back together. We're not so big we can't have a communal life again, with some real experience thrown in. Another dreamer, another poet gone to seed in his head.

The rain is lush and heavy as velvet and the night air cool as it blows in through the windows. The trees are happy. If the suburbs became communities in the real sense of sharing, and the cities returned to us as centers of ideas and visions, and there were men and women who could teach us how to live again with our hands and practical knowledge, America would spring up like some root that lies under a stone. People would turn off their home entertainment and talk on the sidewalk, take hikes in the country, plant flowers and trees along public walks and around our desolate parking lots.

It is early December and the winds come down from the north out of Canada. They are led by tall blue thunderheads that scatter everything before them and then disappear, leaving winter behind. Clothes blow off lines; garbage cans roll down the streets; dogs bark and cower on their ropes. Lights go on and people scurry to wrap outside spigots. A hard freeze will attend this great fanfare of towering clouds. Houses fade away into damp shells; streets grow quiet and uneasy.

My office window looks out over car roofs and fast food joints, the skyline of suburban life. It is the end of the semester, I think with a sigh of relief. A young woman has come to discuss her test grade; she didn't pass. She is pretty and alert, with large blue eyes and lots of blond hair. She is sitting beside my desk while I reread her answers in the blue book. Walt Whitman wrote *Omoo*, and jotted off *Walden* in his spare moments; Emerson was in love with Brook Farm; the Civil War came and went in the middle ages. World War II lay somewhere in the distant future, not a gun yet loaded or fired. On and on, the mush of history sprawled out in her panicky prose, with my remarks trailing behind like a bemused hound dog: "Vague!" "Insuff.," "Wrong!" "Nice try."

Oh well, such is the dreariness of learning these days. She has read America's soul in haste, between bites of a pizza and the drone of her headset; she has not stopped to think that the writers might be telling her truths about herself, her time in history. Has she even stopped once to ask if the loneliness of American literature was real, or that the bitter dreams of *The Great Gatsby* and *Moby Dick* might be her own one day? We had tried to bury our unwanted differences of color, tongue, and attitude; we gave ourselves sameness as a cure for diversity and the strange places we had come from, and now we had sprawl and uniformity from coast to coast. All the McDonalds and Wendy's and Sears stores were alike, and our lives were anonymous. We had traded culture for consumerism, and the writers told us how bitter the bargain has become. She was convinced that nothing matters but the relentless logic of change and innovation, the two elixirs of America.

"Why isn't this good enough?" she asks, her face open and good-natured.

After she left, I recorded the new grade in my book and went back to dreaming at the window. The night was closing over the little well house at Les Martins. The bees were back to the hive, the long lavender field was asleep in its winter bed. I was there now, in the shadows of the stone wall, under the corner light. I was breathing with my wife, waiting for the first cock to crow on the hill.

Chapter Nine

Spring Hath Sprung

T he year closed slowly, my forty-fourth in the world. It was December 20, 1987, and I had landed in the cold gray morning hours of Paris, stumbled along to the Gare de Lyon where all the south-bound trains head down to Provence, dragging suitcases and a duffel bag bulging with Christmas gifts. I had gone overboard on presents to make up for my long absence, our first separation. I had a Cabbage Patch doll, a chemistry set, an erector set, clothes, film, tennis shoes, anything I could lay hands on in the last harried days of packing and closing up the Texas house and my university office. It all dragged behind me and wobbled precariously on my luggage cart at the train station. I was numb, cold, and sleepy; I yawned and felt new yawns coming before I could close my mouth. Everything seemed distant and echoey. An hour into the wheat fields south of Paris, I toddled wearily to the coffee bar and ordered an espresso. It rang bells in my head on the first sip. I was coming to.

When I got down at Avignon and lugged everything to the last flight of stairs, my family stood at the bottom looking up, my son rushing up first to hug me tightly, casting longing looks at all the bulges in my Santa sacks. The girls came up with bashful grins and seemed to take me in a moment before feeling their own rush of excitement. We all drank in the strangeness of that moment in which we were coming together again, and yet still divided. Cathy greeted me with good warmth; she saw at once the ravages of another thirty hours of jet and train travel and took control of the baggage. I was led like a glorious, wounded knight to the car and given the front passenger seat. I eased down into the cushion, head slung back, letting plane trees and clouds close over me on the ride home.

The news was given to me in a chorus of intersecting voices from behind; one story led to others, each bringing in another, fragments passing under and over one another like the branches plaited overhead as we sped along austere winter roads east of Isle-sur-la-Sorgue and onto the N-100, the "Roman road," to our hamlet. My eyes faded in the warmth and love of all this bubbling chatter, and I woke to the crunch of gravel under the tires. We were home again.

The dining room table was laid with a formal service of china and stem glasses; the hooded brazier against the wall was set for a fire, which my son put the match to. The flames flickered higher and filled the white walls and gloomy cabinets with the orange glow of Rembrandt's paintings. All our faces shone in the flames, as the fire snapped and licked along the edges of the hood. Someone had run the faucet for a moment in the kitchen, and the world I had longed for swam through my head and came back real. The oven smelled of roast lamb, a *gigot d'agneau* bruised with garlic and thyme. Wine was poured, a bottle of Cayron Gigondas, fully breathed and ripe. We toasted to our joy and sat to a long meal full of talk and more toasts and finished off with a platter of cheese and a crusty twisted baguette called an *épis*.

I carted all the Christmas spoils to our little bedroom at the far end of the house, and climbed wearily to the mezzanine and went to bed. The journey was ended; my estrangement had shed its skin.

In the morning I sat in the darkened, shuttered room sipping coffee by myself, stirring the embers in the fire pit, coaxing a flame up among the dry twigs and straw. My children were asleep, getting up one by one and drifting in to breakfast. They had learned new ways without me. I could feel my own subtle disengagement from them. Things eddied around me toward their mother, and I could begin to sense all those ancient emotions of the homecoming soldier, mariner, wanderer, prisoner. Life had closed its gap around me and sealed its rhythms in another relation. Slowly, begrudgingly, I would hear my voice intervene and call attention to my presence, like King Lear. My words would startle them, draw a fleeting look of surprise at my interruption of their habits. I was here now, my archaic fatherhood wanted back its throne.

That evening we went up into the icy stillness of Gordes to watch a Christmas play in which my older daughter Maxine had a prominent part. She was the announcer of the pageant and bid us welcome in a lilting, southern French. I had heard snippets of well-turned French in the back seat coming home the day before; it struck me oddly hearing this new speech in their mouths. Now she stood on the auditorium stage and spoke well-rehearsed lines to a smiling audience of parents. The tall, regal figure of Madame Courtasse took the stage to open proceedings, and announced my daughter proudly as her American student, and with a wink asked us to note her southern accent. Indeed, the banjo strings twanged and snapped on "beeyang" for the elegant Parisian *bien*, "reeyang" for *rien*, "rahze" for *rose*, and so on. But the rest was musical and flowing. She hardly seemed my daughter in that moment, standing confidently, her body smooth as sandalwood, pouring French syllables from her mouth. There were the crescents of beginning breasts, her hair was soft and nut-brown, her small lips broke into flutters as she spoke. She had wandered into adolescence while I was gone.

The evening started late and went on fiercely by the hour, acts coming on and fading away into new acts, while a tireless Dominique led round gaggles of children and kept the audience singing, then danced and acted and pranced her own way round and round. It was a wild, manic display of energy that dragged everyone else along with her. Parents slipped away quietly with bundled kids and the hall began to thin notice-ably. An English woman, Florie, parent of two small children in the group, played an electronic keyboard accompaniment to all the singing. She would blow a strand of blond hair from her eyes, give a weary smile, and plug on with the tireless Domi.

By twelve or so, we were done in, even if Domi was just getting her second wind. By then even Florie had packed up and gotten her kids dressed and out the door to the parking lot. We joined her there with big puffs of white breath and stamping shoes. Gordes was dark and glazed, frozen under a clear, moonless night. My wife had made numerous friends through the little school at Les Imberts, including the wife of Peter Mayle, the famous hostess in *A Year in Provence*. Florie was her best friend. Her husband and I stood nodding to one another, saying nothing. We waited while the women whispered and ran fingers over top buttons and collars of the kids. When the voices rose into farewell words, we headed for our cars and drove off into the gray, frosted roads, the fields covered in spider-webs of ice.

I would rise early and make the fire, get the coffee going, throw open the big shutters on all the doors of the dining room and walk out onto the long terrace to breathe the moist, thawing grass of the fields. My coffee smoked in the cup as I walked up and down in the cold, pushing back the nagging thought that I was still alone, still coming home to my family. The ties had altered. I had lost my place. It was a subtle feeling, eluding me as I thought about it. Was I jealous? Did my father undergo these ordeals of reentry each time he came back from his long sojourns in India and Africa?

I dimly recalled my spells of anger against him at his return, bringing my mother gifts from "the field," those "booby prizes" as she called them, looking out of the corner of her eye at a heap of little boxes containing slivers of jade and silver and inlaid bracelets, a tooled-leather purse, silk scarves, fancy little sandals with tassels on them. All this got left on the dining table in our apartment in Beirut as she stalked off sulkily to her room. Dad would shuffle about and remember the knife he had bought me or the little nickel-plated ring, etc. It was all a dreary ritual and by nightfall my mother's pouting would be over, and I and my two brothers would slowly relinquish our male powers back to dad. He must have felt our surge of defensiveness when he came home; it abated slowly, like a tide.

It was my turn to come home. It felt awful. These late risings were my wife's world. She had grown up under a father who worked the night shift at a General Electric plant in Cincinnati, and was used to watching Johnny Carson and the late movies before scurrying up to bed at the scraping of his feet on the doorstep. Her body clock was set for life. The kids were night owls and straggled out of bed by nine or ten some mornings. It was Christmas time, I should be easy on them. I wanted to shout them up. No, no. Best let them sleep. Their beds were by the little stage over the wash tubs. One could quietly poke the fire and do little else. The whole house slumbered under the aegis of my wife, under female rule. I stood outside like a battered, unwelcome Odysseus, drinking mud-thick coffee and relishing its bitterness.

Gustaf and I renewed our friendship. I looked forward to his visits to the house and to walks together. He had taken me silex hunting one afternoon in a field below a neolithic *abri*, where men chipped at scrapers, knives, arrow heads, and anything else useful for hunting and defense in that human dawn. We spent long hours stooped over in a small field looking for thin wedges of quartz that lay almost invisible in the dirt. He was very sharp-eyed and found half a dozen of them while I went around squinting and staring and found none. A collection of his arrow points hangs in the schoolhouse at Goult, including his prize find, a left-handed scraper. What we did that afternoon struck me as a joyous male ritual, something fathers did in their idle hours. At the base of all male vision is death itself, the grim blank at the end of our flesh. All its symbols appealed to us, and all our philosophy seemed to embrace this opening, this abstract question more than anything to do with life.

Coming home to a house that had closed ranks without me gave me some odd intimation of death, or of aging. I could imagine their lives going on without me. Call it self-pity, for that is all it was. I had Gustaf to share my thoughts with, and he was very sympathetic. He wouldn't accept my general notion that men embraced death as their source of power, but seemed more intrigued to think women were the great imaginers of life and fruitfulness. That made sense.

One afternoon as we sat drinking Lumières wine in his kitchen, his wife away on another trip to London, I mentioned my wife's interest in the writings of Krishnamurti and Rudolf Steiner. He gave a quick shrug and rubbed his hands, looking off as he remarked, "When women reach middle age, they turn to such things."

I thought of the middle-aged women I knew and wondered if they had all turned to mystics. I hadn't noticed. I could only remember that a few had discovered a simpler America of quilts and candle-making, herbal teas scented with apricot and orange skin, which had supplanted some of the youthful political rages. But no Indian gurus, not plainly, at least.

"I think you're heading for religion," I said.

Surprise, raised eyebrows, a humorous look.

"I mean it," I said. "Everything points that way in your new book. You are no longer describing, you are . . . meditating." About what I couldn't say; it wasn't anything organized in the way of a doctrine, but he had taken the direction of poetry for a century to its logical end in an open quest for spirit, not as a figure of god or saints, but that spirit immanent in nature, coaxed into visual perception by light and the way matter crumbled under its slow passage from dawn to dusk. *Voyaging Portraits* was about to be published by New Directions; he had given me a typescript of it and I had read it with great care. I didn't look up, didn't want to lose my thread. "All this language is interior, like prayers. It's as if you were talking to some other self within. Prayer, a Scottish bishop wrote once, is the act of talking to the far side of oneself. "When you think of it that way," I said, "your poetry seems part of the long history of meditation in Provence."

"Yes?"

"I mean, Provence does something to men that drives them into their minds. Each feels the need to coax up the god he thinks is hiding in him. Beckett was looking for him while holding out in Bonnelly's barn. Ionesco once lived in Gordes, didn't he? Aren't all his plays about the ambiguity of reality? You know, rhinoceroses galloping by out of thin air and chairs disappearing without warning. René Char . . . Heidegger, they were all chasing after gods.

"I thought Ionesco was mainly thinking about fascism, maybe not," he said, ending the argument.

I left soon after and drove slowly through the hills. Provence has lost its independence countless times. Anyone can come over the hill to claim it, even the tourists. The religious callings of so many who have lived here belong to this history of loss and ruin and rebuilding. The land remains; only the claims to it are lost or usurped. It is borrowed ground, ownerless and aloof but for a few legal threads holding it to some living tenant and his heir. "Home is where you spit," Jean Marie Collin, a farmer, once told me, pointing out his house across the valley. His children shrugged at the thought; they seemed to agree.

The porphyry range that begins inland east of Marseille known as the Esterels is the oldest exposed rock on Earth. Once a mighty range towering over the sea, it is worn down and compact as a diamond from weathering and old age. It is there to remind us that our deeds and boundaries are feathers on the wind. The ruins of castles and farms and Roman baths and shrines make all possession illusory. Buy a few meters of soil for a garden and before long you will hoe up the shards of an arch, a road cobble, a piece of ledge from some other past that was as bounded and assured as our own. An English friend, Mick Messenger, has a Roman milestone in his garden; he points it out with a wry smile, as if time were a kind of humorous comment on our own lives.

If the Esterels can wear away in a blink of eternity, where did that leave us poor mortals? We were all melting away from our bones, feeling a bit older each year. Especially now that our children were growing up and yearning for wider worlds. Here we were presuming to own property and to look after the subtleties of our pampered lives. Self diminished in these hills; it seemed a puny notion against such backdrops of time.

At the Abbaye de Sénanque, which lies in a cleft of the rocks below Gordes, men have prayed for centuries and raised voices in the rich harmonies of Gregorian and Russian Orthodox chanting. The American poet Thomas Merton lived there briefly and joined in the luxurious echoing of voices in the vaulted chapel. It is echo they worked for, the momentary repetition in the corners of the ceiling that gave them the fleeting impression another voice had joined them. And when the echoes accumulated in all the delicate structures of a fugue, the mind gave up its vigil and slept, dreamed, awoke in a visionary landscape and saw things no conscious mind beholds. All this strange sight occurred within the walls of the Cistercian monastery, a plain Romanesque building with a small cloister and cells where the monks slept. The rock sheltered them from passing armies; they lived by vows of poverty and charity, and did all of the menial work around the halls and gardens. They worked specifically to communicate with the life force and the elusive voice of God.

There is something about this famous abbey that stands for all men, representing all their longings to penetrate death and find some voice on the other side of it. No man takes up the question of his brief life without hoping there is some father behind it all, some figure who gives as well as takes away. This is what men try to reach in meditation, or art, or through war and bravery: to touch the force that governs their existence. The men of the abbey stood for anyone who ever knelt and prayed for vision, asking for a glimpse into the secret of life.

What the monks sang in their vaulted hall was essentially a handful of notes monotonously varied until the mind slumbered and the dream state took over. Monotony is somehow the gateway into the sacred world, a foliage of hypnotic patterns that drowns all sense and opens the inner eye. Much of the craft work in Provence is bordered in intricate, mesmerizing patterns; the swirls of color on faience jars is only one hint of that kind of dizzying foliage. Its function is to enchant the eye and lure it inward to worlds hidden behind the literal surface. An actual garden is no different; once lured past its gateway of cypresses or hedge, you may find yourself facing a chalk Venus in some recess, as if to indicate the way of vision.

So be it. All foliage is the dream state; it stands for the hair of our dreaming heads, and for the fur over our genitals, the darkness of medieval woods where fairies lived, and gnomes practiced sorcery and witchcraft. Foliage is darkness, the cedar-covered door to Dante's under-world, the *selva oscura* of vision. And nearly always, that door is not entered until a man reaches middle age, Dante in the "middle of the road of life," Whitman at 36, Christ three years younger. It is where night-mares creep riderless through the moonlit woods, and girls cry out from the velvet obscurity of sleep. The gardens of the world all seem to say, enter here to dream or change your life.

Gustaf's wife, Susanna, is a painter; she says she is not a serious one, though she spends long hours each day in her studio in Lacoste. Her works are small and simply framed. I saw a few in a show at Goult; they were oils composed entirely of half moons and arcs, and a rainfall of other primitive little shapes. It was hard to feel excitement over these little shower-curtain paintings with their monotonous patterns, until I realized she might be trying to graph the processes of prayerful states: all those Lucretian atoms falling through daylight were like the syllables of a repeated chant. Or were they the leaves and blossoms of spring, a rain of petals and moon signs drowning common sense? There is nothing to "see" in such pictures; they are monotonous parades of ciphers tumbling at a slant from one corner of the canvas to the other. But look at them long enough and a kind of sleepy, drugged euphoria comes over you, and you begin to lower into the trance of the monks and the witches.

So this is what the foreigners' wives thought about in sunny Provence; they didn't only run the cultivator in the garden, or paint sills and water the herbs in the potting shed. They aged and mellowed into these ruminative states which Gustaf and I entered from another gate. And they distilled their sources of vision from their own fruit, not from poetry. The Indian writers and western mystics encouraged them to let go a little, to feel another will at work. That was their way of grasping the hidden voice, by letting certain forms of control abate without fear of chaos. They came by their wisdom much as we did: we all seemed to be tending toward the same conclusion. What was all the fuss about in our lives? What did we think we had harnessed by being willful? What lay beyond the reach of this ego we nurtured and protected all our lives? What if we let it go, what then?

Whatever our wives believed, they were tracing paths that led back to the origins of female worship. "*Voila ta Mere*" says the stone tablet under a statue of Mary beside the church at Mane, near the town of Forcalquier. She stands within her fenced boundary like a blossoming shrub; it is her realm and the whole of Mane seems given over to her influence. She grieves, she calls to the poor and the lame and the broken-hearted; she is always amidst the grime and decay of cities with her forgiving face, her selfless bounty. Her blue cloak and white dress are symbols of the sky; her womb is the grove where nature multiplies. She wears the colors of Earth, and stands for the planet in female form.

"Who are you writing for," I once asked Gustaf. I had a notion, but wanted to know what he might say about it. "Who is your listener in these poems?"

A long think. Heavy brows knitted. I had asked a good one this time. Was he deciding whether or not to trust me? The pause seemed overwrought, then came a wagging of the head as all the censors let go an answer: "A young girl."

Surprise.

"Yes. About seventeen or so. I picture her beside me; we are together as I am speaking," looks me over, wants to agree with me and say *thinking, meditating, praying* but keeps to his text, "or reading, and she is the perfect listener. I believe women that young are very wise, wiser than we know. They understand death as well as love. They are fascinated by their own beauty, and sympathize with the men who desire them. They desire them-selves in the same way, admiring each other. They know such beauty is impersonal and passes through them like a season. It's that understanding I want beside me as I write."

But it wasn't a literal girl who sat beside him; it was the girl in himself, the girl as soul that he tried singing to. This lovely figure comes and goes throughout the Latin world, this Nausicaa who comes down to the shore to aid poor naked Odysseus and give him drink and nourishment. This is the elusive principle in men, the life-cherishing spirit in the form of a girl, who sits in the center of the masculine intellect and cannot be called to consciousness other than by lyrical enchantments, sweet talk, guitar strumming. Only then will she appear and counter his talk of death.

The line, Matisse said, has its own desire, follows its own destiny whenever you curve and return to the point of origin. Whenever you escape from death, which lies somewhere off the margins of the drawing paper. Turn and you create woman; curve the line from birth to death and you enter love again, in the shape of the beloved. He demonstrated the point by tracing the figure of a nude on her side, without lifting the point of his pen. There, the line's desire is to capture this figure of the female lying at the heart of all subjectivity, which is the circle. That stroke reaches the "She" in us, the way hills follow their own curve of hip and breast around the flatness of the land, the barrenness of winter. She lies below Paris and fills the city with energy, according to Henry Miller; his celebration of Aphrodite as the goddess of Paris comes in a long meditation in *Tropic of Cancer*. He understood that central principle of cities – they must be animated by a god, and the best ones are inspired by the goddess of love.

In the space of four months my wife had discovered this ethos of the female and had entered it. Her loneliness that fall had been intense, though she had loved her solitude. She hadn't known that silence and intensity of cold days without the kids around for many years. We had never been apart, and now the light, the subtle quiet of fields webbed with hoar frost made her think, perhaps for the first time, of some ethereal dimension that made itself visible as the clock ticked and she looked out from the big French doors with her tea smoking in a cup. In my absence, my wife had grown inward and independent. That is what I felt sitting in the auditorium at Gordes watching women with their children, their nodding husbands standing by looking a bit useless. It was a domain of females who seemed in possession of the life force, whereas the men were admirers, and puzzlers, and mere functionaries at the temple.

But Florie was exceptional among the women we knew, simply the most elegant avatar of the goddess. She had made a fortune in the music business in London, inherited parts of another, and now lived in a spacious villa at Fontcaudette, the hamlet just above us, with her south London husband, a graduate of the local pubs and billiard halls and a hard, basic male lover. We would have lunches together and subside under a deluge of white wine and Cassis poured over ice. She had grace, humor, confidentiality all at once, and a detachment from money only money itself makes possible. We were all important to her, yet it was we who were always listening, asking her questions, waiting for her opinions. She ruled, but always gave us the scepter to hold while she lit a cigarette, took a drink, made a little joke.

And she had a past. A mysterious illness caused by the pressures of the music business, the two-day jags on cocaine and all-night sessions in a studio, the hustle cranked up twenty-four hours a day. She had walked out on it and now had that remarkable charm of rich emigres everywhere, a past she chose, with humor, elegance, even innocence, not to bring up in her friendships. We later found out the "illness" had been uterine cancer, arrested with an operation and follow-up therapy.

Why this was an important part of her charisma, I couldn't say, but it mattered in our appreciation of her. It was never mentioned, but was always present, like the smell of thyme on the wind. It had the effect of raising her above mere womanhood, sanctifying the body through illness. It was no longer a tunnel through which life passed. Now it closed itself and became a stone shaped as a woman, a quartz stone through which a woman's spirit moved, flickered in ghostly purity. She was the secular heir of Mary and the hunter goddesses, women who loved without possessiveness. Her perfume was subtle, remote, like the smell of amber when rubbed, or of marble in sunlight. She gave love to her husband the way she might have funded some worthy cause – generously, without strings.

She was not beautiful, yet her face became beautiful in a moment, in a laugh or a look, as if her flesh were a mask and something larger moved behind it, occasionally showing itself. This is what charmed us, fascinated us about her, the unpredictable graces within her that came to the surface fleetingly but with power, a nonchalant infinity that was swept away with a change of her mouth. I sometimes felt there was a god inside roaming around and occasionally blundering into her eyes or her voice or her hands, then stepping back before being revealed. It was ludicrous to think she had labored in the linoleum dungeons of the recording world all those years, poring over lyrics about puppy love, cheap sex, lacing words with ripples of music, selling the myth of love to dime-store Venuses and pug-nosed Romeos. Now she was out of it, one of the survivors who didn't get caught in its furies; there was time for idleness, and friendships.

Their house sprawled over the crest of a hill and looked down on olive trees and wandering terraces; in the white gravel drive stood a red

Mercedes station wagon and a Jaguar sedan. Who could deny wealth, and yet who would put it between us? She came to our dinners dressed in clothes one rarely saw on the street, the rainy dawn colors of silk, linens that seemed to have sprung out of Mattisse's eyes. This care, this reverence for the body, raised the importance of our evenings together. Under the watery linen, she was young, slender, almost bone and skin, the sticks of her legs barely fleshed by hose and light heels, the hair brushed back and clipped with a girl's nonchalance.

Her husband made TV advertisements in London, a tedious sort of work that demanded a fussy sense of detail. He laughed it all off and beamed at his Venus now and then, living at his own pace in the world beside this rare creature. He seemed a kind of modern Hephaestus, without the limp or the grudges. She was sunlight, and he was the ordinary ground who worshipped her. In the spring, we spent afternoons together under the mulberry branches, stretched out on lawn chairs in the late afternoon, letting the talk drift as we nibbled a slow lunch and sipped champagne. The magic was in having a large soul in our midst, Queen Maev disguised among us.

But all that came later in the year. Now it was winter and Christmas was upon us. The landlord was coming back for his annual winter holiday and we were obliged to find quarters elsewhere for the week. I rented a farm house below Lacoste and moved the family in, set up a tree, arranged all my presents under it, and lit a fire in the huge hearth that we kept going all week long. It was our only heat, aside from a towel heater in the bathroom. The kids were off each day playing with friends while I sat writing at a table I had drawn up to the fire. My subject was Gustaf's poetry and the Provence he drew from.

He was up there on the brown slope of the opposite hill, private, enclosed, an imagination rooted in a few acres of ground, a few villages. My subject was already framed by the cold, silvery hues of winter light. I had only to pick out phrases of poems, summarize plots, draw a figure of the voice speaking from poem to poem to make an essay. And yet the facts drifted through me without connection, and I would sweep them up into paragraphs and liberate them all like butterflies.

Why would a man write compulsively of paradise if indeed he were now living in it? Why was the young girl he spoke to so remote, abstract? Was he merely praying for vision or did he behold what he described? Why is it that Florie, who said nothing lyrical, brought magic into the room with her? And yet this poetry, which I admired almost fervidly, drew me to the intent, the act of, but never the world it tried to grasp.

His poetry distilled the shadows and moist earth of Provence into a lucid trickle of words, the pleadings of a soul unable to grasp life directly. They were poems of male devotion, spoken to a girl who sat in the gloom of her allegorical limbo. She was not flesh and blood, but a thread of silences running through his words. She was an ear, a mute accomplice, a figure of speech, not a living female. If the beaches of Provence were suddenly filled with such verbal lovers, all men would howl and bewail their misery in a minute. I chafed as well. Where was the flesh, the beating heart, the thin wrist with its ivory skin under all these strategic phrases, this music of the mind?

So work plodded on slowly; as a secret sharer of paradise, I was slow to bend to the task of thinking abstractly, when in fact the silvery fields rose and fell outside like an icy sea. It was too exciting, it was too much to think of the bracing air, the wild look of the black hills, the massive tension of ground frozen with stark forms of stone rising from it – all outside my window, calling me out.

My presents were a cheering success with everyone. The fire blazed on our ruddy faces, and warmed the big, stone room with its fat steps going up to the bedrooms. There lay the chemistry set in my daughter's lap, a huge box layered with small vials and tweezers and test tube racks, the very thing for a girl who wanted to know everything at once. She was ecstatic, pie-eyed over her largesse. The Cabbage Patch was hugged and coddled by Maxine, and put to rest among the lesser gifts, the socks and blouse and soap and hair brush and whatever else we thought to include in her looming world. The erector set was already half absorbed into a shiny tower with crane lugging up new girders on its yellow string. By such stealth of heart I had won back my place again, I was dad once more.

Our kitchen was the focus of long dinners beside the little gas fire, where we stuffed ourselves on turkey and lamb roasts, wedges of brie and little logs of *chevre* rolled in soot. The markets had slimmed down their produce to winter vegetables: cabbage, squash, occasionally some spinach from Hungary or Yugoslavia. Spain gave up a few of its lemons, but they were bought up quickly. Our fruit consisted of figs dusted in sugar from Turkey, or the rare orange from California.

On steel-colored afternoons, I took walks and found myself eyeing local ruins with keener interest. I was beginning to look for my own little footing in this brown Eden, this dull, gray fringe of the garden. It was a pleasure to walk in Provence shorn of tourists; there were only the residents now, the farmers, clerks and shop keepers, a few strangers like us here for the whole year. Traffic was thin, and houses glowed in the dark till late at night. Apt was barely inhabited on cold afternoons, with the same faces passing you in the market; stores were empty and the clerks looked up with relief at the sound of the door opening. A clock ticked loudly in the post office.

We returned to our little hamlet just as our landlord was leaving for Canada. We were given a present of a can of dusting spray to use on the floors, with a warning about leaving one's premises a little tidier. A few dust balls under the bed had ruined his lordship's visit. He had tongue-lashed his son about us, whose wife pounced on us with a grim letter full of instruction and a few threats; from then on we lived gingerly in our borrowed house.

I read in the quiet hours and found myself staring at walls while I sat among the ticking clocks and the snap of the logs. It was now too cold for walks; the ground had frozen hard and the creeks were barely moving. The fields were dark brown and moody, with little life in them. The earth seemed almost to creak as the sky lowered and evening came on. There was little to do, and the mind ran thin with thought. I ached for some distraction, but there was none. It was like life aboard some slow-moving freighter where only the gray seas stretched out day after day.

In the mornings we would warm up the car and drive the children to Les Imberts, and stand with a few of the mothers to chat before the children went in. We heard the occasional gossip or planned our dinners with Florie by the fence, or simply stared at the bleak windows of the schoolroom after the children had gone in. Now the slow drive home again, and the hours spent staring out at silvery thin horizons, and the fragile attention that came with writing letters. After lunch the fire would be lit and we would sit in the tiny living room at our end of the house to read, or to stare into the fire. It was an atmosphere of waiting, waiting for the ground to stir, for birds to return, for rivers to thaw and fields to breathe some scent of warmth and flavor once more. For foliage to return and lure us back to dreams.

I could not get started on any of the projects I had brought with me. I sat at my desk under the slanted roof of the mezzanine, cramped into a small space I had created next to the bed, and wrote aimless little paragraphs as if I too were frozen an inch below my hair. I should learn to rest as deeply as the earth, I thought. I should give in to this organic idleness, this simple death. And yet I worked almost feverishly, trying to ignore the stillness, the emptiness. If only there were shoes to polish and door knobs to mend, or locks that wanted oiling and tightening, small things one did in the heart of winter. Instead, drives along the hushed roads led only to the quiet, closed villages, all darkened except for a light in some high window. The garage was full of fire wood and I enjoyed going out into the stinging cold to split logs with my froe and maul. The wood split grudgingly with a groan or a crack, and occasionally stirred some mouse in the soggy hedge, or woke a beetle.

The waiting grew richer as the clouds began to lift and more blue skies lingered over the house. Now one could study the damp grass for signs of shoots, and check all the branch ends in the orchard for swelling. One morning, after the kids went off and the postman came along with letters from home, I noticed the apple tree was streaked with lines. The sap had begun to run, thin honey colored streaks dripping out of scars in the bark. There were little black ridges that had puckered and an ant, the first of the season, sat nibbling on the sweetness. In another few days, I found the swollen end of a pear tree branch had cracked, and under lay the first green belly of a leaf. It was bright and thick, and was a precious sign, a good omen. I called Cathy out to look with me, and we spotted others. It quickened the heart, this promise the earth would wake and life resume.

At school the children were rounded up one bright cold morning and told to prepare for the burning of the straw man, the *homme de paille*, in whose straw body and old clothes lay all the sins of the past year. He was the last descendant of the Celtic wickerman, the great latticework figure in whom cows, pigs, men, women and children were crammed and set aflame to appease the difficult gods that ruled at spring. This little fellow was no more menacing than a scarecrow, but there were latent fears about his meaning, and one hoisted his crumbling body with eerie feelings. There were songs to sing and slow walking through village streets; the villagers came out and provided candy and drinks to the children as they passed. The songs told of the wily spirit of the year, whom they were about to send off to the other world.

As evening came over, we drove out to the edge of Les Imberts where a fire had been set and the poor *homme de paille* was tossed onto it to the jeering and rebukes of the children. Then one by one the boys ran and hurled themselves over the flames, landing in a heap on the far side. The parents and villagers all stood around quietly watching, wondering who might fall back into the cinders.

The evening was clear and starry, and the smoke that came off the fire was as sharp as raisins. We said goodbye to all assembled and went home again to a late supper, and lay in bed on the mezzanine reading. The hard freezes had dwindled away; the roof ticked and birds hopped over the shingles; the creek rubbed along its stones with a sound like weeping. There were small shoots in the fields; the lavender stumps had brightened a shade and were moving like spiders in their furrows.

This is the Provence the tourist rarely sees: the private, old-fashioned ways, the plodding routines. Winter is long and moist and offers few comforts to the visitor. But for those who weather out these long sieges, there is a feeling of brotherhood among us. We have seen our faces grow pale and weary from all the idleness, and we look hard into each other's eyes when we pass on the roads. Solitude has strengthened us, and we are now thorough searchers of our minds. Time gave that to us; we are masters of wood fires and know the will of the small flames that ask meekly for fuel before the ashes claim them. We are connoisseurs of moss and dampness, and bathroom mold, and the mildew of our closets. We know to take our time, to walk carefully over the ice and to be patient with our bodies wrapped in layers of wool.

When friends arrived, as they sometimes did to a clatter of stones in the drive and the headlights filling our dim rooms, the intensity of a visit was breath-taking. Talk seemed such a waking up, and we felt tense and self-conscious to have other faces in the room. The silence no longer owned the house; our voices took over, our laughter rang strangely in our ears. The night seemed overlong with the visit; there was comfort in the signs that someone would leave soon and bid us farewell as the door swung open on the glistening night. Then silence again, warmth, the fire smoldering, the bed waiting with its novel on the night stand. Winter was dying, and we were low in spirits.

As the winds veered round and the new season came in slowly, our lives grew more complicated socially. We had begun to meet people in the hamlet, most of them English-speaking guests borrowing houses here before the season. Once, I heard voices behind the locked shutters of the dining room and came out to find a woman of about forty-five standing on the terrace with her eight-year old son, Ben. She had come to pay us a visit, had heard we were Americans. She was Australian, with alert eyes, a sexy mouth that had faded into tiny wrinkles, a small, tense body she divided with a wide belt. She spoke with a nasal drawl, a boring voice that whined at the end of long paragraphs of complaint. You could tell she had bitched her life away, and her son had suffered for it.

Ben stood beside her working his handsome mouth, muttering little broken sentences under her tedious monolog. She ignored him while he stood there twitching and blinking, hyperactive and explosive beside her. Finally, he drifted off and began searching through the toys and junk under our children's beds. He found something to wind or knock against the bed frame, and got a few nasal volleys from his mom, Sylvia. She stared straight ahead but sent her warnings behind her, as she sat in the dining room talking to me. He kept right on working with nervous frenzy, mercifully obsessed for a few minutes.

Cathy came out and took a seat at the dining table as we listened together to a tirade on bad husbands, the corruptions of French bureaucracy, her dancing and music hall career in London, the houses she had bought and sold at various times, the falling price of houses now on the ferry route through Folkestone, where her last property awaited a buyer.

She was sharp, fierce, cynical, and her eyes drifted around and flirted occasionally. She still had it, the old magic; she had kicked around a lot, knew the bohemian quarters of Sydney and London, Paris, too, I gathered. She had been quite a lover; now she was a mother and a loner, working above us on a little stone house she was turning into a *gîte* for paying guests. "Ben! Stop it, *please!*" she shouted behind her, the last word like a nail scratching on a blackboard. The whole French nation was hounding her and holding her back; they would hear from her. Her son went on relentlessly pulling apart dolls he had found on the floor. She finished her second cup of coffee and left, but not before inviting us up to see her place.

We met members of the circle of our hamlet and people from the American arts college at Lacoste. The old timers were drifting back to Provence from winter houses elsewhere; the shutters were coming down from doors, gardeners were out trimming and sweeping, maids hanging out bed linens on the sills. The season was stirring, the postman was going around pasting name tags on the mailboxes. The burglars were cruising by in rusty, banged up Fiats, taking mental notes.

Kitty Taquey was an eighty-year old heiress of the Arm & Hammer baking soda fortune. She could trace her lineage back to the *Arabella* on one or both sides. She was an earthy, humorous woman who took to my wife instantly. They fell into the roles of mother and daughter, a relationship that bound them until her death years later in a Paris hotel. Kitty held forth in a low, gravelly voice, a glass of white wine in hand, seated out on the little cramped balcony of her house, "Les Quatre Vents," concealed among the slopes of a vineyard near Oppede le Vieux, where the ruins of another De Sade castle stand. The rooms were crowded with older couples sipping cocktails or wine, talking in low, murmuring voices about business and politics. It was dull work standing there nodding to banter about falling stocks or incompetent officials.

The only compensation was Kitty's humor, which put a barb on every story. She had been raised on various estates in Pennsylvania and Cape Cod, and had all sorts of tales about the brats and scoundrels of her class. The Rockefeller "boys," whom she knew well, "never had money in their pockets. They had to borrow from *me* to get their supper." Poor George Bush, W's dad, was always trying to live up to his father, whom she also knew, "and never quite could."

She had an honest laugh that shook her breasts and sent her jerking around in her chair. You laughed with her, as she stared back at you with blue, moist eyes sunk like spiders in a web of wrinkles. She was littered with skin cancers, she told us, and was the hit of any dermatology exam, when all the interns piled in and went over her like a map of the moon. She was full of moles and lesions and little brown patches that sent them into the corners to whisper, she said. She loved it, propped up naked like a ruined Venus. Death didn't frighten her in the least. She would end up in one of those "black holes Stephen Hawking writes about. That's where I'm headed when I die." She died in an elevator descending to the lobby of her Paris hotel, without a whimper or struggle.

The only other presence in the room was a tall blond from Paris, Madeleine, married to a man from a prominent Boer family in South Africa. He had quit his business there and now ran a small factory that turned out all the shutters and window frames for the houses of Gordes. She had the ambiguous smile of Meryl Streep, the same lips puckering slightly at the taste of a lemon. She taught French to the foreigners here while her husband looked after his cabinet business. The face was almost too elegant for the easy way she talked, smiled, ran long fingers through champagne-colored hair.

These were the women we came to know as friends; some, like Florie and Madeleine, we knew because we all had kids attending the local *primaire*. Others like Kitty came into our lives more slowly, as she grew to trust us. All of them, one way or another, came from the taste of money and lived well. It was a world of women, all of them strong in some element of their nature. They seemed to come up out of the ground on Persephone's shoulders. They were here for the blooming of the fields and the long, green summer. Some would vanish in the fall and leave the hills bare and empty. As the weather turned fertile, they wore the colors of the apple, the cherry, the blood-red grape, the brown of the warm earth, now moist and feverish with seed.

Apt had become a festival of the female, a celebration of the life-bearers. Everywhere in the narrow streets were spring dresses and delicate shoes, straw hats, purses, frilly lingerie. The pharmacies brimmed with lotions and posters of bronzed girls sleeping naked on the beach. Breasts were their glory, their symbol of authority. Beauty was a god whom they honored with their sensuality. How deep the cult of beauty went here may be gauged by the masked woman of Gargas. Some thirty or forty years ago she, like many of the farm women of Provence, distilled her own *pastis* in the *cave* beneath her house. The volatile mixture caught fire and burned and disfigured her face. She gave up the world until she came across pictures of Japanese porcelain masks, simple, unadorned faces where beauty had frozen into stone. She ordered several and began to wear them to answer the door, to cross back into life. She wears them now, I hear, and her house, on the road into Gargas, a vast mansion surrounded by orchards and plane trees, is where one casts a long glance driving by – the house of the masked woman, the disfigured Aphrodite.

The women of Apt passed me wearing flimsy halters cinched with a loose string, their breasts swinging heavily inside. A girl in the music store came to the counter wearing a mesh sweater, the meshes wide as fishnet with her nipples poking through. The clerk hardly noticed as he took her money. The girl at the ice cream stand leaned down into the freezer to scoop ice cream into cones, unconcerned that her shirt fell open to large white moons below.

This was the summer foliage, the green earth dressed as females, and they strolled in twos and threes down all the streets, talking and looking, their bodies scented and luminous with spring colors. They were Persephone's daughters. Catholic girls, working-class girls from the *confiseurs* and the *potiers*, from the dim world of work and tedium, free at last in the sunshine of early evening. I could not take my eyes from them as we went along, following the crowds, picking up our bread and *pâté de campagne*, our *banon* from the *fromagerie*, the newspaper. It was a breathless feeling of excitement to be out in the air, in the honey-colored light, surrounded by girls and women who felt beautiful, who laughed and stroked the gleaming hair of their friends, and admired the swells and hollows of each other's bodies. It was a celebration of the flesh, a joyful recognition that life begged for increase, and all consented to its urge.

I had laid to rest some squabble of a year or more about my own life. I knew I would put my foot on a piece of my own earth one day. As I walked the streets, I stood long moments studying the photographs of sale houses in the *immobilier* (realtor) windows. I was hoping to find the one small pile of stone that would allow me to slip unnoticed through the gate.

Chapter Ten

A Hole in the Wall

There are many books and pamphlets on how to buy a house in France. The reader is advised to look elsewhere for advice on the process. It can be tricky and there are many ways to lose money or be lured into the wrong choice. Houses come on the market slowly, begrudgingly, after the heirs and relatives have had their court battles and resolved not to come to blows over its disposal. Sometimes even the gardener, entrusted for years with the upkeep of an empty house, may have a lien on its ownership, which you do not discover until you try to close the deal, or move.

An English couple we know bought a modern house that had been the dream of a man for fifteen years; he labored slowly on it, fetching water from the well at the village bar, hauling the bottles up to his dry land for drinking, some for mixing plaster. When his wife left him, he continued on, out of habit until he could go no further. He let it be known he was willing to sell the house on its cliff edge overlooking a deep canyon and the village beyond. My friends put up the money, closed the deal, signed an inch thick sheaf of documents, and began working on it. Only to discover someone else had proposed the *idea* of buying it to the owner years before and had a letter to prove she had *intended* to secure the place when it came available. She hired lawyers and began a legal *procès*, a suit, to make her claim. Work was halted on the house and for the next three years Phillip and Nicky spent far more than they paid for the house to defend their ownership. The case is still pending, though the woman, who has sued them, her previous lawyer, masons who worked on the house, and anyone else passing below her windows, has now struck the presiding judge as quite mad. Still, the wheels of the law grind on and leave the verdict suspended in Cartesian twilight.

Whenever a house comes onto the market, a picture of it goes up in a dozen agencies scattered throughout the region. Everyone has a chance at selling it, and quite often when it has been sold, other agents continue to show it, work up client interest, and almost seal the deal at the point of discovering someone has already moved in and begun to paint and scrape.

I became an avid student of agent windows and knew almost all the available houses by heart. Some of the photographs were more artful than others, but I could always make out the same properties by noting the surroundings or the cracked window, the missing tiles of the roof. I chose, wisely or not, to go around the agents and to beat the countryside on my own. My reason was quite simple: I had too little money and wanted, if I could, to avoid the heavy commission agents charge their buyers. If I could find some little ruin that others had missed, and cut a deal directly with the owner, we might just pass most of the price under the table and save on taxes.

Wrong from the start. There were no idle properties gathering heat in the fields. The agents had combed the hills and found every inhabitable bump in the earth. Nothing passed their notice. They spent their idle moments over cocktails kibitzing on obscure bits of rock that might keep a human being dry, just to see if others knew about it. I had overheard such conversation at parties and finally gave up on the idea I would ever find something by myself.

Gustaf took interest in my plight and led me down to a meadow one day to show me a tiny, vine-smothered building. The heat shimmered off the broken roof tiles, and the vines had pulled the walls apart at the corners. Huge roots sunk into the rock and blistered the thin stucco. There was a pipe jutting from the earth which suggested water, perhaps not. Nearby was a farm house, newly built, with laundry dancing on the lines, and a few cars parked forever in the side yard. A baby was crying and a skillet landed sharply on the floor. Dogs roamed in the dusty yard and sniffed the water pan before leering over at us. They would be our neighbors if I chose to buy this little piece of ground.

It was for sale. It was cheap. And it had no right of way to the house. It was a dingy little cell with only one broken room inside, and sat in a muddy declivity that captured the heat and sent the cooling wind high over it. We stood in dead heat and the plane trees thrashed their limbs overhead in a steady gale. The right of way would have to be negotiated separately, he said, smiling sympathetically.

Though Provence has its quaint face and meek manners, behind the comely appearances rage bitter feuds among the dwellers here. They stop short of murder (almost always) to win a suit against a neighbor's transgressions. Without a secured right of way to a house, you are likely to find your path of entry blocked by a family waving rifles and holding back hunting dogs.

I know an English woman, then married to a Frenchman, who

bought a large house with property, but not the adjoining *remise,* the added portion, that extended from the house on a lower terrace. This was bought by a Parisian couple who discovered they owned the little strip of ground running before the large, formal driveway into the house above. When my friend came down to the new co-owners to ask if she might purchase the strip of earth in front of her entrance, the answer was a flat, ill-humored no. To emphasize the point, shrubs were planted there by the Parisians and legal action threatened if anyone trod on them or budged them from the iron gates. To visit her now, one must find a little patch of weeds to park in and come through a side gate, narrow and inconspicuous behind the arched, formal entrance out front. There the puny little privets struggle to root in the dust, and spread their branches with proprietary arrogance.

I didn't relish a fight with surly farmers, so I let the property go. But not without driving out there with my wife to look it over once more. It stood down in its little grassy depression like a burial mound, tightly wound in its vines, imploding slowly from heat and neglect. Why did I still long for it, standing there in the blazing sunlight, with the baby crying thinly under the gusts? I wanted my foothold, my handful of earth, my own pebble in this tiny province of the mind. But I turned and left, and went on looking.

Our strategy was mainly to waste time and enjoy ourselves driving through hamlets and nearby villages, filling the car with smells of garlic, fennel, and cinnamon. We would get down to walk the neighborhoods, stop in at the local café, sip coffee and calmly endure the eyes of villagers poring over us inch by inch as we sat there. Sometimes a hand-painted sale sign flapped on a wall or faded in a window, but it usually gave a far-off telephone number in Nice, or Toulon, or Marseille. If we called, a withering staccato of southern French poured out of the receiver and our single "Comment?", thick with American innocence, would end the conversation. The line would click and we would shrug back to the car.

Once in the little cliff top town of Saignon, which sits above Apt and the Calavon valley beyond, we came into a square burbling with a large fountain. In one corner was a narrow house with a sale sign on it. The landlord was standing nearby and we were shown around inside. The rooms all faced the square and the narrow street; none looked beyond to the sunlight. The stairs were so dark we had to feel our way up to the next floor. The shutters were unbolted and a thin bluish haze came into the bedrooms. The odor of rotting wood stung our nostrils. By twisting painfully over the sill, you could see a sliver of the fountain, but it would take some personal risk to get a better view. Once, he explained, it had been a fine house, with the whole rear portion looking down on the coveted view of Apt and the villages beyond. At night, ooh la la, the lights, the sunsets! But alas, over the years, the previous owners (his own family) had sold off room after another with any market value. Now there remained this apple core of darkness and crazy angles, of leaning walls and crooked tile floors. Downstairs, the only ventilated room opened onto the street. To have light at all, you were required to sit there, I suppose, in the full view of every passing villager.

The house reminded me of the little cement dwellings of Mexico, with their naked windows and sheepish inhabitants pretending to live privately under their glaring light bulbs. The price? A mere forty thousand dollars. Plus an additional thirty or forty thousand to . . . well, to *restore* this gem to its former glory. Any chance of buying back a few of the other rooms? "Never," he said, scraping his shoe with annoyance. That is the past. This, this tower of blue air and soft, crumbling wood was the future. I left the house to someone else's dreams. But now, many years later, it sports blue shutters, and bright new windows. A patio extends the side door, and what were sealed windows were pierced and framed to bring in lots of light. It is the jewel we hadn't seen in our mind's eye. At today's prices, it can't be had for under three hundred thousand dollars, possibly more.

I wanted a house, I looked for one, I kept notes and learned the different areas where one might find one. My budget was meager, a small sum I had saved while teaching in Malaysia. It amounted to forty thousand dollars. It would buy no more than a porch or a shed or an apple tree with a scrap of roof under it. No matter; I looked in every little byway and village corner for my dream. And all the while a voice inside nagged me with doubts and misgivings. Why buy, it asked? Why own an idea? Why not remain a guest, a visitor, a passing admirer? To own, what is that? Shovels and rakes, paint brushes and broken glass? All the tedium and labor of ownership, the greed and avarice of possession. We were a duet together, these voices in me, urging and banning, pleading and denying, as I stretched my little nest egg to the limit of its purchasing power.

Summer was upon us, the first long rays of June had already struck the roofs of our hamlet. Sleep grew thin and restive under the tiles. The bees buzzed and zig zagged over our dinner under the mulberry tree. The grass grew thick and tangled in the yard; the little pond was sinking below a wobbling rim of wild flowers, fiery *coquelicots*, blue bells, dog rose, and wild strawberry.

The cherry trees were heavy with fruit and we walked the road to St. Pantaléon at sunset, sometimes stopping to pick a cherry to eat. Our neighbor's orchard came to the edge of the road, and she watched as my son pulled off a cherry and ate it. Her dry shouts, her crackling rage from two fields away, singed our ears and we backed off as if we had robbed her of her jewels. But it was wrong to pick the trees before harvesting. I was sorry we had done it. Afterward, there were always branches and whole trees left full of fruit for the gleaners and birds. Worse is to venture into someone's vineyard and take grapes; there are powerful superstitions against trespassing. The vines are easily disturbed; the guardian spirits might be chased away.

I was now an authority on the market for houses that came in at eighty to ninety thousand dollars. I knew intimately what that included in the way of rooms, views, gardens, village locations. Shave a few dollars off and you found yourself in the dog patch end of a village; add a few and your upper windows looked over the neighbor's fence into the spacious freedom of a valley. The French are masters at pricing an object; there were no accidents, no flukes, no bargains, no undiscovered diamonds. A house in the dusty little town of Robion, where the Luberon tapers to its end, stood baking in a narrow street, a sale sign flapping in the wind. I called and made an appointment with a crisp, clear voice on the phone. When we returned, there stood a dark-haired man with leather jacket, his wife dressed in a stunning pair of blue slacks, the BMW humming on the curb.

They opened the door and led us into what seemed like the lobby of Dante's *Inferno*. A short, blunt room went nowhere, not further into houseness, or space, but just there, a corridor that slammed you into solid rock. To the sides, like vents, low, narrow doors led off to other stumpy chambers, each crumbling and sad and built, it seemed, for undressing the dead prior to heaving them into the pit. The rooms above were deadlier, the front ones had windows tightly shuttered and lined with strips of molten sunlight, like blast furnace doors about to blow off. The back, such as it was, formed a series of crushed closet-sized rooms that were windowless, but for some reason known only to itself, each of these back rooms, black with soot and nightmares, bore a massive, noble door of entry. The doors were the only indulgence in the entire structure. We sighed, and touched, and crept along behind our well-dressed hosts. At the end of the inspection, we stood in the living room, behind the crumbling shutters, and surveyed the cracked, peeling walls, the rotten ceiling beams, the loose brick of the hearth, the crazy floor disintegrating with broken tile, and smiled politely at the price, a hundred thirty thousand dollars. Another hundred thousand would make the place livable, they suggested, while we made more serious plans for renovation later. Not bad.

They drove off again in a nasal roar of tuned mufflers, leaving us standing on the curb. It was his house, I surmised; he had done all the talking, seemed to know everything about it. No doubt he had grown up in it, had suffered all the winter drafts and knew all the creaks and shudders of the back rooms. He would have nothing to do with it now, except to milk the cash from it. He lived in Cavaillon, where he ran a company. He had escaped from the peasant past; it was all a dim memory now. Few of his generation could bear staying on, living on the same street on which they grew up. The other children of the street had gone long before, perhaps to live in all those stucco-clad cottages that ring the major cities of Provence. There, at least, one could start afresh, live in modern surroundings, invent new customs or accept the ones from Paris and Lyon. But the villages, they belonged to the elderly and the foreigners.

We admired the handsome fountain in the square, where several men stood about with their horses. There was still a dirt street, and the church leaned on its blackened stones in the shade of giant chestnut trees. It was a place full of the relics of paleolithic people. It moldered away at this end of the Luberon, solemn, indifferent, enclosed within itself. It would be difficult to live here; the spirit was deaf to all strangers. The bar was rocking with American music; it was crowded with men hunched over the tables playing cards.

There were other houses of a similar darkness and morbidity scattered throughout the villages. These were *maisons du village*, the townhouses of Provence, built primarily by farmers who had moved up in the world. Their habits and needs were different from anyone else's. Peasant families preferred to live in tiny, well-heated parlors and to sleep in remote little rooms that would conceal their love-making, their children's whimpers, and the dying of the elderly. They wanted no more sunlight than their eyes absorbed in a day's plowing or planting. They chose to wall out the world of light which others worshiped at every sill. The peasant had had enough of the world by the end of the day and preferred life under a naked light bulb, his gloomy furniture, the dark walls, the cold, uncarpeted tile of the floors, the sooty little hearth with its tubercular back drafts on a windy day.

It had been our privilege to find this peasant world intact before the renovators got to it. They were coming, and we were only a month or two ahead of their ladders and paint buckets. But here we were, creeping from vault to vault of a way of life that went back to the caves. Some of the older peasant dwellings jutted out from overhanging grottoes; they snuggled into the rock which formed their roof and sometimes their walls. You can see a few of them along the N-100 at Les Baumettes, a town named for its shelf of grottoes above the road. There, tucked under the overhanging sandstone are clean little cottages with a steady temperature of about 65 degrees throughout the year.

The rock house in Robion was essentially a cave with rooms built out. Its back wall was the granite face of the Luberon, which passed down through the house and below the street. One communed directly with the mountain, which came down to the foot of one's bed. For the Celtic peasants who grew up there, this was a comfort, despite the cold and damp that leeched out of the rock each winter. The same gloomy darkness filled the pilgrim chapels and abbeys of the region. It was the darkness of the *bories* and caves, which had not changed in hue or temperature in five thousand years of domesticity.

Of course, any time you peeked into one of these sepulchral dwellings, the agent or owner would rush ahead pulling at shutters and window frames, tearing out the darkness as you came in. It was always pointed out to us where we might break through to more light, or gash the roof with skylights, or enlarge a little side window into a balcony. The only force stopping us, we were told above a whisper, was the mayor, who along with the regional architect controlled the design and revamping of house exteriors. You could turn the inside of a house into a purple psychedelic scream, so long as the outside remained beige or ocher *crépi* or bald rock and mortar, to conform with the village.

Balconies required special dispensation, as did roof terraces, those attempts to peer over a neighbor's roof at a few inches of the Luberon. Terraces were fine so long as they could not be seen *from the street below*. In fact, almost any village looks as it once did a hundred or two hundred years ago, except for streetlights, meter boxes, and telephone wires. But get up behind the village on some overhanging cliff and you will discover swimming pools lodged in crannies between houses, myriad terraces, solar panels, satellite dishes, sauna closets, all the luxuries of contemporary living kept out of sight of the tourists.

To find a house at our financial level meant taking the house directly from the peasant culture and converting it on its first round of use, i.e., making it minimally comfortable for middle class habitation. That meant stripping out dark painted plaster, antiquated wiring, lead-pipe plumbing, broken floors and ceilings, rotten roofs, and leaking basements or *caves*. It meant installing a bathroom with tub and toilet, and refitting a kitchen for modern appliances. A peasant family got by with a *bidet* and a sink for all its cleaning purposes. A French peasant could manage a pretty good bath while seated on a bidet, a not unattractive proposition if there were hot water present, which in many cases there wasn't. A better class of peasant owned a zinc portable bath (with fire box at the prow) for luxurious bathing. The kitchen sink bore the brunt of most family uses, from cleaning vegetables and washing hair to doing dishes, rinsing mops, scrubbing babies, late night emergencies when it was too cold to step outside.

Getting rid of the inconveniences of simpler living is what doubled one's investment overhead. There were those among us who enjoyed being first at the task of conversion; a certain psychological type liked pulling up the boards and setting a shiny new toilet onto ground that had never known one before. When you took a house on the second round of improvement, you paid for the primary renovation and perhaps for the psychological burden someone shouldered changing over lifestyles. On the second round of purchase, you put up with the needs and desires of someone else, with whom you might not always agree. The "improved" houses in the villages of Provence often came with cable service, multiple bathrooms, storm windows, central heat, burglar alarms, occasionally some tacky paneling on the walls, carpeting everywhere, lots of traverse rods and fancy new light switches. And an inflated price.

As you went up the ranks of renovated village houses, you came upon a forking in the paths. One path led off into the vision of an artificial cosmos, with the house as fortified lunar module tied in a few ways to the Earth, but mainly self-sufficient, artificial from roof to cellar, and fitted out for a life of exile among strangers and the polluted environment. This house sold quickly, often to Parisians who wanted their sun and views *au naturel* and their interior life as automatic as a Skinner box. This type we had learned to sniff out from the wording on the cards in the agents' windows; we didn't need a photograph to warn us.

The other path led toward some conscience-driven tolerance of primitive domesticity. Things were left almost as they had been: a *real* well left intact in the *cave*, a *grenier* with hay and bird shit and rotting stone walls going off directly from some luxurious, tiled bedroom, a kitchen with the Provençal wood stove still in place, the *potager* still functional in the niche of a wall, where soups were warmed over embers from the hearth. The lintels would be original, the walls would slant and wander around to small, low-ceilinged rooms, and there would be fine blackened cabinet doors hanging in lime-washed walls. These houses went for more, because they had preserved a semblance of Provençal authenticity, and had carefully done away with the look of suffering that may have come with farming in these hills.

In this housing market, and at our income level, one had to choose between ruthless modernity within a shell of stone, or the hypocritical standards with which others had been renovated. The latter sort, going at prices I couldn't hope to pay, had varnished peasant life into a Currier and Ives dinner plate. The polished wood and fine ceilings that drooped down over little rooms with hearths, the cane settles and bits of quilting, the rustic clocks and casement windows, all this fabrication of an idealized past spoke more to the longings of a middle class trying to escape from paper work and abstractness than it did to actual Provençal life.

As you looked and pondered, and ran figures on your calculator, you learned a little more about the depth of your own convictions. I wouldn't budge, couldn't bring myself to settle for a house at either end of the spectrum of renovation. I began to think it was beyond our means to buy a house. The pure product was too gloomy to live in, the refitted ones were confections of one school or another, and I disliked both.

One rainy day in Apt we were running our chores and I stopped instinctually at one of the larger agencies to ogle the photographs. Nothing new. Same bungalows, *gîtes*, sheds and mansions.

"Why don't we go in and talk to someone," Cathy asked innocently.

"Nah, that's cheating," I muttered to myself.

She took my arm and led me in, stood me before the desk of a woman who was as tall as she was wide. My wife could still only speak a few words of French, and these came out of her with a curious Midwestern purity which the French could not comprehend. So I was required to do all the talking. I was soaked, and inside the long, tapering room, bare but for a small desk and a little office raised a step at the rear, I felt chilled by the air conditioning, the sudden dryness of the air. I sniffled, and wiped a drip from my nose, waiting to be noticed.

The agent at the desk was busy talking on the phone, gesturing with great precision as she spoke, writing something down with the other hand as she held the receiver in the folds of her large neck. She resembled Humpty-Dumpty a bit, with small brown eyes, the face lodged within the shoulders, her hair tumbling down to enclose the head even more smoothly into the shape of a great egg in a chair. Her voice, as is often the case with fat women, was musical and expressive, a wonderful organ for selling things. She hung up, jotted down an appointment in an impressively crowded journal, slammed this shut and appeared to be getting up to leave. Instead, this rather fussy set of motions was her effort to rise from her chair, which she did with the help of the desk and the window sill behind her. Erect, she was very short, about five feet at most, and held out an arm that was as blunt and round as one of the branches on our mulberry tree. She gave me a firm handshake and a bright smile. We were gestured to sit down. She sat with a large sigh from the cushion beneath her.

"*Alors, qu'est-ce que vous désirez?*" she asked brightly.

"Eh, well, ..."

"Ah, you are Americains!" she said with brilliant eyes.

I thought I could disguise this fact by muttering indistinctly, but no. She had us pegged even as we stood outside, I think.

We explained our plight, our money, our interest in older houses, our desire to live in Provence during the summers. She noted all this without speaking. She merely smiled to herself, like someone working a crossword puzzle. Finally, she looked up and fixed me with a very strong look. I squirmed.

"You don't want any land around your house?" she asked.

I told her about the gardener at our hamlet, the one who came once or twice a season to tidy up, days, possibly hours before the owner came back. And was paid for diligent service weekly across the year. I didn't want to be made a fool of, I told her. I didn't want to depend on a gardener to come in and work for a frenzied three or four hours for what should have been done gradually year round. Ah, that struck a note.

"And why else?" she said, as if we were flirting over a soda at the drugstore.

Because, I explained to her, when the grass gets high and the damned gardener is off hunting ducks or something, the thieves know the place is wide open and break in. They can do it in minutes, merely by climbing a roof, peeling off a few tiles, drive up the moving van, unload the whole place, including toilet bowls and sinks, and copper pipe, and light switches, and have the wind howling through a vacant, windowless, doorless husk in no time. Yes?

"You've been getting around, eh?"

"I listen at parties," I told her.

"Gardens are okay, if you want to show off. People like Provence because gardens are, well, easy!"

She looked down again, conferring with her muses again. Was it over? Should I get up? We heard the rain sizzling under the tires of passing cars. The cough of the owner came through the glass door; a cigarette was burning in an ashtray, the phone was off the hook, the desolate white paper of some deal lay all about her, and she coughed again. Life creaked on its hinges, wheezed a gear into the next tooth.

"Voila! I will show you some houses," she said in English. "I speak Anglish," she explained, "a leetle. I learned it in Paris. I come from there. Come? Came. I came from there. You meet me here tomorrow, at same time? Eh?" looking at both of us for a nod. We nodded. "But you must speak French to me, okay?" Laughter. She lit a cigarette, blew a thin trail of gray vapor from her lips and laughed again. We got up and left.

The next day she led us through the streets of Apt, smiling at everyone, nodding to some, stopping to give the *bise,* three pecks on the cheeks, the requisite number in Provence. In the north, it is abbreviated to two. She knew everyone. They looked at us with a mixture of sympathy and friendliness. We felt childlike next to this great sphere of flesh bouncing on small, fat legs. She carried an umbrella, her cigarettes, a notebook. She breathed hard and in short gasps. She seemed a little unsteady at times, leaning against a wall to catch her breath, laughing quietly to herself. She would tilt her head and purse her lips to indicate we were not far from our destination, just ahead, she seemed to say. That gave her another moment to rest. Then on we strolled, taking small steps, while she chatted away in little quick exhales of words.

There wasn't much to see in the range of three to four hundred thousand francs, my top limit. A few places, nothing terribly interesting, she confided. "But, then, you are different. Not my usual customer." That meant we could enter into the Arab quarter without quaking, and this we did around the next turn. Kids in the street, a ball going off someone's brown toe, graffiti here and there, the little plaza like a scene from a Ben Shahn painting – poor kids playing against a big wall. I liked the atmosphere; a tea salon to one side, the Maison du Parc on the other. Years ago it had been a combination of things going back to the middle ages: a hen and egg market, a tiny Les Halles where produce and meat were sold under a glass canopy. I had seen photos of it, the Place du Postel, with men hawking eggs from crates full of straw; chicken cages piled on the sidewalk. The canopy had been taken down a dozen years before. When they pulled up the foundations, they found the stone bleachers of the Roman amphitheater, and left them exposed in the large concrete square. Arab women peered out from doorways wearing veils, clutching crying babies in their arms.

A narrow house lay down an alley next to an abandoned church, a convent chapel, I think. The streets were small and dense in this ancient quarter, squeezed together by the constraints of the *enceinte,* the town walls. Nothing much had changed over the centuries. One of three stone towers stood at the end of a nearby street, at the foot of which was a little restaurant. The murmurs and cries rising from all the neighboring windows was a sound unique to Arab towns. It brought me back to Beirut, that inimitable babble of life followed by peals of dark, moist laughter. The smells were different: mint, chickpea, parsley and onion, Turkish coffee, tobacco. Good odors for a neighborhood. Queasy feelings about the sound of the place; too much chattering, too many eyes staring out of curtains and shutter slats.

The house we were shown had been wedged in among other gnomic dwellings, only this one had its back to an air shaft, which went all the way up into the blue sky, protected by a fiberglass roof. An odd, flat light, silver and gray, came into the kitchen from the shaft. The rooms were all squeezed onto a circular stair. The only other light came from the front, through two small windows on each story, one for the ground floor. A hot, desolate little house, with only the air shaft as a surprise, a place for a new kitchen, with room for a cypress or a vine or two. We could almost imagine living there, but not quite.

Price? Well, how about one hundred thousand francs? We looked again, climbing up and down the tortuous stairway, rediscovering the air shaft, the "study" room above, the humorless dead rectangle of living room. But at that price, we could afford to travel, to primp the place to the nth degree. I went to the top floor again, looked down at what was surely an artery for foot traffic into the darker regions of the quarter behind us. And a place to hang out on hot nights. Heat! There was nothing between us and the naked tile of the roof, and nowhere for heat to go but into the house. I liked the top because there were new beams in the ceiling, and the walls had been plastered. A workman had left his tools and buckets in the corner.

I began to gather courage about the house; I asked to meet the owner, to have a key to go back and ponder the place a bit more, alone. Yes, fine. We did go back alone, the next day, and found the work had proceeded nicely on the top floor. In fact, there were signs of life on the bottom floor too, a few boxes of appliances and some clothes were piled up in a corner. I had better move fast, I thought, and hurried back to the agency, to my friend Bernadette. I was getting ready to leap. When I came to the desk, waited my customary ten minutes while she spoke on the phone, sat down with a look of eagerness and conviction, she lit a cigarette and informed me she had just talked to the owner.

"The house is already sold," she said. "*Voila.*"

I gave her back the key, quietly, contentedly resolved to give up the whole ridiculous enterprise and let ourselves stay rootless and itinerant. Our agreement on the rented house was up in a few months, the end of June, and it was too late to do more than find a summer rental, here or in Italy. Provence would recede like Brigadoon back into the mists and I would go on with my life. I must have thought all that out in my eyes and my mouth. She read me exactly. She patted my hand and said, "There's better houses. I didn't like that place, anyway. It's not a good neighborhood for kids."

The next day she led us up the steps of a back street of Apt, and round through a warren of alleyways to a little row of houses hidden behind garages and sheds. It was a secretive little mews, blocked at one end, jammed with tiny houses that were heavily draped and fortified, creepy little places with a look of fatigue and age on them. We entered a door into a tiny kitchen/dining room stuffed with a huge fireplace, its only amenity. Behind it was a damp, airless living room, and up a stairs were several merciless sarcophagi to sleep in. Behind the house, across a slab of cement, was an addition, the former garage, made up like a mobile home with gaudy yellow drapes and cheap furniture, a thick shag rug. It was like a house in Brooklyn, with the same gray skies caged in a maze of wires and poles and cables and laundry lines. I smelled lye and mothballs in the back yard. We got out and breathed deep to shake off a feeling of decrepitude.

"Nice? You like?"

"No, I hate. Detest. If I had wanted this, I would have moved to New Jersey!"

Not what she wanted to hear, but the smile was Cass Elliott's, the voice Kate Smith's, the odor of her dress a combination of all the fat women I had ever known growing up in Philadelphia. If I didn't shake loose of Bernadette, I feared I would round a corner in a moment and find my mother waiting for me, her green coat snugged up to her chin, her hand ready to grab me and drag me home for being so late from school. I was very depressed.

"Come back tomorrow. I think I know what you want," Bernadette said, a querulous note in her voice. We were coming back down the steps again. The sun shot out from a cloud and warmed the dark, gray walls rising on either side of us. The gray ivy turned deep green again, the birds fluttered. Sun came down in a thick braid of gleams and shadows. I was just about to say we didn't think there was time to go on with this search when I looked and found her disappearing before me. Her face had turned an odd angle, the mouth dead, and she was sliding instantly below my sight. The next moment Bernadette, her great bulk suddenly melted into a glob, lay outstretched on the steps before us. She had fallen as if all the bones in her body had snapped at once. She was a puddle of velvet and cheese-colored flesh. But she was talking, she was a boneless heap talking mildly and matter-of-factly to us, counseling our calm, bidding us to take a seat beside her.

"I am quite all right," she said, looking up like a pixie at us, an uncontrite and unbroken Humpty-Dumpty. We sat down on either side of her. We actually chatted with her, rather amiably, I recall. I mentioned the turn in the weather; my wife said the house wasn't so bad, with the right furniture it might work, etc. And there was always the villages to go to, Bernadette said. That's what we would do tomorrow. Someone was coming up the steps then, and looked at this scene of two people sitting beside an immense rotundity of flesh chatting away, and caught his shoe on a riser. He coughed, stared, kept to one side of us, and passed us with a few jerks of his head back at this sudden intrusion of Lewis Carroll into his life.

Finally, rested and reassured, she asked us to get her up. We did, feeling a little like Celts about to erect a dolmen. She came up rather more gracefully than I thought she would. As soon as she was upright, she was bolting down the steps on light feet, well ahead of us, bidding us to come tomorrow, same time. She had errands to run, she said. Bye!

The fall had cleared something between us, I surmised. She believed we were different from the ordinary run of customers. We hadn't embarrassed her but had taken her little accident in stride. So, she owed us a favor. Perhaps she might pull something out of a magic barrel. And she did. She found us a house. Now she wanted to know about us, to get some particular sense of what kind of writer I was, what were my interests, who did I read. We no longer filled our time with Berlitz-styled chitchat. It turns out she read widely, and read poetry and plays for pleasure. She was part of some loose circle of intellectual friends at Roussillon and Apt, serious people who kept that side of their lives out of their business. We had gained entry to it, a small glimpse of it.

Okay. So we left Apt, which was a dead end as far as buying houses, and headed east, the dreaded border of the respectable Five Towns. This was no-man's land, the undeveloped end of the valley. It hardly existed in the minds of the wealthy Gordes circles. We drove along for fifteen minutes or so, took a left up into the foothills of the Vaucluse Plateau, and wound around for a while until we came into a rain cloud and colder weather. It had been cool all day, but now there was sleet in the air, and a few snow flakes. We had climbed to about 1500 feet altitude, and in the distance were the sandy-colored walls of Saint Martin de Castillon. She said nothing, but it was a *real* village, modest, sedate, hidden, above all, unvarnished. We stopped on the road to let a herd of goats pass by; the shepherd walked slowly ahead with his crozier, which he raised to show where to turn down into the fields. His cape was wool and was sodden with sleet. My heart almost broke for joy at the sight of the goats, their smell of dung and gamey milk. I loved it.

Ahead lay the village made of bread crust. It's name, which it shares with some five hundred other villages honoring the great 5th century evangelist, also joins itself with the ancient duchy of Castillon nearby, razed in the religious wars and whose citizens, long haughty and superior to the mere Saint Martinais, begged to be allowed to live inside their walls. I would grow fond of Saint Martin, whose fame reached far and wide when he gave half his cloak, the part that didn't belong to Caeser, to a beggar in the road. He may have authored the notion of giving a stranger the shirt off his back. The church on the hill has a statue of St. Martin offering his cloak to a kneeling figure.

The houses were leaning this way and that as if whispering to one another. Nothing was gussied up. Even the shutters were bald and peeling, the walls left raw with patching concrete, the street asphalted and unglamorous as it bumped down through the center of town to a little bar at the far end. We drove along the peripheral road to the bar, interrupted a crowd of farmers having a morning *marc* together, and got a key from the barkeep.

The sleet went through us; an icy wind wrapped our pants around our ankles. I felt a sore throat coming. We pried open a big ugly door and went up the dusty tiled steps to a single room with a narrow window, a bar counter thrust up into the center of the room, nothing else but white walls, the bar, the floor littered with dust and bits of paper. It looked like the sad end of a bachelor's dream, something he had run away from after touching bottom in his life.

We gave up on it, headed out, down to another house for which she had a giant key. It stunk of mold and pesticide, and the walls were covered in a dead green mildew. There were no good windows here, only the remains of another house whose better half had been sold off in the lean years.

"So, let's go home," I whispered to my wife. "Forget it. Nice village, lousy houses."

"There's one more," Bernadette said, surveying our despair in that sleety, desolate moment. "Come."

We followed meekly, our coats dusty with ice. We went down the *Grand'Rue* to a house that jutted out at an angle, just where the *Impasse* began. A tile stuck into the stonework announced the little blind-end as the *Impasse de la Grand'Rue*, a suitably dignified oxymoron, a good address for wanderers. We got the front door open, pushing and shoving it along the floor, and found ourselves in a long, triangular room full of tables, chairs, a wall thrust up arbitrarily under one of the beams. The ceiling was *old*, the real plank and plaster stretched over huge beams, two of them hand-hewn, the other two telephone poles. A fire place trickled black rainy soot down the sides; a hole went through the floor to the right of the hearth, where cold air rushed up. It was a hay trap for feeding horses. A trough stood in the *cave* below. This had been a wheelwright's house. Hoops were piled up in one of the three *caves*.

A bedroom had been made out of part of the living room, hence the odd wall that backed up on the front room. It was a thin sheet of plaster and lath; a sledge could knock it down in a few minutes. The bedroom held the other window, a good-sized double window with the swing-latch on it. A bathroom stood behind the bedroom, long, large, gutted to make another bedroom. Both had been left as if peasants had just gotten up for the day's work. The mattresses were dented from sleep, the covers thrown over, the battered crate had an ashtray full of butts. Saucers, glasses, clothes were strewn about. The stairs led up to two other bedrooms, a *grenier* or hayloft running down the other side of the central wall, entered by a little door. The bedrooms were large, with windows over the *Grand'Rue*, one larger and given double use as a TV room. A broad bed lay unmade in one corner, a huge ugly modern table stood under the over-head, matched with six big chairs and a sideboard, all made of the same veneered blond wood. Rain was running down the wall into a hole in the steps; it was cold inside, damp, dark, forgotten. I went to the living room again and looked at its miserable proportions, the hole in the floor, the floor tiles cresting slowly like a wave and descending at a slant to the front door. The floor was going.

Under the *grenier* was the *remise*, covered in straw and strung up with broken feeding troughs for sheep or goats. A door clung to its iron hinges, the wood rotten and falling to pieces but for a few nails and a slat. I dusted off my pants and went back to stand on the stairs, trying to imagine life in it. The rain was cold and flew off the step and sprinkled my face. The roof was probably rotten.

It was another dead end. I started to leave, but Bernadette went out into the rain to "have a look around," to let us talk, in other words. She had a look of expectancy as she went out. "Nice *caves*," she said with a wink.

"Well," I asked forlornly, hoping we could get back in the warm car and go home to a fire, a glass of wine, a long, leisurely talk about our flight plans home.

"Let's take it," I heard my wife say, her eyes bright with excitement. "I like it. It will be beautiful, you'll see."

"Take it? Take this heap of rubbish? This, this . . . this miserable cistern of a house?"

"Yes," she said, and started framing things with her hands. "The wall would come down, we would have a big room then, and the kids would go in the upstairs back bedroom, your study would be at one end of the bedroom. O Paul, don't you see? This is a great house!"

I couldn't see, I didn't believe, I thought she was teasing me. But she wasn't. She meant every word of it. I looked again, I tried to imagine the larger room, a red tile floor, bright sunny windows, a dry stairs, my computer humming on a desk under the bedroom skylight. Well . . . maybe . . .

Bernadette came back. She led us around on a more refined tour, pointing out the authenticity of window frames, tiling, etc. She was *selling* the house to us now. "Get more light in here, more direct sun. Build a terrace, open the roof, buy the back lot and make it into a garden. It will raise the value and you can resell at a big profit," she said, facts, figures, details tumbling out of her fleshy lips.

On the way down to Apt we talked money. The house was part of a trust under the protection of the notary. There would be no agent's commission, just a little *baksheesh* among friends. Some could be paid, well, *sub tabula*, to shave off some unnecessary taxes, yes? Price? It's available for two hundred seventy-five thousand francs. Groans from the front seat.

"But I can talk to the people, and get it for you for *two hundred thousand* clear."

At the time, that was thirty-five thousand U.S. dollars. I liked the price, but it hardly mattered. There would be forty thousand to put into it to make it livable. I had forty altogether. Talk, talk, winding roads, talk and more talk, faster and sweeter talk until we got to rainy, darkening Apt.

"Here's the key," she said, getting down from the car. "Go back and look at it again. You'll see."

We did see, and the next day we felt the clutch of a decision gripping our bowels. Bernadette led me to a bank and we sat on the margins of a vast desk, talking rapidly with the loan officer, a thin, hollow-cheeked woman of thirty or so, tapping a new pencil on a new pad of paper. She wore a tweed suit skirt, a blouse of creamy vanilla cloth, her body shimmered inside it, and she calculated fast with Bernadette, her buddy in many previous deals. We got up finally, shook hands, and went out to the street.

"When will we know if the loan is approved," I said, having caught half of the conversation.

"You're a professor," Bernadette said emphatically, "you had it approved the moment she heard that. It's done. The house is yours. We'll do the paperwork next Monday in the notary's office. Okay? Bye."

We drove home in silence, the pit of our stomachs warm with fear. What have we done, we each thought in the rain, under the cold gray folds of sky. Did we ever think it would be like this, buying a hole in the walls of Eden? It hurt, it dulled the nerves of the heart, it fell like lead pellets through the veins, it smarted behind the eyes, it squeezed the conscience to think most of our little nest egg would be cabled across the Atlantic and shrink like plastic on the hearth by the time the bank got through converting it. We were cooked, we were inked in, we were homeowners in Provence.

Chapter Eleven

A Home of One's Own

This is a suitable chapter for discussing the burdens of owning a home in Provence; one can easily go bankrupt trying to make a pile of rock and sand habitable once more. I came close to declaring "chapter eleven" several times in the months remaining to us before moving out of our little hamlet and into the village, and from there, in another few weeks, home again. The moment we had signed our deed papers and the loan contract – all thirty pages of the loan papers, in fact – we faced the formidable mazes of French bureaucracy.

But let us not rush past the ceremonial nature of deeds and loans. The office of our notary was in Apt on the *Place de la Bouquerie*, where the two branches of the Calavon once met. There the Café Grégoire sits with old fashioned tables and chairs, and a row of older buildings looks out to the bridge crossing the river. Our *notaire* has his *étude* there, his palatial study, where we sat with our agent, Bernadette, to transfer the property. Fifty thousand of our francs (outside the stated purchase price) were counted out on the big desk, with door shut against nosy secretaries. Winks, nods, and handshakes closed the procedure, and we were rushed away. Bernadette shut the door behind us, on our very heels, in fact; we descended to the street door wondering what all the secrecy was about.

We had already come from the bank office, where a bevy of clerks and accountants and bank officers surrounded us in another large room, grandly appointed and with immense windows reaching up to the high ceilings. There we were given great sheaves of paper to initial with the statement, *"Lu et approuvé,"* read and approved, as though we had pored over each page when in fact we were fanning pages and scribbling initials hurriedly. All smiled as we looked up from our copy work. When done, we were again treated to handshakes all around, and given to know – through formal little smiles – that we were up to our ears in debt and legal entanglements.

In Europe, more than in the U.S., one's signature is a crucial instrument of identity. Putting one's name to paper constitutes an act of soul transference to things. And should a signature ever change its scrawls by much, as mine does almost daily, it can mean the difference between refused credit, scrupulous comparisons with other documents, grave suspicions of treachery. We signed carefully when our names were required in full. All done, we rose from both these rituals with a new weight upon us.

Beyond, lay the great scheme of French bureaucracy, the model of government "systems" everywhere, designed by Napoleon to run his armies. It retains his military aspect even now, as we soon learned. That universe of dingy, numberless small offices, each with a clerk and a battery of stamps and musty file cases, beckons you in with your first errand – maybe a water connection or sewer service, or the electricity. You venture in with checkbook, notary paper, your passport, a grin you wear to make you appear humble, naive, vulnerable, sensitive, earnest, worthy of a small break when the red tape begins to strangle. That grin becomes an ache in the cheeks, a spasm of the lips, a paralysis of the whole face by the time the first round of negotiations is completed.

When you have finally figured out where you are to go to get the water turned on, and you have stood for half an hour behind a customer who is in some obscure way related to the person behind the little grilled window in the basement of the *Sous-préfecture,* and then step up to find the wooden shutter being pulled down for the two-hour lunch break, you go home again, and return, and wait once more, and humbly advance to your turn at the grill. When you finally arrive at the window, the face behind it frowns at the sight of your papers, and then a voice softly, untranslatably murmurs instructions for some intermediary phase of the process. You are turned away with your papers once more – left standing in the clean, dull hall as a line forms at the window without you, and you suddenly come to the limit of your endurance and quake. You discover in that crushing moment that the French are different, that they extend from sources deep inside Celtic Europe and the Roman imperial world, where symbolism and mechanistic logic take their seat in the soul beside Eros and laughter.

With that lesson branded on your heart, you plunge off into the bright streets once more in search of someone who can help you figure out the next step, which involves descending to a lower maze of windows and getting the little faded circular stamp with initials squeezed into it at the bottom of your *blue* paper, and then you return. You are once more back in the limbo of a long corridor, advancing one step each ten or fifteen minutes toward the far-off window, where the face, pinched, yellow, tense with scrutiny, awaits you.

You arrive finally with a few minutes to spare before lunch again, and present your papers, looking away to avoid the pain of seeing those eyes grow dim, the brows arch, the mouth palsy into a scowl at some missing stroke of a pen somewhere in the blotchy wastes of your documents. Only this time there is the erotic thud of a *tampon* striking your document, and the scratch of a pen across the last seal of approval. The paper slides into the little brass depression and you feel as giddy as when you were handed your diploma or your first driver's license. You have your water service now, and you go out feeling as if you had taken on the Minotaur and won!

That is how I felt sitting in the café later, having a little *café simple* to celebrate my triumph. The paper lay on the table with the stamp showing. I hoped the waiter might take a peek at it over my shoulder, and get the measure of the man he was serving. This one can get *water service!* He came and went without looking up; the coffee, as always, dark, delicious, slightly burnt. As I sat savoring my victory over the legendary public system that had crushed more resilient contenders, the water man was rushing up the hill to open the valve into the house. I had no idea he would be sent off this quickly, but in France anything related to the kitchen and to domestic comfort is loosely equivalent to state emergencies.

So there I remained, enjoying the front page of the *Herald- Tribune*, sipping my second coffee while the key turned in the valve in the street, and the water raced into the first bend of the pipe and pushed a column of air ahead of it, which escaped with a hiss out of the tiny fractures of the bedroom pipe – which ran along the floor and fed a bidet and two sinks. The water filled up the toilet reservoir, the downstairs sink inlets, then mounted the vertical pipe into the bedroom, squeezed all the air there was from the last links and found the little rents in the copper tubing, caused by a hard freeze a few winters before, where it built up a fabulous pressure and burst out in an arc of five or so meters. Rusty water ran down walls and windows, and then stairs, and a milky little waterfall slid under the front door and down the steps into the street, where the water man stood with his key. With a flick of the wrist he closed the valve again, packed up his tools, and came back down to Apt. Errand over.

When I finished my second cup of coffee and prepared to leave, I felt smug and tipped the waiter an extra franc. I can handle this, I told myself, looking at the next ordeal – electricity, I think. I decided to drive up to the village just to have a look around before going home to the hamlet. As I walked down the *Grand'Rue*, our new address, villagers stared at me with a mixture of interest and sympathy. One even shook her head and seemed to say, "What a pity!" I got to my front door, saw the damp steps, and thought someone had bothered to wash them down as a kindness. When I pushed back the door, a stench of wet dust and plaster stung my nose and eyes. Pools of dirty water stood in the hollows of the brick floor; the stairs were still dripping. The heavy beams were slick with water that had seeped down from above.

I shut the door behind and stood alone in my moment of disaster. I was out of money; if the plumbing was ruined, I wouldn't be able to have it fixed. I stood in the middle of the room with the gray water dropping on my forehead, smelling the dead house, its decay, its soulless destitution. If a beam broke in front of me and the ceiling cascaded down around me, I doubt I would have blinked. I had bought a dark shadow, a pocket of time, a little envelope of rock that held a ghost. It did not want to be filled with the living again. I felt better letting the whole tragedy of the affair come down on me.

When I turned around at the sudden shift of light in the room, I found an old man gesturing to me anxiously, trying to explain the problem. He took me by the wrist and led me upstairs, into the big bedroom, where we knelt and he pointed out the little slits in the copper pipe. From a winter freeze, I think he said. I stared down into the little cracks, no bigger than the print of a thumb nail. All this water from here? Was the water turned on *already*? Ah! A plumber can fix this sort of thing, I asked? He can, eh? Cheap? Yes, then the water will come on again? Wonderful!

When Serge left, a handyman who worked for the mayor, I sat on the cold bedroom floor, exhausted. I was either happy or sad, I couldn't tell which. It was a long white room with a skylight and two windows full of tarnished light, and the floor sparkled with little pools of water. I could get this fixed, but didn't know of any plumbers around here. And when I got it fixed, where did the man with his meter key go? Would he ever come back and turn on the valve again? I sat listening to the village through the closed windows: the velvet murmur of voices in neighboring houses, the ticking of a dog's paws on the pavement below, the notes of a flute or recorder followed by a laugh, water gushing into a sink, a baby coughing and being shushed by a croaking syllable. I was a little boy in my loneliness, and these sounds comforted me.

I sat meditating on the murmurs and sighs of the village, the wheezy clang of the church bell just above our roof. These were the quaint sounds of a lost time, and it would not have been impossible in that moment for me to suck my thumb. Failure always reduced me to this numbness, this state of quartz, as Emily Dickinson would say. The sounds that rose up into the windows were those of helplessness – of elders soothing the pain and fear of those who lay in their cribs waiting, throbbing, hoping.

Failure. It is the purest emotion; it strips the flesh from the soul, it empties the mind. All failures leave the father triumphant, the son in pain. All battles are the symbolic reenactment of father-son rivalry. The hero who returns swells with fatherly fertility, and is showered with paper rose petals and kisses, and flowers, and passes through the vaginal arch of triumph to his rewards. And here I sat, under the cooing pigeons of the church eaves, hearing babies sigh and fall asleep under the soft humming of their grandmothers.

In this serene neutrality, it struck me that we had no bathroom. The room where a tub should have been contained an unmade bed with a rubble of bric-a-brac crowded onto a little end table, a mound of greasy peasant clothes piled on a chair, a small closet in which stood the only toilet in the house. If there were no tub, I mused, then there is no hot water heater either. There was no evidence of one, as I went over the rooms in my mind. There was no comforting bulge of white enamel in any corner, hung up on any hook above a plumbing fixture. If indeed a tub had once been in the house, its place had long been cleared out for another bed. The rooms below, the stubby little kitchen-living room, the tiny bed-room behind the false wall, the bathroom-bedroom were all shaped out of the dwindling resources of a man with too many sons. He must have torn out all the amenities of life to make room for his tribe.

I got up, dusted myself off, went down the cold damp stairs to the "bathroom," peeked in at the sad little cot with its depression from the last sleeper, poked the objects of his night stand, the ashtray with crinkled butts in it, the shoes left waiting under the dirty counterpane, the sad little rag that hung over the window. Pipes led down and crossed over through the wall, which I followed to the next room – and found them supplying a little sink and bidet. The last tenants of the house had sat on ice-cold bidets to scrub their bottoms, and to sop water from the sink onto armpits and faces, and then went out into the stunning cold of winter to work the fields.

Or so I surmised.

We had forgot to ask about a tub or hot water. It hadn't occurred to us to even think of such a thing as we stared up into the dripping roof and down at the holes in the living room floor. The water heater was a thing one might *suppose* to have existed, if not in the house, then in the *cave* below. I went down, pulled the rotten barn door loose and stepped into the warm, black vaulting to feel around for the gross belly of a water heater. My heart raced for that sudden welcome roundness. Alas, a slick pipe ran along the moist stonework and disappeared into the ceiling. There wasn't even a valve to open or shut the water supply in the house. It ran from the street valve into the house with nothing to slow it down or heat it up. The house was a bare sepulcher of peasant ways; we had given our souls to a stone box on the mountain side. It offered us nothing but its own solemn decay.

I shut the door, which hung loosely on its final rivets and rusty hinge, and locked up, then drove down slowly into Apt and west toward our hamlet. A letter awaited me from a friend, whom I had pestered many times to come visit us. He now accepted our kind offer and timed it for the moment we moved into our new house. He would come with his wife, who had gone to great expense to buy plane tickets and rail connections during the tourist season. They were looking forward to their visit – to luxuriating in our spacious new home, to basking in the warm sunshine and washing off all their dullness in the glistening depths of our bathtub. They were coming soon, in a few weeks, roughly a day or two after we moved into our little mansion on the hill.

In the meantime, Sylvia and my wife had become close friends. I would come home from shopping or a hike into the hills and find her seated in the dining room, her nasal complaints rasping over the world like a rake gathering up broken glass and pebbles. Her son would be milling in the corners of the room looking for loose stones to pry out of the wall, or for some clever way to blow us up. He paced the perimeters of the dining room like a newly captured cheetah, hands swinging, face brilliant as a sunrise, eyes furtive and unquenchable. Before long, Sylvia insinuated herself deeper into our lives – she knew a black market labor force who would work for cash, less the value-added taxes. These were always young, well-built men with strange pasts, a vaguely criminal eroticism simmering in them.

These were the mortals whom Sylvia would cast under a spell and make work for her for peanuts, for the rare compliment that might brighten her face among the jingle of pinched francs she dropped in their hands. She would berate them horribly if they slacked off, and then soothe them with a kind word. They would work frowning and cursing in whispers to themselves, but the job would get done somehow, a patched roof, plaster on the walls, stone in the path, whatever she might need.

Mario showed up at our house with a thin, sickly woman and a taciturn brute who never took off his expensive leather jacket. They brought a radio and turned up the volume to a screech and set to work on our little false wall – it tumbled into a mound of plaster and splintered lath, and sat there in the middle of the sloping floor for weeks to come. Walls got plastered, the second window suddenly leapt to life in the living room, the walls of the "bathroom" got a new surface. Then the tempo slowed, and Mario became restless for the road again.

Sylvia grilled me on the job he was doing; I caved in and showed her a few spots where the trowel missed. She would collar her little serf and drag him around to each spot like a woman housebreaking her puppy. He would scowl at the mess and curse audibly, then come back the next morning and slop more plaster into the hole. But he was temperamentally finished with us; he couldn't hold back his rage. The ceiling of the bathroom was still a mess of naked rock and patching wood used to hold up the floor above, and he whacked his trowel into the corners a few times, then gave up on it. He hauled away the mound of broken plaster from the living room in the back seat of his car, and reached his limit. I paid him for work done, and the next day there were his buckets and trowels, but no Mario, and no cohorts. He was gone. A few days later he got his tools back and went on a spree with his money. Only then did Sylvia inform us that he had "quite a record" with the law, and an "awful temper."

Meanwhile, we had been carting all the junk in the house down to the trash cans, and dragging a multitude of chairs and bedsteads up to the hayloft. The junk was a remarkable archive of the previous family: plastic table covers, a rotten scrap of needlework that had been pinned up around the mantle, some moth-eaten strips of netting to keep flies out, lots of plastic dishes and bent or broken forks, rusty butter knives, dented and leaky pots. The pantry still bore traces of their dinners: cartons of flour, a few sacks of grain, some spice jars and a few bottles of unidentifiable dried herbs. There were mounds of work clothes, run-down shoes, piles of damp, yellowing magazines. Nothing bore the trace of a female among these bachelor farmers. The grate had long ago given way to a small iron brazier and a rusty stove pipe; it had served as heat and cook stove, to judge by the cake of greasy soot lining the back of the hearth.

The more we hauled out, the more we entered into their lives. I began to imagine the long nights in those darkened bedrooms, after the fire had gone out and the candle alone flickered on a night stand. The sounds of the village would be muted on such nights; the house would be filled with snores and muttering. A dead cold would stand in each room, and the sleeper would be snug under a pile of soiled blankets until morning. In the gray hour, someone would toss a few sticks of wood into the brazier, some charcoal, and get a blaze going for coffee and a hunk of cold, stiff baguette before work. Others would clomp down the steps and drag the door open into the only warm room of the house. Their clothes would smell of sweat and damp as they warmed themselves in the little cane chairs, the ones now standing at our dining table. Their feet would drag over the upturned, cracked floor bricks. The cold rotting cellar below would seep up through the hay trap beside the hearth. The walls would sweat and fill the room with damp lime smells as the stove heated. Harsh cigarette smoke would mix with the tang of boiling coffee; the bread would be turned over the flames until hot. The men would eat or smoke in silence, as morning dripped and the heavy overcast sky lightened a little. A tractor would go by down the *Grand'Rue* with two men hanging on it, talking. It would be time to go down into the vineyards soon; or to ride into Apt for some other form of work. It would be another winter morning toward the end of an era, a few days or months or a year before the father died, and the sons scattered into the streets of Marseille to live some other way. They would go out the door with all their belongings and past left behind; the last one would draw the front door shut with a wheeze, and not look back. It was over, the era of farming and communal life was closing. All those ancient photographs that adorn the walls of the Foyer Rural over the bar, where men and women in black work clothes helped bring in harvests, stamped the grapes, beat flax, put up the cherries or cleaned almonds, gone. Finished. An era, an epoch of life culminated with the wheeze of our door, and the turning of a large iron key.

Twelve or thirteen years later, we would push open the door and Bernadette would gesture brightly at the quaint details of the ceiling, or the little stick one pivoted on a bracket to lock a Provençal window. We would interrupt the silence and the ghosts and come in like creatures from another world, looking to occupy this strange shell of human ways.

Slowly, indirectly, the ancient form of house began emerging. We were spending very little money in the process, doing most of the hard labor ourselves. We dared not look up from our scraping and peeling, the sweeping, nail-pulling, rag gathering, or we would have given up; the work stretched on, the list grew as we finished one corner and moved to another. At the end of a long day, we would sneak a few glances at our work and head home to a hot shower and a quiet supper. The children would come home from school at Les Imberts full of stories and an occasional song to sing – merrily unaware of the purgatory we came from.

In the evening, after wine and cheese, fatigue would weigh us down and we would climb the narrow mezzanine stair and drop into bottomless depths of sleep, wake sore and stiff, come to slowly over coffee, and by nine be ready to speed off to the village for a day of hard labor again.

By now, it could be seen what sort of house we had bought. It was no longer a dark pit in the rock, but an actual house with windows and white rooms. We bought a stove and installed it with a bottle of cooking gas; the plumber had come and given us a proper water valve and soldered up the leaks. Water ran free and cold through the taps. The lights worked. The toilet flushed with a vigor that shook the floor. The living room floor got a thin coat of cement that leveled it up for tiling. When the shutters were pushed back from the living room windows, the light entered the room like the cold glinting beams of a glass of water. It was the pure ancient light of Provence, sieved of its honey by the mottled walls of the opposite house. It was lovely light, thin and fragile, falling through the overhanging eaves of the *Grand'Rue* and down into the stone street, and into our windows.

The stones are alive, as everyone will tell you here. They breathe, they remember, they speak to you. Wherever the bleached sandstone runs in Europe, that is the road of Celtic migration. And left behind is their religion of the living stone, the gods that inhabit this ocean floor, this sediment of time. By the time we had scraped and gouged our way down to the rock in our walls, and beheld the rose and beige highlights of its boulders, we could feel the house regain consciousness. The walls lined up again, the space within seemed to organize and define things once more. Light filled their shapes and a certain beauty, rustic, primitive, elemental, came up through the ground and filled the place. I couldn't believe so little handiwork as we did could bring back the spirit of such rooms – the small, compact reality they enclosed, the delicate geometry of light that ruled there.

By now, the major walls were resurfaced and painted, and the ancient character of house returned. Our rooms were much bigger than in most such houses, almost double the size of the little cramped chambers we had seen on our house shopping. Our own bedroom could well have been made into two or three of the standard ones. The hall upstairs was generous, and the *grenier* was a future addition, a study and another bedroom waiting to come to life. Below, the *remise* would be reborn in a year or two as a proper *salon*, with a door going off our living-dining room beside the hearth. I was joyful over the work, over the rough diamond we had begun to polish. Cathy had been right all along, she had seen the ghost of house under its shabby dirt.

I wasn't completely sold until one morning I came in alone to face the light coming over the roofs into the window. It was old light; it was ivory from another century, veined with gold. It lay there in a puddle of radiance on the sill, and etched the wood of the frame with tiny filigrees. The dust turned in the motes, and I was somewhere else, in a dimension that belonged to the deep silence of graves, the formal silence of statues in an empty church. I felt time on my hands when I reached out to the window, to hold the light. I looked behind me, into the white plaster room, with its dark beams, its collective memory of hands shaping wood and forming these spaces over many centuries. I was no longer myself in that moment, but the tenant of a borrowed and transcendent space that gave me the momentary, fleeting right to be there. I took a deep breath, as if a pain had stolen over my heart and made me think of death.

We began moving in – with a few suitcases, some dishes and utensils, a box of pots and pans, some towels. We made up the heavily-timbered walnut bed in the children's room and propped up a set of wooden lockers that had been left in the hallway upstairs. I pulled down the curtain some-one had tacked over the skylight, dragged away rotten sheets and blankets, the broken vase and chipped ashtrays, the framed religious pictures, calendars nailed into the plaster, hauled down the sprung sofa, the big old-fashioned TV, everything that could be bullied out of the narrow door frames. The giant, veneered sideboard that lay against the far wall of our bedroom refused to budge; it weighed three hundred pounds and was too long and wide and ugly to go anywhere. I thought of taking an ax to it and burning it in the hearth, but without any closets it was at least a place to cram our clothes, so we kept it.

The time came, in other words, a giddy moment of suspense and anguish, in which the kids climbed into the car, and the trunk came down on all the stuff I had squeezed into it, and we took off for our new village. The kids looked back once at light and serenity, a garden and pond, at lavender fields and crunchy gravel drives, at peace and hot water, and watched as the road led east up into the mysterious blue slopes. When we pushed the heavy front door open to the living/kitchen/dining room, with its new depth and brightness, the kids held their breath.

They ran upstairs to their bedroom, examined the shell of our "bath-room," used the functioning toilet, sat down in the living room on the little bed we had made over as a sofa. They sat and stood and milled around, looking, probing, touching, smelling, while the parents waited for a reaction, waited to *smile*. And there was a ripple through their bodies that told us it would be home, if not now, soon. They accepted the place, they put fingers to the wall or the doors or to the window sill that meant they would possess it. We hugged and sighed and babbled happily. The

Images of Provence

Photography by Paul Christensen

Private entry to a house just off of La Grand' Rue.

Above: Entry to the village from the car park, with its "one-way" sign and alert that horses use this passage. **Below:** Just inside the entry to La Grand' Rue, this little-used passage leads down to other houses and steps leading back to the main street.

Above: Further down La Grand' Rue, where the house walls tilt out at crazy angles from old age. **Below:** The author's house, jutting out at the intersection of La Grand' Rue and the Impasse, a private court shared with a neighbor to the left.

Above: A turn in La Grand' Rue (Main Street). Note the notched stones of the arch to protect against earthquakes. **Below:** A typical housefront on La Grand' Rue, halfway to the bar.

Above: A view from the old "dryer" above the wash basins, looking down on La Grand' Rue and the valley beyond. **Below:** The back way up to the top of the village, where the castle stands.

Above: At the top of the village looking out over the Calavon Valley to the Luberon. The little garden takes the place of a house long since razed. **Below:** The Bar de La Fontaine is the social hub of the village. The stone arch has two pipes flowing with water year-round from the Durance River.

Above: Along the corniche road below the village is this old garden gate. **Below:** The house in Croagnes where the journey began.

Above: Gustaf Sobin's writing studio perched at the end of his property among vineyards and scrub land. **Below:** The little fountain with four swans in the Place Carnot in Apt. Beyond is the Church of Ste. Anne and the public library.

little refrigerator left by the previous owners worked well and was full of our supper things; that was the coup de grace. Milk was poured, and cookies were spilled onto a plate. We ate our first food under the new roof, in a silence of deep reflection.

On the first evening in our own house, the girls crawled into the big bed, and my son into the little iron cot I had put against the wall. We talked, and I told them an episode of our endless saga of the "Magic River," and shut the light, drew the door closed, and crept downstairs into the living room. A streetlight stood over the door and cast a soft glow into the windows. It was the first time we had seen the room at night. I uncorked a bottle of dark Bandol, rank and earthy with *mourvèdre* grape grown along the coast, and jiggled two glasses together as we plopped onto the mattress-sofa we had pushed against the back wall. We drank in silence, and shivered at the sound of voices in the street, villagers passing below our windows, ancient voices whose syllables were worn down and flowed together like mountain streams. We were Americans, the only ones for miles around. We were deeply grateful. We were *home, home at last.*

In the morning, church bells bonged in our ears and woke us at seven. The kids were already whispering and getting out of bed. They ate breakfast at our rickety table and took off into the village while we sat back and savored our first cup of coffee from the *cafetière* we bought. In a few minutes the kids returned with a new friend, a small, black-haired girl of eight or nine years, with a chipped front tooth that gave her smile a reckless candor. She cautiously approached me and kissed me three times on the cheeks and then turned to my wife to do the same. Musical French poured out of her slightly lisping mouth. In another moment, the older sister, a plainer version of Mathilde, came in and also kissed us, then introduced herself as Sonia.

The kids went off together and we cleaned up slowly. I took down the shutter from the door and stood face to face with a woman standing outside. When I beckoned her in, I was greeted with three kisses on the cheek, and waited as my wife received hers. This was Mireille, the mother of Mathilde and Sonia. She was a short, attractive woman with an early spread on her hips, wearing loose, drapey clothes to hide it. Her mouth was small, humorous, her eyes brown and darting. She was taking us in at some dizzying speed, talking slowly, a careful, lucid French I caught every word of. She was raw, brilliant, wild as a hare, still young enough to look me hard in the eye until I blinked. She sat, drank our coffee, gave me a little nod of approval on the taste, and went on with business.

Business was welcoming us, first of all, asking of our needs, a dark, purring voice full of marsh salt and tangy grapes and cigarettes and the confidence of a southern businesswoman. If I had known her a month ago, when I sat alone in the miserable flooded bedroom, she would have led me by the nose to a plumber down the street, or had one there in ten minutes, wrench in hand. We were given clear instructions to ask her for any information whatever, and if she didn't know the answer, she would find someone who did. We were given a steady, warm, open smile that fluttered our stomach muscles.

Every nerve in her brain strained to drink us in. She was radiant with interest; we were Americans, I was a writer, my wife was a college instructor, these were signs of a wider world, a culture mythologized on nightly TV. Perhaps we were rich, hiding out from publicity hounds and disguising our importance to nosy villagers. She would love to know, but only to slake a thirst for what existed beyond her own horizons. We must meet her husband, Jean Marie, one of the farmers of the village. One of the heroes, she might have said, the last men of a dying tradition; when they roared up the village roads in their tractors, you felt a darkness ripple through the women who watched them.

In another hour or so, with the light bleaching into noon, we heard steps under the window, and saw Mireille's face appear in the door again. She had brought Jean Marie, her husband, to meet us. He was short, stocky, lantern-jawed, with mild, protruding eyes and a leathery sheen to his forehead. His brow rose abruptly and the back of his head flattened like a cliff down to his weathered neck. He had a small boy's meek expression in his eyes as he extended his hand and warmly shook mine, and then my wife's. He spoke in the banjo-plunking twang of Provençals, most of which passed over me untranslated. He wore blue jeans and a plaid shirt, and sucked at a gap in his teeth, while Mireille rambled on in a mixture of slow, clear French and some English.

We sat, I offered a glass of wine, which Jean Marie accepted with a grin of approval, and we stumbled forward into small talk. Jean Marie eyed me now and then, wandering if I were a rival to be dealt with. Mireille was too animated, too radiant to be taken for granted. Jean Marie's lips flattened as he went inward again, to his own thoughts. He was nervous, timid, lost in this brighter world of chatter about things beyond his knowledge. But he sat patiently, drank his wine, and rubbed his knees as a sign to leave. Mireille ignored him and he got up and went home alone.

A few days later, we were invited down to their house for dinner. I bought a good bottle of wine and we dressed up a little, then all five of us strolled down the *Grand'Rue* to their little house in a bend of the road. The table was bare, a naked light bulb hung down burning into the cluttered corners of the room. The hearth smoldered with a heap of kitchen garbage, egg cartons, foil wrappers, tin cans, and wads of paper. A black dog scratched its fleas on the cracked floor. There were cooking noises in the kitchen, but we all stood stiffly by the door, wondering if we should creep away again.

Mireille spotted us as we turned to go, and the whole house erupted into arguments, shrieks, pot clanging, doors slamming. Everything leapt to life at once, as we were pulled down into dining chairs and given glasses of whiskey. Immediately a distracted, rambling small talk took over, as the two girls labored away in the kitchen, dropping dishes, snapping at each other, calling for Mireille. Finally, in one menacing bound from his chair, Jean Marie sprang to the kitchen, routed Sonia, and chased her into the dining room brandishing a kitchen knife. He lunged one way and then another behind our chairs, trying to catch her. Sonia was white with terror, and shouted in a thin screeching voice, while Mireille blindly struggled to maintain our small talk.

Though short and thick, Jean Marie was as agile as a goat as he scampered behind one chair and then another, the knife, a dull kitchen carver, held awkwardly in his hand. We knew this would not end in murder, but the game depended on a subtle balance of real terror and fits of laughter, as the chase went on, grew angrier, subsided into silly exaggeration, and then died out for lack of plot. This show of manly rage was meant, in part, as a caution to me; it was also a glimpse into the frayed relations of a stepfather and his two daughters. Clearly Jean Marie was a jealous, spiteful little boy in this marriage and would drive off one or both daughters to command his place.

The ruckus ended and we could stop smiling nervously at the imminent violence. The poor girl retreated to the kitchen and prepared the first course, a steaming plate of spiced mussels, which we all ate with forced merriment. That platter was whisked away, and another brought out, something Sonia had thawed from the supermarket and resembled large kidneys, but which were in fact a bit of flesh stuffed with a *farce* of ground organ meats and herbs, called a *caillette*, or "little stomach." The outer rubbery jacket was hard to pierce with a fork, and I worked to keep the thing from skittering off my plate into someone's lap. I half feared poor little Sonia, pouting still, though wicked and darting smiles all around, would do something to rouse up *papa* again. The meal creaked on with a few polite oohs and ahs from my wife, and my own smacking of lips over the sour, thin, pinkish wine he had poured for us. Our rich bottle was uncorked and stood in a corner of the cabinet awaiting a sign from the gods when it should be poured.

The meal began at ten o'clock, and from there moved sluggishly toward midnight, each course ending with a long pause at the table while noises built up in the kitchen. A new course would emerge in the hands of Mathilde or Sonia, and each would carefully go around their father, whose arm's reach defined a danger zone. Once he did strike out and pinch Mathilde hard enough to make her eyes glaze, but that was in humor and we chuckled abstractly and went on eating. Our wine was poured at last, with the second meat course. At close to one o'clock, our eyes sagging in our skulls and our bellies leaden, the tempo had slowed enough over brandies that I could signal Mireille it might be bedtime soon. She acknowledged this message with a glance at her husband, who sat stonily at his end of the table.

The barriers of culture had slowly built up again and he had retreated to his own thoughts an hour ago. I saw now that all decisions, though made in part without him, would ultimately have to be passed *through* him, like a ticket at the *Metro* stiles. Mireille's murmurs stirred him out of his reverie and he poured me another brandy. Our children had begun yawning openly at their seats. They toyed with the last little bit of their chocolate cake, something out of a box that Sonia had not quite warmed to its frozen heart, while I took deeper gulps out of my brandy glass. Finally, hand firmly on the top of my glass as the neck of the brandy bottle came toward it again, we stood, a quiet group at this hour, and kissed and shook hands and backed out of the room into the street.

In the morning, the walls of our bedroom glowed like a buttercup; birds chittered in the eaves of the house opposite, the church bell bonged its deafening report into our ears. I dressed and went out for a stroll down the *Grand'Rue*, and took a seat at the little bar on the end of the village. A coffee was brought out to me and I sat, squint-eyed, in the brilliance. I ran my eye over the ridges and black splinters of the Luberon, that mysterious lump of trees and granite and buried springs. It changed its meaning every hour of the day. One never tired of its ambiguities, its vast, slumbering spirit.

I sat thinking about it while a big, slow-moving Mercedes cruised by, a family of German tourists eyeing me carefully as they passed. I was a subject now, a small part of the strangeness of the hills. A dull thrill went up my arms as I realized my new identity – *a villager*.

In a few hours I would drive to Avignon to pick up our house guests, and spend the hour coming back giving an impromptu tour of the valley: the Fontaine de Vaucluse, where Petrarch first laid eyes on Laura de Sade, an ancestor of the infamous Marquis, whose castle, I would note casually, is right up there above the village of Lacoste. Here is the Pont Julien, built by Julius Caesar's engineers on his Gallic campaign; there is Bonnelly's farm where Beckett hid from the Germans during the war. There are the ochre cliffs of Roussillon, and the iron sand runs all the way to Rustrel east of here. And so on all the way along the Calavon, where Hannibal marched his elephants on the way to Rome, and up into the foothills of the Vaucluse Plateau to Saint Martin, our little sandy crown on the brow of the hill.

When they did arrive, flustered, weary, smarting from encounters with hostile Parisians and the extortionary bills they had paid for hotel and meals, I could hear their spirits clink down a drain when I informed them we had no hot water. We would go back to the hamlet and take showers each evening, if that was okay? It was, but a shower *now*, to scrape off the road dust, the cinders, the sweat and smoke and weariness . . . I drove them over to the hamlet after a glass of wine and they sunk deep into their ablutions.

The days faded into nights and mornings again as our last week in the house came to a close. Our friends took off one afternoon on the Apt bus for a trek into Burgundy country and back to Paris. The children had bunked together in the living room all that week to give our guests a private room; now they watched with mild interest as we reorganized the bedroom for them. Life returned to normal, as the long, warm days disintegrated into August and all the impending burdens of departure. Already, we had put the hamlet house back to its original state, filled the kerosene tank with fuel, dusted and mopped and scrubbed, replaced the bottles of wine I had pinched from the larder in the dining room. Our mooring lines were severed one mid-day without ceremony, and we left without a look back at the long, low house with its white gravel and shimmering pond.

Mireille offered to keep the car for us, and to look after the house. Sylvia wanted the use of the house for occasional nights away from her little bungalow. We suspected the beginnings of an affair with her neighbor, a handsome, decaying farmer whose children forbade him to marry again. We gave her a key. We would take the train up to Paris and go back by way of London to Dallas and then down to the prairies of Central Texas.

I was now a lounger of the village bar, and a stroller of the streets. I nodded to everyone in my path, the women strolling by twos, the men heading for a game of *boules* with their cronies. I knew the layout of the place, and had traced the original town walls, the *enceinte*, and found all the ancient gates. The shape of the village began to make some sense; it had grown outward like a tree, one ring encompassing another, on down the hill and into the meadows on either side, filling, expanding with the centuries, dropping battlements and ramparts as peace lengthened, and farmers moved to the valley below.

Saint Martin has a long history, but it began more or less in the 6th century when sisters of a Benedictine order opened a small hospital, a rest stop, for pilgrims on the way down from Rome to Campostelo, Spain. By the time they had cleared the Alps and come through the passes of the Durance and Calavon, their bunions and calluses had hobbled them up, and a good meal and clean bed were waiting for them here. The Greeks had been here long before; there is evidence of a *agora* where the church stands. Dolmens have been found in the area, and the caves were occupied by Paleolithic migrants. And now it stood between its canyons pointing almost due south toward the sea, with the Alps on its left, and the rolling hills stretching out to the Atlantic on its right.

Gustaf had come up to the village a few weeks before to look over my purchase. He approved the moment he saw the rough beams, the mortar and planks that "tudored" the ceilings, the narrow stair that climbed up into the upper story with its creamy plaster walls. It was a suitable house whose foundations, according to Mireille, went back to 1500. We spotted our house on an 17th century map that hangs in the Foyer Rural, the village's photo-archive.

All this measured up to an authentic gesture on our part, as Gustaf came down into the street again and began to tell me of the World War II exploits of René Char in these villages, his leadership of a band of farmers he had organized into *maquisards*, a Resistance force. Char, a poet as lean and pointed in his lines as was George Oppen, moved to Cereste, our neighboring village to the east, where he ran his anti-Nazi operations. Told that the Germans had begun to suspect the farmers of hoarding gun powder on their farms, he used a poet's logic and had the powder dumped along the sides of St. Anne Cathedral in Apt and covered with tarpaulins. The Germans would never suspect good Catholics of endangering their principal shrine. The weeks went by with the powder safe, until the heat began to cook it and throw off a heady scent. When told the odor was becoming suspicious, he had the men piss on it regularly, which offended

German decorum. The Nazis stayed away from the tarps and the powder was left to serve its purpose – blowing up German supply trains.

I had proprietary interest in these stories, as I leaned against my own stones to listen. It all happened here and in the hills above me. Char on the run, face blackened with soot, his men dodging the headlights of German trucks as they scurried into the oak woods to a rendezvous. It was like Vercingetorix' men fighting Julius Caesar at the battle of Alesia two millennia before, or like the Vaudois of the 12th century fleeing before the Pope's armies, and again in 1680 when Louis XIV crushed the Protestant rebellions. The oaks grew out of spilled blood; the bones were buried deep in this country of broken hills. We parted warmly, his long, loping figure going up the *Grand'Rue* for the last time. Our friendship would break soon after over the essays I had written about him. He had warned me he was tough on his critics, and I was now among them.

Here, now, spread the amber light of summer, falling like rose petals on my shoes. The air was tinged with savory and thyme. I could feel the wind entering the silence, beginning to rattle loose rain gutters under eaves, spreading rumors about the coming of winter. It was dry, and the ground lay parched and brown under the long sunny days.

A young woman got down from her car and stood shielding her eyes as she looked out over the valley, which swung down the slopes in a long, leisurely curve, and spread out along the shadowy footings of the mountain. The wind bore all the sighing of the fields toward her, and wrapped her white cotton skirt against her thighs, as if to caress her with its scented breath. She bore the principle of love, and the wind pressed against her like a ghostly suitor.

On our last day in Provence that year, Mireille drove us down to Apt to catch the bus to Avignon. It was a day of thin realities – even the shutters had closed like a lid over daylight, casting the dining room into a dark dream that forgot our voices. We were strangers again, heading north where the earth grew hard and practical, and the female tumbled back into the unconscious like Eurydice.

Chapter Twelve

Deaths and Entrances

There is a funeral this summer morning; my wife is getting dressed for it as I putter in the kitchen. I got up earlier to see the kids off to school, which involves building a fire, laying out bowls, spoons, the pitcher of milk, grating a few apples for apple sauce, sitting quietly, abstractly as they dress in the bathroom, eat, hoist up large backpacks full of books and trudge down the *Grand'Rue* to the school bus. It is dark then, and cool, and the fire is full of reds and blacks and flickers dancing over the ceiling. I had drifted off to sleep again, woke at ten, all thumbs as I drank burnt coffee. She had come down by then to put on make-up.

It occurred to me I should go up to the church as well. I could see the elders turning up the *Montée de l'oratoire* dressed formally, going stiff-kneed up the stone steps. Another link had broken with the woman's death. My wife and one of the widows of the village had gone to see her a few days before in the Apt hospital. They brought fruit for her, but bronchitis had eaten up the tissues of her throat and now pneumonia filled her lungs. She lay stiff, hollow-eyed in bed, her teeth out, as the two women talked to her, promising her *promenades* in spring, company on the boulevard wall at sunset. We had all seen the woman sitting out in the sun on summer evenings. Once, a month ago, on a cold, bright afternoon I passed her in the street on her way to the vegetable stands, which were set up each Thursday on the boules court. "I am going for my provisions," she said in a sweet voice, her face clear and vital days before she fell ill.

After the visit, my wife was bemused. The woman had made peace with herself, she told me; she had that radiant innocence of someone who wants to die and can't be talked out of it. She listened intently to the words spoken at her bedside, but there was an iron will that desired to be joined to her dead husband and son, and to give up the cold windy mornings when she went to the front of the village to wait for the bakery van from Viens.

I remembered her standing there in the gusts coming up from the valley, the wide blue Luberon stretched out on the far side draped in morning shadows. She and a few other village women would lean into the wind and talk sparingly as they glanced up the road. Sometimes she would sit in a doorway behind the village gate, to keep out of the stinging wind. She would brighten at our approach and seem like a little girl caught at some mischief. Behind the sunken lips and loose eyes, a small ray of energy still glittered. I liked her, and was sad to see her go.

Earlier in the year the bell clanged wildly to call the town to order, and the lines formed and straggled up the cracked steps to the cemetery, where a crowd formed at one of the graves and someone we did not know went into the ground, ending another generation.

I pulled on some gray trousers, my sweater and sports coat, and smoothed my hair. We got down into the sunny street and went to the church escorted by one of the village dogs, Belle. We could hear the priest saying prayers in the bare, echoing nave. We were late. When I opened the side door and stepped in, the church was crowded. Men were standing in the back, and all seats had been taken. The village elite, the men and women of property, had gotten there early and had the front pews. The rest of us stood loosely at the back. Gray heads, bald heads, dyed hair and pompadours, they moved like a field of winter grass as the priest made the sign of the cross and prayed over the dead. A coffin, varnished and trimmed in brass, with a crucifix on top, lay on trestles at the head of the aisle.

I was surprised to find so many here; the whole village had turned out. My wife and I were among the tallest heads. This was the peasant race of France, blunt, dark-complected, with small faces and pronounced eyes, and mouths that had long known the grape and the olive, the *chèvre* and communion wafer. Napoleon had shortened French men by four or five inches through all his wars and bloody campaigns. The aristocrats kept their height by buying commissions in the officer corps. The peasants ran up against the cannon fire and took the musket ball and sword end. Their voices made a muffled amen together, and our woolens crackled as we passed fingers over forehead and mouth.

The doors behind me, the big wooden doors of the church, rattled noisily and I stepped back. Someone came forward and undid the latch and four short, stocky men appeared wearing blue uniforms, shiny and ill-fitting. These were the undertakers, officious men who waited a bit and then marched together up the aisle to take the coffin. There were no family pall bearers. The coffin was heavy, and the small men grimaced as they trudged back down the aisle to the van, which would go ahead of the crowd up the road peppered with sheep droppings to the cemetery.

I stood to one side to watch as everyone passed. I recognized many and nodded to them; the crowd whispered or mouthed prayers as it went by, and recognition was limited to a nod or a brief smile. Others went by whom I did not know – dark, small faces, the descendants of a long line for whom death was as practical and rhythmic as birth. They were clear-eyed, and walked heavily with the motion of something eternal in them, like waves coming to shore. What they saw in me, I don't know – a man with a goatee, wisps of gray at his temples, a height that excluded him from their world. Their faces softened and a nod brought their eyes down as I smiled back; I fell in line behind them going up the steep, twisting passage to the road.

Cathy had been pulled from the crowd and an arm slipped into hers; it was Rosette Saint Martin, a Corsican woman with whom she had gone to the hospital on her visit. Rosette was the mail carrier in the village back in the fifties, who kept one of the larger houses in the village, a winter apartment in Apt, and owned property up and down the land. She wrote the obituaries for the local paper and composed a poem or two each morning, which she would read to Cathy in her airy little kitchen over tea. Cathy would drive down to Apt and take her shopping once a week, and bring her vegetable soup if she were ill.

She too had a large crypt in the cemetery which she looked after diligently. Her beloved husband lay under a bright marble slab strewn with porcelain regret signs from relatives and friends, a pair of iron urns and a stone vase laid on its side, and trays of painted geraniums she would rearrange from time to time. The two women walked ahead of me chatting, as I followed, nodding to some of the men who had fallen out from the procession to smoke.

Earlier in the week I had gone up to the cemetery on one of my solitary strolls; I often walked around the streets with a map from my neighbor, André Fulconis 's book on the history of the village, checking wall foundations and following little passages where they hooked around and came to dead ends. Each had a history, most of it forgotten now. What was the *Rue Sacoche*, I wondered, coming along the footings of the castle? It meant money bag or purse, and were there pawn shops here, or was this the lower shelf of the agora? The relic of an outdoor theater lay moldering in sun just below the sheep barn. The rank odor of sheep and dirty fleece scorched the air, tangy as cheese rinds and onions. The amphitheater built by a *lycée* teacher back in the '40s now held an audience of hollyhocks and wild blossoms among its crumbling stone tiers. Houses sagged along its outer aisles, as if weary of waiting for the play to start. There were other corners of this tiny village that were part of the folk lore retold by the women, like the house of the *Musulman*, in which a rich man built a private chapel to honor his own dead for burial in the cemetery, but the bishop refused to consecrate it. I doubt he was a Muslim at all, only someone who tried to elbow his way into the village graveyard reserved for native born. The story was passed around to new-comers with relish; it shows how well this village can snub the outsiders.

I found myself at the cemetery under the empty winter sky, the day eerily warm and breezy from the west. The tombs were all blazing in the light, with their little grilled doorways breathing out the cold, moist air of stone. Vines had gotten in some of them and had twisted around the crosses and straw baskets, crushing them in their wooden coils. Time did not wait in these sanctified chambers, but tore at the mortar and the roof tiles and pulled down the little timbers from the ceiling, or forced walls to teeter back slowly as a crack of light seeped in like molten gold.

They were all here, the Renauds, Catalas, Brémonds, Fulconises, Bellos, the roll call of village families. It was the other set of mailboxes, with the name incised in gold or black lettering onto stone. Where tombs had weathered, the name still hung on, fighting off eternity. The flower jars were tumbled or broken, but in no instance was there outright neglect. Some of the monuments had about had it, and would fall in a few more winters, but for now they drifted on, like bell buoys on the waves. Someone frail came up to sweep them, and put out cut flowers or more porcelain regrets, and to look longingly at the memories lying below. Soon, soon they too would lie there, joined at last. And who would come up the hill to mind them and pay respect? Who indeed when all the young were living elsewhere.

The survivors were modest, habitual people doing their work, driving old sedans, playing boules in the pitch outside the bar on summer days, and here were their roots enshrined on the hill, under the passing sun. I was a stranger here; my ancestors lay buried elsewhere, and I was given no second address among the enshrined. If you are not given a second home on the hill, you are forever a stranger here. Under our window last spring came the man who looked after us with tools and advice on fixing the house. He brought along some visitors who toured the street with him. "*Voici les Américains,*" he said, with a voice that seemed to relish this exotic fact of the village. We would never be much more, though the village had adopted us by now. We were *les Américains*, forever and ever. In this second village, the eternal one, houses and crypts lay side by side in a smaller version of the town below. And at night, under the silvery arc of satellites wheeling by and the stars glinting in ragged luster, lay the souls of history calling the living home.

Cathy had even asked me this week if I knew where I would like to be buried! I had looked at these tombs and had actually felt the need to have my burial place among them. And suddenly, on this bright, unseasonable afternoon found myself drawn to the graves wondering what it must feel like to know that one of them will shelter your dust. To turn away without a piece of ground to rest in gave me a shiver of loneliness, a fear I would leave no trace behind.

Now we filed into the narrow stone gate past the oldest tombs, over to a far side where earth had been piled up before a large slab. A hole went down in front of the crypt, and a man inside raised his blue sleeves to receive the coffin, which was lowered on ropes as soon as half the crowd had gathered. The family of the deceased had been placed directly in front of the opening, where a stone slab had been broken free and the tomb exposed. The coffin was pulled in onto a shelf; an older coffin lay on the opposite side, its brass tarnished. It was her husband's coffin, buried in World War II; her son lay there as well, though I could only make out the ends of two coffins, the one bright, gaudily new in its dusty quarters. Instantly, the slab was put back and braced with a timber, and the men began shoveling earth into the hole. Another mixed concrete in a rubber pan and prepared to seal the tomb. The family went to the gate to receive condolences.

I shook hands and recognized one member of the family, a relation on the husband's side. The faces had a prepared look of somberness, not open grief. The deceased had lived a full life, drained to the lees at eighty-nine. Her death had come easy, with little suffering. A long life of many winters, many winds, many silent days of eating alone, the sun beating on the shutters. When my wife joined me again, after her friend had gone over to talk to the family, she told me the woman died rich, had left several houses and much property behind.

I looked back at the man I had consoled at the gate, with his round, small head, his sensuous mouth rolling r's as he spoke to well-wishers. He would be sitting in the *avocat's* office tomorrow or the next day to learn of his estate. I had watched him at the New Year's Eve party held in the village a few months before, a man of simple tastes who had filled his glass with the cheap local wine and drunk it thirstily, eating his fill of the fish and rice, the *civet*, the dessert pastry, sitting with his wife, elemental, gnomic, a primal Celt at the new year. What would he do with his new wealth, I wondered? Be its custodian for the next two or three decades and pass it on as well, augmented by a little?

These were all the closed circuits of life I stood among, as my wife came down the road with her arm in her friend's. I walked on alone, moving through the crowd as it dispersed back to cars and to houses in the village. Two cats fought in a sun-glazed patio, large, gray animals with yellow eyes, their thick paws boxing in the silence, then rolling back onto the stone with little growls. They were the life force gathering strength for its spring rituals, as we crept down out of the land of the dead.

Time was not one river but a whole system of currents running in all directions. Change roamed down a great capillary network pushing the living into a thousand shapes, some of them backwards, others forward, like myself. In the big, ugly room above the bar, the Foyer Rural, where we had had our New Year's party, hung all the pictures of the town and its citizens. Someone I had gotten chummy with last summer, who kept a summer house near the bar, dragged me over to a photograph of children sitting in rows before a house, taken sometime in the 1930s. He and I stood there in the roar of the crowd, already loosened by *apéritifs* and spiked punch, as new comers arrived and heaped their coats on a railing behind us. We shouted to one another in French about the photo; it looked exactly, *exactly* like my son, he was saying, the mist from his mouth landing on my forehead as he spoke. He was a tall, willowy physics teacher from Bordeaux, a good boules player from all that knowledge of ballistics and trajectories in his head, and a good dancer, the best in the village. He leaned over me with that archery bow of a body, and claimed and proclaimed with wine-musky enthusiasm that this indeed was the very likeness of my son!

I agreed, noting there was a vague likeness, though the forehead was too round and the eyes too vacant to persuade me further. The chin, the mouth, the strong legs were my son's, yes. But a thrill bumped up my arteries as I realized the compliment I was being paid – my son, my likeness, my blood was perceivable in the archival recesses of the village circa 1932! What could it mean, what could it say about me? Had I found my place through the trick of photography, through a *trompe l'oeil*? I found myself nodding more vigorously now, shouting back that the likeness was uncanny, almost eerie. And as I did, a voice like my own conscience spoke behind me, and identified the face as belonging to Maurice Reynaud, the farmer at the end of the *Grand'Rue*. I saw it at once, the old man in the young boy, the unbreakable continuity of village life. Here was time unfolding the petals of the rose from face to face. All those grimacing young boys in shorts and shirts, squinting at the sun one spring morning in front of a house that stood just as it does now, were as brief as last summer's flowers. As I peered into the photo, I saw other faces of the men shouting behind me – small, budded replicas of their round, loose-jowled faces now. The boys were a garden of shoots and sprigs, but the fruit hung ripe and withering as I looked around the room. We were not among them in any archive; not yet, anyway.

But we were becoming part of the village, part of its outer skin at least, known to the faces of the summer fetes, the church services, the Apt market, the merchants in the surrounding towns. I could walk down the streets of the village on a summer day and be made to stop, chat, shake hands or kiss cheeks with almost everyone I passed. The village was friendly, open, bound by its customs, not yet thinned out by death or the flow of tourists and foreigners. Our stay as residents had peeled away a layer of formality to more intimate glances, more searching eyes, more direct questions about our lives. We had worked at being accepted, and slowly, like water over stone, a groove of welcome had worn its way into village society.

Every morning at six the swifts flexed their small brown wings and left their nests under the roof tiles to play a dangerous game of dart and dive through the narrow streets. The *Grand'Rue* in Saint Martin is no bigger than the width of a sedan, with mirrors pulled in. I know, I have scraped a few fenders negotiating the curves of that Main Street to our house to unload wood or crates of wine and bottled water. Down those narrow winding passages go the birds at full throttle, in a competition so fierce only the bravest and most agile mastered the full circuit. Now and then I would find a dead bird in the street, its neck broken, eyes still wide to the oncoming wall that killed it.

In a village that traced its roots as far back as 500 BC, longer if you count the cave dwellers, one life seemed hardly more durable than the leaves on a tree. We were aging with that effortless soaring of birds into a clear blue canopy of time. Hardly had we unpacked our bags and made our home here than the phone began ringing at odd hours, with chirpy adolescent voices asking for Max or Signe, or in another winter or two, Cedric. The parties began in our "new room," the northside dining room we converted from the straw-floored *bergerie,* where the door closed behind such initiations like smoking one's first cigarette, taking a swig or two from the whiskey bottle. That allowed the stereo to be cranked up, the furniture rearranged to accommodate the needs of kids flung headlong into the awkward age.

My spindle-legged Maxine soldiered forth into that treacherous world of teens, and got her ego trampled now and then. The school yard at the *lycée* in Apt was a proving ground where girls created the culture and the rules by which others were to live and behave. The boys obeyed, and the girls imposed a nearly fascist control over the hormone-driven egos that assembled and competed for places in the various tight social circles.

Maxine survived; Signe was next, and her first day in "the yard" found her sitting alone at lunch, the two-hour break in the day, while girls surveyed her appearance and made their giggling judgments of her. She weathered out her exile and one by one kids came to her to assess her worth. It was a game of wits and possessions; the name brands of socks were just as crucial as the book bag logo. Hair was a measure of potential, and a pocket book with a cigarette or two, some matches, a willingness to scale the back fence and climb down onto the muddy banks of the Calavon for a forbidden smoke was like coin of the realm. She passed all her tests and found a seat among the better sort, while other girls trudged through their days without identity. Sometimes the pressure was too much for one of them and she took her life. The rest lived and found their niches in that terrifying bureaucracy that is the mirror of the adult world.

The anarchists were few but their attitudes were already apparent in their rags and rasta dreadlocks. Apt smoldered in the spring months, and by May, when I arrived back from teaching to begin my summer, the books were scattered over my daughters' beds, the heavy book bag bulged with notebooks all puffy with laborious note taking and the infernal *dictées*, those grinding routines where you wrote down what a teacher read aloud, and then he or she corrected accents and agreements. And gave you a four out of a possible twenty, and added this to other grades in an unceasing tide of numbers rumbling to the end of the semester and your fate as a student.

Meanwhile the boys sauntered into my children's lives, and awakened Eros and Aphrodite in the back of their minds, where the heart sleeps. Books blurred in their eyes as they remembered some remark that was teasingly suggestive and aloof to translation. How hard it was to grasp the meaning of events at thirteen; I remembered how much I suffered as I tumbled through my adolescence and landed more often on my head. The sexual arena was more frank and cut throat here than in America, where, despite the same urges and drives, we are shyer to express them. French girls emerged like moths out of their cocoons and took to the air with very little hesitation. My girls were less demonstrative, more likely to think things over. A bridge over the river separating the town from the school was the kissing place, where a girl might be seen grappling with her young lover in a furious embrace, mouth agape, cheeks burning. Maxine found it all humiliating and demeaning, though she looked twice when we passed couples on the way to our car.

The serious flirting went on during sports class, my daughter later told me. That's when the teacher, in gym shorts, would spin around on the athletic horse while the kids allowed their eyes to roam and fix on someone's face and hold that moment in deepest suspense. The voice of the adult would drift into the springtime radiance, while the bodies gathered around her were as ripe as the cherries on the trees. Nothing could stop the bees from trembling in the buds, and the girls to make the first move and hold a boy's hand, or touch his hip with her own. All this solitary adventure into life while I got my coffee from the office urn and heard the gossip of who got the biggest raise, seven thousand lonely miles away.

The rhythm of summer had been set since 1992 when I began to teach alone in Texas and come for Christmas and the summer. Cathy stayed on to raise the children, and made sure they talked to me every few days on the phone. We had a fax machine, phone, regular mail through which we kept in contact. And e-mail when it became available. But my voice on the phone, coming in waves through an ocean of air, made me seem all the more distant, a voice in another world, while Cathy faced all the tribulations of our kids growing up with my empty seat at the table each night of the fall and winter, broken by my arrival at Christmas, and my return in spring.

The phone would ring, or I would get a fat envelope in the office mail with pictures of my son riding his bike, or my daughters at a house party with the streamers hanging above their heads, tallish boys making faces as Cathy fired the flash and the music thumped in the speakers. I would put the picture up against my desk lamp and sit in the afternoon light of my office, the cold gray sky closing in and deepening the shadows around me.

Back in my role as father, I witnessed changes in each of them. My oldest daughter coming home from a hard day at school, with homework she couldn't finish before midnight. My other daughter reading novels in her bed, with the light bent down an inch from the page, her cookies and juice on a crowded night stand. My son poring over the pictures of his new magazine, studying the luster of a fat black motorcycle parked on a cliff, with a couple beside it laughing over lunch. Each had a world now, a French world they had grown into and left us partly behind. Their voices were more sure of words in French than in English, their jokes and dreams cast in southern French dialect. Their hearts were tormented by French boys, and the romance of French films. They had secrets, and myths and illusions that sprung from the dry bed of the Calavon and the drab corridors of their school.

But what would they become? I who had made them and plucked them out of one path and set them down in another. What right had I to play a Greek god with these mortals, these children of simple Texas earth? They couldn't work in France, they would arrive at America's door step with a French baccalaureate and a fistful of report cards of inscrutable meaning to an American university dean. What had I done? Oh, what had I done to these innocents who twanged like Django Rinehart's gypsy guitar when they talked on the phone?

Little by little, the decision Cathy and I had made on a stone wall in that far off highland station in Malaysia formed itself out of the local rock and mortar, became a reality of sturdy beams and irreversible winds. My children were of two worlds, with the one rising, the other fading ever so slowly into the background. My son clung to his Americanness and insisted that we speak only English at home, the base of his memories. The French world was at our doorstep, at the back windows, on the phone, in the messages scrawled at school and crumbled into balls in his book bag. He would hold the waters of his Red Sea apart as long as he could, not knowing that his own developing powers of French would engulf him, capsize him, drown him.

Their appearances changed and took on the local colors, the pungency of the kids around them. No one could tell them apart from the most rooted scion of Provençal tradition. One day in the playground, as Signe stood about with her best cronies, each girl told where she had been born. This hamlet, that village, this dale with single farm and two lavender fields, that cherry orchard and granpa's *bastidon* or *mas*. When it was Signe's turn, she said she had come from Bryan, Texas, in America. The others merely laughed at the joke and asked again: which brook, which knot of pines, which cairn of tumbled limestone had she been conceived and delivered in? Texas, Signe said, not one to dissemble or tell fibs. No one bought it. Again, where was she born? America, she said. The girls demanded proof she was American. Who was the first president, where was the capital? How many states in that fabled nation? When she answered each query with correct answers, her dearest *camarade* burst into tears. Signe told me how confused she felt at her sobs. Even though her

French was as pure and tangy and fruit-ripened as anyone's in her group, she was the stranger.

That momentary alienation had nothing to feed upon and in a week she was back to her old self sharing her soul with everyone close to her. But the moment in which this split identity revealed itself troubled her, even if it left the rest of the process of transubstantiation into a new identity undeterred, like one of those torrents, dusty and strewn with bleached rock, that gorges with water and bursts its banks in a momentary rain storm.

My son Cedric, the adamant American, wearer of jeans and American sneakers, a boy as eager to play ball in a Texas town as he was to eat a burger from Mcdonald's, was perhaps the most transformable of the three. His French was more instinctual and authentic; the girls, being older when they started, learned their French to utmost efficiency, with Signe the scholar and historian of the language, and Maxine the voice of the street. Cedric's tongue was in the culture of rap and hip hop, honed to the nuances of his peers and so completely his own when he spoke it, he didn't realize he was trading in his American speech for every new word and phrase he gained on the other side. He was a changeling in spite of himself; a boy slipping off one set of clothes and, as if asleep still, putting on another. When he was fully dressed in his new Adidas shoes, surfer pants, sweat shirt, he was a gamin of the streets of Apt.

And the Apt that taught them, provided their pizza slices and *pain au chocolat*, later their half-pint of Kronenberg *pression* (from the tap) to share out among five friends short of change. At noon they got a *merguez-frites*, spicy sausage and fries on a baguette, and languished in the heat of the day under the bar awning among friends whose powers of sitting were boundless if the talk flowed, and there were Marlboros to bum from an older student at the next table. These immersions into French bonding went on daily; if one decided to *sèche les cours* (play hookey), the day framed itself around St. John's Pub, or the Aptois, whose tables were across from the kissing bridge and welcomed all strayers from Plato's grove.

The house of English on its village hill shrunk in proportion, with an American mother eager to perpetuate the old identity as much as to embrace the budding new one; the father, gone much of the year, was a weaker glue to hold them to the map of America. I came, I saw, and I was vanquished by their magic acts and quick changes.

One bright afternoon at the end of Maxine's *troisième*, the third form, we stood before the fluttering papers of the school bulletin board.

It was the end of her *collège* (junior high) years; one entered the *lycée* where older kids had more privileges and could leave campus, dine at their own tables, and generally take on adult pressures and obligations, like the even more dreaded *bac*, the national exams, oral and written, for getting the degree that enabled one to have employment and a decent life. Beyond lay the universities, reserved for those who were permitted to enter the academic track, based on the grades of the *brevet*.

The names of those who had passed the *brevet* were casually posted on the portable bill board set up outside the campus gates. Here was the work of the French Revolution at its most essential: those who had the brains and the stamina to pass the *brevet* were entitled to their chance to rise higher; those who did middling or poorly on their tests were channeled into the trades, like oral hygiene, sales, maintenance, and factory work. There was no shame or disgrace in taking this second, practical line of education. There, too, the French Revolution had put its mark on the French psyche – a man or woman wore a uniform with pride, did the sometimes tedious work of repair or counter service with skill, and considerable care to detail. It was no dishonor to serve France in blue work pants or highway reflector jackets, or to push those plastic green brooms to clean the gutters of Marseille or Paris. But the dividing line of the classes was here, writ on A4 typing paper, names and numbers in columns for parents to consult and for children to approach with trepidation and sometimes tears, or shouts of joy.

We scanned the lists and there among the passers of the *brevet* was our own Maxine. Our joy made us stagger around for a moment while we went back and stared at her name. Some names we knew were not there; they had gone into the other paths of life here, but our own daughter, the American far from home, had passed soundly, undeniably into the higher world. We had not erred, we had helped her survive our dangerous gamble. We had all come through. We knew in our hearts, without saying it, that the others would also pass and move up, and no one in the village could snicker over his beer that the poor Yanqui kids were just not up to the rigors of French learning. They would have to snicker at something else, for the bar was the clearing house of opinion, good and bad, on all who lived there. We were strong, we could do it. We knew that now.

Signe came home one night after spending time with the neighbor's children, Manon and Estelle. Manon was a nervous, edgy girl who worked late into the night studying, and who bit her nails down to the quick. She came over to study English with Cathy, who helped her write her English homework. Signe was a middling student up to then; she had passed the *brevet* strongly, and was now in *seconde*, second form, among the older kids bound for college. When she watched Manon go up early and start her work while her younger sister romped in the TV room, she followed Manon and asked her why she worked so hard. Her father was a substitute coach in an *école primaire*, an elementary school; his wife also taught. She told Signe she didn't want to live like them; she was going to study political science and become a journalist like her uncle. With that, she shooed Sig from the room who came home in a bemused state. She had never heard anyone so young state a clear vision and goals for the future, partly driven by what her parents didn't or couldn't do. She couldn't say her own dad was a slacker, someone who got his beer out early and watched TV for the night. She had no such easy foil for her ambitions – but she came home and told me, in a flat voice, that she was sick of being average.

"I'm going up to study; I'm going to be as good as Manon." And with that statement she changed her life. Her grades soared, her serious-ness was permanent. She bought her own books at the *bouquiniste* in Apt, and her teachers grew fond of her. She was smarter than the serious, driven Manon; she had elected to follow in her father's academic footsteps. Cedric kept his powder dry; he too would unfold and show his hard, clear intelligence on the *bac*.

My summers were marked by blossoms and harvests. When the lavender grew dark and velvety, like long blue caterpillars along the hill-sides, it meant mid summer had come. The wagons loaded with sheaves of lavender were pulled to the presses. First steamed in underground vats, then hauled up and pressed for their juice. Great clots of dry stalks were piled high behind the presses, and arranged along ditches. For days the fields were deeply perfumed with lavender oil; the tractors rumbled along leaving a heady wake of scent.

It was July, and the grapes were turning on the vines; the long tendrils of new vine snaked along wires in the vineyards, meeting other vines. They trembled in the wind, and glistened in the sun with morning dew. By early August, the grapes would dim from green to light purple and then turn black, whole clusters like heavy sacks of marbles. The wild flowers which began spring in their yellows and whites shifted to red and blue by mid-summer, in time for Bastille Day, and the more muted orange red of the dog days. The trees were dense and wrapped in dark-ness behind the vineyards and along the mountain roads. The oaks will have weathered some dry weeks, their leaves thick and tough as frogs' feet. And heat rolled off the fields into the dry river bed with a smell like my mother's old steam iron.

Each shift of season told me the summer grew shorter, the fall advanced on its cold feet from the north. My kids were increasingly submerged in their social worlds; parties and sleep-overs, and dates for Maxine. She had begun to pull away from us, lured by the wild streak in the boys she met at school. Martian was thin and sinewy and ate only what he grew in his garden at his parents' house. He served her a meal of fresh salad, slipped off his clothes and danced with her naked in the empty house. The shiver of anarchy ran through her bones; she had discovered another world where the doors hung open to the night air, and the rooms were lit by a kind of sinister energy that pulled her apart. She succumbed to her feelings and came home wiser in at least one facet of her life.

She was discovering that she was an artist, and her hand began to move on its own down the page, with her eye barely controlling what the muscles in her arms already knew. She had decided to join the program in *arts plastiques*, which would take her into the studios where clay pots were drying on warped shelves in the window, and paint tubes were half squeezed out on messy palettes. The kids in that class wore self-conscious rags and mops of hair; her teachers noticed her talent and encouraged her. For the first time she prospered in school.

Cedric discovered his genius in humor, the kind that provoked mostly rancor from his teachers. He was class clown in a school where no one spoke unless called upon, and where the rules had been fixed by mind-numbing repetition for many years. His remarks were brash, unpredictable; if his English teacher mispronounced a word, his hand shot up to correct her. His fellow students smirked and giggled behind the raised lids of their desks. He was class critic, and paid dearly for his candor when we trooped in for the teachers' meeting at the end of the year. They agreed he was smart, but once said, the roster of faults and flaws was long and we twitched in our seats. Irony, skepticism, indifference were all tools of his trade as student provocateur, and he had a knack for peeling the skin off a teacher's nose with one-liners. But he did the drudging work, when he had to; and he was teaching himself on the sly. He styled himself an anti-intellectual in our house, and only when Cathy pulled off the sheets of his bed would she find a book hidden under a mattress, or behind his shoes. We said nothing. His reading, by the way, was good French novels.

The French classroom was old fashioned; too much starch in the teacher's attitude, not enough freedom to think or feel among the students. But every day students were made to recite something from memory, and to write long pages during the week that were rigorously corrected and handed back without compliments. Students took it all in stride; all three kids had calluses on their writing finger from pushing a fountain pen all day. No ball point pens allowed, thank you. Classes dragged on for hours, in colorless rooms with old fashioned florescent tube lights to cast a depressing winter light upon these southern imaginations. Books in the library were dog eared and used up; the histories were all about French glory and pride of nation. The notebooks were soggy with ink written on both sides of the page; the class book all students were required to bring to school bore lunch card, class schedule, and notes back and forth from teachers to parents.

All this Napoleonic rigor was aimed at educating the common man and freeing him from church and superstition. And little by little, in that drained atmosphere of droning teachers and half-dark corridors, the ordinary clay of France acquired not only speech but a surprising eloquence and freedom to express. We marveled at our children's facility with words; writing was routine to them, and they wrote often, in diaries and letters, as well as homework. They had a certain freshness about them when they spoke, from long hours of standing in heated classrooms where rote learning was enforced daily. The memory was stocked with songs and poems, with passages from Rabealais and Diderot, and of course Descartes. Montesquieu and Montaigne supplied models of prose and lucid argument, and Hegel provided the backbone of French logic with his dialectic. All essays flowed like the channeled waters of the Durance around a thesis, an antithesis, and finally, as the channel widened to supply Marseille's thirst, the synthesis in which all sides were accounted for in an elegant, slightly Rube-Goldbergian coda.

There was no room in this chock-a-block curriculum for free-flowing conversation, or any of the other American reforms in which the inner self, that angel with small voice, was lured out by colorful textbooks loaded with pictures, counselors eager to smooth out psychic wrinkles, computer labs for the technical, and luxurious gyms to enhance the competitive spirit. In France, where education is free from the *crèche* (pre-school) to the *aggrégation* (Ph.D.), gray paint covered the halls and doorways, hand-cranked windows let in the light and air, and the chalk boards hadn't changed technology in a hundred years.

We noted how fluent ordinary people were when stopped on the street to speak to TV reporters; quiz shows and talk shows were popular fare on French channels, and the talk flowed in all directions. The art of speech was perfected in this culture, and the ability to do so was ground out of reluctant throats by all those stern-faced, unrelenting task masters who loomed before them when they were toddlers, and who gave them merciless instruction until they left school with *bac* in hand.

I felt like a sculptor with my children half emerged from the stone I chipped at. An artist, a scholar, and a wry, perceptive mystery in my son – who seemed to take a tack different from all the rest of us. But who appeared to be heeding some voice within him that lured him toward history or politics or some other line where social power and influence lay. Perhaps he was using his double nature as an American abroad to study the raw power that shaped people's attitudes and ways. It would be many more years before I would know for sure that he was headed into international work and would win a seat in the prestigious Paris school, the *Institut d'etudes politiques* where many of the ministers who ran France got their degrees. But that is near the end of my story. I am still chipping at the three rocks in which my children hid their true natures.

My hand on the hammer was intermittent; and as time went on, my wife did much of the chipping, until finally our hands were no longer needed in the process. Things took over without us; peers and teachers, and a few of the older students trimmed and polished their edges. And one or two townies tried to break their hearts. But they grew up; they strolled along with confidence in an Apt I knew little about. They saw France from the inside; the gossip of the village flowed in their veins; they cast French shadows alongside our American ones. The French, living and dead, raised our children to think like them, speak like them. When it was apparent that they had learned their lessons well, the nation seemed smaller and more intimate to them.

Neither Cathy nor I suspected how closely our kids were supervised. But I did know that if Cedric were missing for dinner, I had only to go out my door and ask the first villager if he had seen him, and if he hadn't, he knew someone who had – minutes before. I never had to worry where any of the kids were – eyes were everywhere. In fact, our children grew up under the disapproving glare of the old women who judged young flesh as it passed in front of their knitting kneedles under the *tilleul* (lime) trees. It was customary for these crones to comment on each girl, native or foreign, with a succinct word or two. When a girl reached puberty, the word was whore, *putain*, breathed just above a hiss, and loud enough to be heard. My daughters were not spared; they were accused of sleeping with strangers in the back seats of parked cars, and worse.

The gossip was cruel and unremitting. I felt annoyed every time I heard someone say my Maxine was no better than a street walker, or my Sig was sowing havoc in the creaky world of the village. Her friends were equally indicted, and one of them, a smart, witty little brunette who was my daughter's soul mate, got the worst of it. And she was the daughter of one of the five powerful families in St. Martin. But then, the moms could remember when they had turned fourteen hearing the very same words flung at them. *Plus ça change, plus c'est la même chose.*

"Not to worry," Mireille told me; "it's the tradition around here to condemn the girls when they reach puberty. It's nothing personal." I believed her; she was wild herself, and had an inquiring, suggestive eye even now.

The girls *were* experimenting, kissing the boys at the summer festivals, going down to the open field called *les aires* to stand in the dark of two tall pine trees to smoke and twist tongues with the reedy Lotharios of that generation. The adults watched them march off beyond the village street lights and the carnival bulbs, and come back an hour later blushing and feverish. The farm couples would be two-stepping to a combo on a make-shift stage in the boules court, shuffling along with their arms touching shoulders, while the girls came in twos and threes followed by the boys hiding their beer bottles and Marlboros, each slinking along like Renard the fox behind the chicken shed.

The village had seen it all before down through the centuries of summer time; the field had witnessed so many rites of passage it yawned among its stars and high grass, and patted a few heads with its low hanging pine boughs. The *mopeds* passed down from older brothers to younger ones, and the crackle of unmuffled two-stroke engines throbbed against our bedroom windows all July long. The older ones came along in deep voices with hard snorting laughs while the girls whispered and pulled them along to the front of the village, or up beyond the church to their houses to whisper in the dark. Love in its time-less cradle of stone, with eternity peeking down among the house eaves and chimney pots.

Who needed a watch when love was in the air? The girls felt the thrill of their freedom and one by one were deflowered in gardens, on terraces, in cars, and fields – disappointed it wasn't more mythical and sublime, but glad it was over and adulthood could begin in earnest. In a way, the old women knew that when summer came, girls went blissfully astray and their dark words echoed both a wisdom and a yearning in their own hearts.

August 15th marked not only the Feast of the Assumption but the end of summer heat and tourism, as the village went back to its autumnal mutterings and empty streets. One by one cars were packed and went off into the afternoon light, to Nîmes and Bourdeaux, Lisle, Paris, Strasbourg, Mulhouse, and all the other cities where money was earned to pay for summer in the south. The shutters were closed, the rain guards placed over the front door, the flowers removed from the sills. The very next day, a cooler wind blew down from the north, and the dry weeds on the hillsides rattled like skeletons. Fall was near, and winter lay behind it. And silence and long nights were coming over the steep escarpments.

The stores were full of school bags and new clothes for the *rentrée*, the return to school. The pencils smelled like cedar chests, and the paper was stacked in the aisles, among the crisp new erasers and pencil bags. You forgot the tedium and punishment of last year, and saw all the bright new products and yearned for the moment you could walk into class with new shoes, a new skirt and blouse, a smart new backpack with a U2 or Rolling Stones picture on it. Friends to make, friends to welcome, different teachers and books, a sense of motion and change to obscure the dread of another long year of pencil pushing. I could feel the turning emotion of my kids as summer got long in the tooth and endless freedom had lost its allure.

If the years were as quick as the flight of swifts, they carried me to the end of each summer and gave me back my suitcases and my sad farewells, the drive before day break to the airport near Marseille, its runway jutting out into the backwaters of the Mediterranean, where I would soar off into the night sky home to Texas alone.

Chapter Thirteen

Belonging

My neighbor's son jogs down the *Grand'Rue* on his way to work. His feet barely touch the ground, as if he defied gravity. But he is rooted to the bedrock of the village, like one of its wild flowers or gnarled oaks, so made of the soil and the wind nothing, or almost nothing, could free him. And yet he flies along down the street on sturdy legs, in baggy shorts and T-shirt, sneakers gray from long work over plaster tubs and piles of sand.

It is one o'clock of a sheer June day in 1995 and the village is empty. Six years have gone by, with stays with my family growing erratically longer from my efforts to land various jobs in Europe, like the year (1989) spent teaching in southern Austria on a Fulbright lectureship. Or, five years later, the semester-long teaching stint in Tuscany, at a branch of my university. Each time the kids were thrown into the local schools, and learned a bit of southern German one year, a sprinkling of Dante's Italian half of another.

Each time I got to look around, deepen my sympathies with another stretch of Europe, different from, yet continuous with how France formed, and where its ancestors lay. The Teutonic roots of France go deep, to the people who lived here or migrated here in the early Middle Ages, and who fought and drudged for Merovingian and Carolingian kings, then under the Capetians, each time sloughing off a bit of East Francia's (the future Germany) more guttural tongue and refining, shaving, chiseling out the consciousness that would shape West Francia into France. The hills looked the same in Austria as they do here; the farm houses were heavier and squatter against the long alpine winters; the villages more intimate and informal in Tuscany, but in either case, France's soul was perceptible through a gauzy screen of history and evolution. I could feel my sense of France sharpen, like a blade on a whet stone, as I wandered over the Old World and lived here and there, discerning out of German gravity and Italian passion the sensuous, more balanced French psyche.

Jackie, the name of my neighbor's son, seems sure about his life, and is taking over his father's business a little more each day. An older brother left home to cook in a restaurant in Germany, fed up with village life. Father and son were following ancient patterns of these hills, handing on to the next generation the skills that had come down from the Romans and had simmered in the bottom of the mind all these centuries since. To pass something down through the blood was different from almost any other way of cultural transmission – it came mixed with love, authority, jealousy, secrets so grudgingly given they rendered the student powerless in accepting them.

They were restorers of houses, builders, roofers, plasterers. The father, Giovanni, came west from a village in the Italian Alps, near the mountain town of Cuneo, a decade after the war with a few *lire* in his pocket, a willingness to carry hod and clean the fallen stones of bombed or abandoned villages. He got on, saving his money, keeping his own counsel. He had wandered over from an Axis power which had given Nazis access to the border into Nice during the war, but the passions of that calamity were spent. Besides, the region is woven with Italy by blood and history. Provençal villages are filled with names like Isaiah, Picano, Grossi, Bello, Sacco, Novela. Testanière is a common name here meaning "black head," a southern Italian. Giovanni kept to himself, slowly buying land from farmers and those who no longer wanted to live here.

He bought stone *cabanons* in which to store the roof tiles he removed, the cut stone he hauled out of gutted buildings. He saved floor bricks, fixtures, whatever he could salvage in those early years. No one cared much for the past that had gone wrong; the villages fell silent, weeds sprouted in the doorways, lintels fell down and became ramps for creepers to climb. Many villages stood empty in the barren hillscapes, and men like my neighbor came along and mortared, roofed, dug out rotting floors and reconstructed them.

Did he have a hunch the Calavon valley would one day rival the Côte d'Azur? Perhaps. The money accumulated in sufficient dribbles to give him a foothold. Towns like this one went begging for residents, and he bought a ruin for almost nothing at the base of a sandy cliff on which the church stands. He dug it out and began making a house with his salvaged beams and rafters and lintel stones. He was hard as flint; nothing deterred him from his visions. But he couldn't simply build, he had to create with stone, adding the soft curves, florets, wandering lines that brought stone to life again. Clean, cobbled walls rose straight against the dark, almond-colored sunlight. Behind the walls was a citadel of smooth plaster and oiled beams, a place where wife and sons could begin to rise in the world. A daughter would come along in a few years, a tall blond who rode down the *Grand'Rue* on her pied mare, golden hair falling down her black velvet riding jacket, the symbol of her father's success. The parents went on humbly working, with a night out occasionally dressed in the mauves and wheat colors of tailored clothing, the village eyeing them as they passed.

The son stopped schooling after his *bac*, apprenticing himself to his father. I could hear rock music in his ground floor bedroom, opposite our manger – but the stone swallowed most of it, letting out base notes through the little transom over his door. Inside, in that pocket of cliff-space, with its two-foot thick walls, he spent his idle hours listening to the sounds of rootless youth in America, crying for freedom, for sexual liberty, for the right to explore the ragged edges of human identity. It was the sound of generations cutting their ties, drifting into America's material ethic, a landscape luminous with desires. He couldn't imagine what life would be like in the suburbs of Detroit or L.A., days spent idling over football, driving the endless maze of superhighways looking for something, calling home now and then to keep in touch with family he hadn't seen in years. All that lay on the far side of imagination, a lure of potent meanings never real enough to seduce him into leaving. He was like some flightless bird who might beat his awkward wings, but never leave the ground.

Once, at a summer *fête* in Caseneuve, a village up the road, I saw him holding the hand of a thin, homely woman who seemed indifferent to him. He had come with his racks of cassettes and seemed to have a side-line as a DJ at these village street dances. The towns were always hiring someone with a stereo system and some fast gab to keep teenagers bobbing up and down on the boules court for an evening; it was cheaper than booking rock bands. I saw him study the face of the girl for some erotic glimmer. She went alongside him mechanically, and then they left. I felt sad for him; he worked hard, and his love-life was empty.

The news in the village was that he had become engaged; that part of his life was even more protected from village scrutiny. I never saw his wife, though I heard later that he had divorced. He would give me an evasive little greeting from time to time, keeping his distance. He was always hurrying off to his next errand, pressed for time. So be it. The father was kinder, wiser; he knew it paid off to nod, have a few words, dawdle leisurely over weather talk. His mother is Breton, a sturdy, implacable domestic force whose shopping and cleaning ran on an adamant schedule. I could have made a calendar from her movements – the duvets hung on the sill at eight a.m., the clatter of her feet as she wheeled provisions on a barrow from the parking lot to her door a little after eleven on Saturdays. Her dinners on Sunday for Jackie and his girl, terrace parties with trusted friends in July; her two or three good dresses for dinners out in August, just before leaving for her long vacation in the Alps. Hair always the same, short, curled around her round face, dyed blond, her voice flat as a duck's.

The daughter was growing up as well. After a year at the university in Aix en Provence, she came home to spend her time sitting in doorsteps on summer nights, letting the boys flirt with her till one or two in the morning. She seemed a bit lost; her future was as hazy as the sky before a mistral. She had an inheritance to count on, and like so many kids in Provence, she felt no particular compulsion to leave the region or start a career; she would have a house and property, some money in the end. She bided her time and took her brother's bedroom when he moved to his own house on a hill opposite the cemetery. A motorcycle was parked near her door at night, and now a softer rock played in the evenings, and the lights stayed on late into the night.

The years were going by; I had watched Jackie growing up for six of them, and his face was filling out, his body growing thick from labor. His arms were powerful. There were days last winter when I saw him patching up rock walls along the Caseneuve road, smiling briefly as I drove by. Occasionally he would bring his car up the narrow street and lug in his stereo and cassettes, a basket of food for a party he was catering. Sometimes he roared off to town with his mom beside him, the music rumbling through the closed windows of the car. She was serenely maternal in all that jangle of pop music. His family heeded the father's rules – to work hard and charge a good price, to eat and drink well, to have beauty in one's life. Iron gates fortified their entry; they were locked each night as if the world were given over to wolves while they slept. The windows of the house gleamed like mountain pools, and behind them lay the fruits of labor and vision: warm evening lamps, a few paintings, tall goblets along a shelf, the long table for all rituals.

Several times each winter Jackie drove a tractor up the narrow street towing a wagon of sawed logs and lime-caked rafters for the hearth, along with trash oak and whatever else could be salvaged from their work sites. They didn't buy cut wood off the market – it was overpriced. Sometimes the wagon came loaded down with vegetables from the fields; a pile of Cavaillon melons, crates of cherries in early summer; small dazzling yellow rows of apricots, little green plums. The trees of their hillside land were bountiful and generous, and occasionally, if Giovanni were in a flush mood, we would get a small bag of fruit from his harvest, or the invitation to pick the remaining cherries in his orchard. Sometimes the old man would wheel his barrow up the *Grand'Rue* with his demijohn swishing full of wine. His wife would wait in the cold for the butcher or the fish monger from Apt, and she would buy their best for the family meals. Lunch in the salon, under the herb sprays and dry flowers, was the main meal of the day, a joyful rite to break up the winter days.

The son fascinated me; he seemed at times a living fossil of medieval life. What transpired in his subjectivity? Did he have doubts, hidden desires? Was he ever anxious that his life might not be large enough? He left whole areas of self unexamined, lying there like the blood in his arms and legs. But there were signs he was unhappy; for what reason, I couldn't say. Perhaps, as an American so used to self-immersion, I thought that mere labor and obedience to village dictates would eventually make him snap from boredom. As an apprentice, Jackie did the stoop labor for his father. Like most *maçons*, Giovanni had given up picking up heavy stones or wielding a trowel loaded with plaster. After forty, a *maçon* suffered from bone splinters if he was not careful; he either hired street labor or trained his sons for the heavy work, who in turn would know to give up the grunting by middle age.

Fathers and sons in the village were embarked on a dangerous journey together – passing a fragile world made of the past into young hands distracted more and more by the lures of the city. Did the gods come with the stone? Were the oak lintels still part of some Celtic world of spirits? Or were they merely the objects with which one fashioned a living? What did the young believe in, and did the fathers give more than the knowledge of how to build? Was there more to a building than its four walls and roof? I don't know. I wasn't there at the first lessons. I couldn't say if beauty were part of the curriculum of Jackie's first rock work. But something had crossed over from Giovanni's instruction; Jackie was precise, had the "eye" for good stone, and even if he didn't believe in Givoanni's gods, he had some latent understanding that "good" involved more than shape or durability. He wouldn't build with cheap materials; he was a traditionalist and kept to his father's standards.

Nature was a slow and ill-humored muse in early spring and late August. The droughts burned up whole vineyards of starving tendrils; the wind broke the wheat and trampled under the delicate first shoots of carrot and onion. The lavender if left too long in the field ate up all the useful minerals and left the ground sterile. How could youth master such dialogs with weather and the precarious life of fruit trees? Cherries would ripen early and hang thick globes of red from their branches, only to swell from an unexpected rain the night before harvest and be worthless. Did a young man have the patience to serve such a cruel master as the weather? Most did not; they took their chances in the human world of cities, and labored under the more predictable cruelties of human bosses and market places.

Was it any better having to endure a father's rages at the supper table when things went sour? Farms are not democracies, nor are the economies that pay *maçons*. To live by one's wits and hands is no easy task, and the soul can become hard in the process. Fathers beat their sons and passed along the hard hand down through the generations. Many of the young fathers in this village beat their sons out of habit, showing the same lack of mercy they had received. The subtleties of the self were not in evidence here. Things worked, people obeyed, life went on or didn't. Not because psychology had some part in the equation of survival, but because a father labored against the odds and endured, and taught his son accordingly.

The daughters came up the same way, trained by mothers to do the cleaning, the shopping. At the supermarket, I watched pairs of them go by with eyes darting over the poultry, the cut meats, the fish on ice. A girl might touch the head of a gutted perch with tentative fingers, and the mother would point out the faded eyes and turn up her nose. The girl did likewise. On they moved to the vegetables, smelling the melons, squeezing the peaches and green peppers. There was a trick to knowing ripeness from rot, or the greens that would never ripen after being gassed or forced in factory hot houses in Spain. The nose knows, mom would say, and the girl would wrinkle up her pug nose and twist her lips in imitation of her mother.

It isn't always this way, of course. Microwaves have been replacing stoves for years; many a kitchen now is modernized to the point that few meals are made in them, just heated and served. Girls grow up all over southern France as ignorant of food and nutrition, thrift, and re-use as any suburban American girl. There are no courses in home economics, no basic training in consumerism to help save a few hearts and livers from abuse. Obesity is on the rise, and heart ailments are becoming frequent. France is a leading center for heart surgery, which would indicate that fewer people understand the so-called Mediterranean diet or how to balance eating in the old ways.

Still, Signe's old fashioned kitchen where pies were made from scratch and cakes were decorated was Mecca for village girls forbidden the use of the kitchen without a mother's supervision. Modernizing had only been around for two generations, and the grandmothers still cooked or knew how to teach the art. That mystery of the recent past was opened and explored by Signe and friends, and the secrets of herbs, oils, spices were being rediscovered. Our table was a great lure to friends of all three kids, since we took the time, pains, and patience to bring out food cooked from fresh ingredients.

The arts of sewing, mending, and decorating the house were disappearing; mercers and bead shops were a rarity, though the bead shop at Isle-sur-la Sorgue was still something of a female temple and many girls could be found poring over the bins of tiny colored glass beads, and buying them by the gram. The big low-cost Swedish house wares store, Ikea, in Vitrolles, near Marseille, was supplying young couples with ready-made drapes, slip covers, inexpensive napery and flat ware, glasses, and all the other necessities. An "Ikea house" was now common among the bungalows of village outskirts, and was becoming more familiar in the stone dwellings as well. A certain varnished, molded, laminated feel was stealing over the countryside, replacing the expensive walnut, rosewood and oak furniture that still bore the hack marks of an adze or chisel and plane. These authentic pieces were heading for auction houses and *brocante* fairs, like the one at Isle-sur-la-Sorgue, where English, Dutch, German dealers all came to buy up rustic farm furniture, and hand-made goods. Increasingly Americans were dismantling Provence for re-sale in California, where a "New Provence" has long been emerging in wine country. Such faux Provences were blossoming in places like the Hill Country in Texas, and in planned communities in Arizona and New Mexico.

The thread that held fathers and sons, mothers and daughters together here was frail, fraying fast in this dangerous age. Jackie's life was a reminder to me of the strength of tradition as well as the threats bearing down on it. I watched as Giovanni laid more burdens on his son's back – more errands, more runs with the tractor to bring food or fuel, or to begin work on a neighboring stone ruin that he had bought for his other son, the German chef. Jackie plied his trade under his father's all-knowing eye, took the criticism, bore the brunt of his father's advice and lectures, and generally endured the travails of a son in yoke. The rewards, concrete and in the offing, were enough to compensate for his ills; the house he lived in now was spacious, rambling atop a sloping field with views of the back hills and the Luberon, and almost beyond price. He was lord of his small domain and more was coming, if he could hang on.

But the years were mill stones; something was wearing out between them. The old man had no sense of compromise, I suspect, and the son's signals went unnoticed. Seven years later, at lunch, Jackie stormed out of his father's house, slammed the iron gates behind him, and took his first steps into alien air. He had had his scene with dad, and refused to lift another finger. Thereafter I heard no tractor putt-putting up the *Grand'Rue*; saw no brown legs in short shorts strutting away after one of his mother's good lunches. He was gone, up on his hill, plunging into a world where fathers were no longer in power. King Lear was bereft of an heir, as Jackie tore the rest of the threads away and declared himself independent.

Now he could stand with the world of sons who had left home and not looked back. Was it better now? What were fathers in this age? What did they provide for their sons that was still of use? Order? A vision of the soul at peace with the world, not in contention with it, or at war with others? Fathers were monuments, shabby figures in rags with their noses bent, their chins wattled, their backs almost broken from labor – did they have spiritual gifts for their adult sons? Jackie would find out what real solitude was. His mother would remain loyal to her husband and not conspire or send secret gifts up the hill. He must come back and make his amends in the proper way for there to be peace. But a year passed, and the son was resolute, growing used to his new life. He might never return. If that were so, then the gravity of tradition had weakened in this last reserve of medieval bonding. I began to despair for them and for me.

The father was stoical and went about his errands with a wheezing persistence. Having breathed all that plaster dust and cement over the years, he suffered from emphysema, which gave him a halting walk and a sad, woebegone look. But he gave in not an inch. He even labored on the work site next to his house, and visible from my study window. He would mix his concrete, adjust the supports holding up the new floor, go about the hard grind of masonry work with a rattle of trowels in the tub, the pouring out, the hammering in place of wooden molds. He grunted, he tottered on his ladder, he shut the wooden doors up at night with a grim face and trudged up to his dinner. The lights burned brightly in his dining room, but the joy of life had ebbed away.

Why had he bore down so hard on his son? Was his love demonstrable at the critical moments when Jackie wavered? Were the criticisms mixed with admiration for his son's skills? I believe Giovanni did not feel threatened not by his son's divided loyalties between work and the world that lay around him of night clubs, disco parties, fast cars, a few joints passed around. He must have felt that the world itself was slipping away from him and he took it out on Jackie. Who else was there to rage at? The values he lived by were eroding visibly by the day, with pink cottages sprouting up in symmetrical encampments requiring only a blue print, ready-made materials, and a team of Arab laborers to throw the thing up. It was a world of hovering helicopters and ravenous real estate agents looking for spare property to "develop." Giovanni was a hand held up against such progress, such dissolution, and if the son came to work in dyed hair and an ear ring, was this not a sign of further dissolution? He used his dull tongue, his heavily accented French to draw a rasp against the son's nerves, and it finally cut a nerve that bound them. Their crisis was as mysterious as it was blunt, revealing something they dreaded and admired simultaneously.

My own son was coming of age in this same village, and I found in Giovanni parables to apply to my own life. What held me to my son now? What were the bonds between us, if I had neither land nor trade to deed to him? What did he find in me of use, spiritually or otherwise? He sometimes thought I had favored Signe over him, that I could only love the scholar or writer in my children, and since he professed no interest in either, what did I offer to him but obstacles and misunderstandings? We talked, but the tensions grew between us – partly because I had missed his crucial growing years, and now came around to confront and perhaps block his pubescent leap to freedom. He confided in his mother, not me. He got his spending money from her; my payments were formal, and bore clauses of cause and effect. I struggled to enrich my role, to define it better. If anything, I gave him his consciousness of class, his sense of a place in the hierarchy. He knew we belonged in some secure way to white collar society. I taught the future managers how to think and express themselves; so did my wife. He was preparing to enter into that professional realm one day himself. But how much instruction did this require from me? What was there to know that he couldn't learn from an institution?

If Giovanni had failed his own son, with property and livelihood heaped on the scales of loyalty, and a thousand years of family tradition behind him, what purpose did I fill in my son's life with nothing to put into the scales but love and protection while he was young? Provence rose up before me as a paradise gone sour, with exile and disharmony shaking its rocks loose and tumbling the houses down the steep hills. Tales of disintegration seemed all I heard now. And before us, casting its long shadow over the world, was an America that stood for total freedom. Didn't the stores, the superhighways, the TV shows all supply the language of that dream of autonomy? Shows like *Friends* and *Seinfeld, Sex and the City, Six Feet Under* portrayed lives that couldn't stick to anything but the image in the mirror. Selves at odds with the outside world and incapable of lasting relationships. Our American dream was driven by curiosity to know the soul's distant edges and depths, not the nature or worth of community or the compromises sharing would demand. Our quest of the end of self was a journey fraught with terrible dangers and crises to our psychic life, our moral and spiritual existence. But on we drove ourselves to know the absolute degree of independence from everything.

My son was born and raised in the framework of that culture, Jackie was not. And yet both sons were drifting from their fathers. I had come to Provence partly to satisfy my longing for a childhood image of beauty formed when I had lived in Beirut. Marseille was close to my memory of that other city, the Paris of the Middle East. But as layers of Provence peeled away over the past few years, revealed below the pretty surface of earth with its scattering of groves and quaint houses was a dark mirror in which I stared into my own unexamined beliefs.

With my neighbor only twenty feet away, I couldn't have lived a more remote and alien life than if he were on the moon. Giovanni's blood ran with Roman coins and the relics of saints; his breath stunk of wine musk and his dreams were littered with fossils and volcanic rock. What had I tasted of the earth but a few bricks in a row house in Philadelphia, screen doors banging in summer, the stale air of planes droning over the Atlantic on my way to my father's next posting. The smells I remembered were of pencil shavings, new book bags, erasers held to the nose on a crisp September morning hours before my first day of school. I remembered toast in the morning, and hamburgers frying in the pan at night, the tangy aroma of my mother's spaghetti sauce, the rattle of plastic plates on the 4th of July picnic. I had never plunged my arm into the earth's entrails or come up with a handful of nature's blood. I had not ordered the lamb slaughtered for Easter, or taken my hank of boar's meat for New Years. I had not swallowed my spit gritty with the newly plowed earth, or bitten into the mistral at morning, my hands stiff from plastering. We were opposites he and I, and yet we were failing fathers.

But I could go to the mirror and see my father's face emerging in my own. By fifty, my face had rounded, my chin had doubled, I wore the bushy eyebrows and bags that were his. Like him or not, I housed my father's image in my flesh, and carried around his tics and habits. He was neither generous nor stingy with me as I grew up, but made giving a big deal. I got money from my mother simply with a whisper; dad required a deal, a promise of repayment. He gave me more than she did, but it was colder money and I didn't ask for it often. But he had descended from a father who gave no money at all, and my grandfather had come from a house in Rock Island, Illinois ruled over by a Norwegian ogre who threw him out into a winter night with threats of death shouted from the porch. He was hidden in the window seat when the father started to snore. Those were my fathers, the cold men of the north, the hard-edged silent types. I was them and passed their legacy onto my son, who politely refused as much of it as he could. The tradition had lost its force in me; I was not cold, but my attitudes had been made for me and I wore them.

Provence warmed us both, and fed us with something like southern nonchalance. The olive and the grape were heady fruits and melted down the hardest stone. The earth was shaped by wind and water, soft voices that cajoled the mountains and pleaded for yielding when they came down out of those soft heavens. To escape the iron will of the desert, and the harsh justice of the Middle East, even Pontius Pilate took passage here and retired at Vienne, to the north of us. Mary and her mother left Golgotha and came here as well, to live out their lives in this consoling place. Shouldn't the magic of Provence melt even me and dissolve my fathers' ways? Wouldn't it melt down Norway in me and give me heat and some of the love that had blossomed in the courts of the Troubadours? I hoped so, and prayed that my son would forgive me and find in me something worth loving.

It must have been in spring of 2004 that I saw Jackie walking slowly out of his parents' house eating a heel of bread. A child was beside him, his son, about three years old. I didn't even know his name; the seclusion he had sealed himself behind had left the essentials blank. Now a family man, he had come back to reconcile. Some force had bent his will, the way fire bends iron. He had come back home, made his peace, shaken his father's hand, kissed him on his cheek. He had found the words to amend the offense, to forgive the insult. He was elegantly dressed in soft black pullover and loose slacks, and his son was smartly attired as well. They made a handsome pair, and now, he had returned, but on his own terms. He would never be his father's slave, but his friend. He had started his own company and his name hung on the village sign, with phone number. He was his own man but also a son, and the Provence that perched at the edge of the ancient world endured.

It occurred to me that sons are given this nugget of fire to place in their guts as they turned fifteen or so, and the fire gnawed at all they knew. It made them thrash at their limits, and kick at the authority that would tame them early. They were wild and dangerous at sixteen, ready to kill anything that would deny them their feral liberty. They were easily seduced into violence, gangs, into that moment in which a father could be struck, a house torn to pieces in rage. Only the aging father offered some hope to such a young man to quiet his soul, to know that there was an end to anarchy, that destruction could give way to building, to participating once more. Jackie told me as much as he moved along, his body calm, reassured, his hand affectionately clasping his son's. His father was upstairs at his table, relishing the last drop of wine in his glass after a dinner of peace making.

Chapter Fourteen

Weaving and Unraveling

The land abounds in symbols of woven life: the fields are the oldest cloth, woofs and wefts of green coursing through the earth. When the pickers come to pull down the fruit from the trees, they move like dancers through a stage setting of orderly, unified nature. The houses that border the fields are mosaic shapes, a ripple of fragments that cling together, as if to say this is the right use of energy. Nature always moves forward, pushing its energy in a stream ahead of itself, forming, opening, budding, closing the tiers and ranks of its creations, and here they were mirrored in the fields, and in the houses my neighbors built. We were all riders on the wave of beauty, plunging through space in our stone dwellings, with the fields gathered around us like the troughs of some coherent, magical sea.

You cannot improve on this innate world; there is nothing one can add or take away without debasing it. Many newcomers try. All would like to bring their own experience into this life, since they feel too much like strangers when they arrive. One night several years ago, as we began our evening walk to the fields, we stopped to greet our Swedish friends who had moved into the village two years before. They had been renovating several houses in the center of the village. Leif, a sculptor, was very thorough and masterly as a builder. He was awaiting the arrival of his brother-in-law, who was stuck in some colossal traffic jam at Lyon, as truckers protested the new driving permits based on a punitive point system. All the auto routes were halted with trucks, and now there was little chance his guests would make it for dinner. He invited us in for a drink.

The little house he finished first is pristine inside; white walls rise in banks of snowy brilliance. The edge of the trowel scored the plaster here and there in a rustic style, which Leif had done himself. The *maçon*, he told us, didn't know how to do it; he only dragged his float around in rough, overlapping circles. "Terrible." The little stair led up into the kitchen, with counters and new appliances, a clean window with a gray cat sniffing the planter. The stair turned sharply and climbed to a bedroom on one side, and to a small salon on the other. The stairwell was railed with plain black tubing and panes of glass. A Chagall ink drawing hung over the desk; a drawing of a bird dominated the stairwell. We sat on a white divan drinking wine from the Sylla vinicole in Apt. We admired his immaculate dwelling.

Our house seemed dull and dusty and shapeless by comparison. The stair was a marvel of intricate triangulated steps, each tiled with razor-sharp precision. We stayed for an hour and left. I told a story to the children and went off to bed, but by one or so, was aroused by insomnia, what the French call the royal disease. Leif's house came back to me, tilting out of dreams and worries, to stand before me with its knife-edge staircase, its glassed-in well, its bird crying in the void. It was a Swedish house, full of ice and snow, and Calvinist anguish. The stairs had erased all the matriarchal lineage from the house. It rose like a conscience to the bedroom, where two single beds lodged in opposite corners, with an iron floor lamp standing between them like a parson. Poor Leif had dragged his whole regional world with him to set up inside a stone shell. He had killed Provence with his miter box.

Because he would not hire the local *maçons* and did all the shopping for materials himself, word got around that he was unfriendly, not a true villager. He began to notice that the supply shops were running out of things too quickly, that he had to drive to Cavaillon for plaster or bags of chaux. Soon, nothing was available at either of the big warehouses. He was being froze out; the village was taking vengeance on him. The whispers grew louder at the bar, and the more he tried to ingratiate himself with others, the colder the stares. When no one would sell him goods to build with, he slowed down to a stop. Then he threw his tools into his tubs and packed up. He went home, and the house he had made such an expression of northern austerity remains shuttered, gathering dust. His other projects were finished by local *maçons* and are used now and then, but he never came back.

Each house in the village is a story unfolding with fathers and sons gripped in a furious battle of wills, raging against and for continuity. As each generation comes of age, Jackie's for example, something gets lost, and the past is transformed or diminished, oozing forward in the arms and legs, the attitudes of the son now father. The house contains mother-daughter sagas as well, a mixture of repression by stern mothers and grandmothers, a slow relenting toward freedom by a father or uncle, as the past is squeezed and twisted and the girl wanders into the future, her fingers red with cherry juice, her mouth humorous and ironic as life beckoned to her.

The errors and tragedies are part of the story; the son who leaves, the son who is rejected and molders away in the dungeons of the asylum at Montfavet. The girl who gets pregnant and lives with her boy friend in a small dark room in Apt, and helps cultivate his marijuana crop in the nearby woods. She too is the story. As is the alcoholic aunt, the retarded girl who goes with anyone to the woods for quick love, and is a standing joke at the bar. The wife cheaters and the husband cheaters live in their dark houses and drive off at sunset to a rendezvous. The widows stand at their windows as the shadows creep across the Luberon at sun set.

Each family lived a tale, a Greek myth in miniature. There was no escaping the plots of jealousy, rebellion, hate or love. A man blew out his brains in a farm house on the Caseneuve road; the *pompiers* (fire men) showed up and put him into a body bag and off they went again. Madness had claimed him; the mistral and the winters had claimed him. The house is gloomy and alone on its hill; the gate leading up is chained and the weeds have shot up in the ruts winding their way to his door. Even the stalwarts grow old and die, leaving the next generation the task of replacing roof tiles, painting the shutters, watering the kitchen garden, throwing the shuttle in time's loom.

We are all actors on this sea floor stage. Even strangers like myself have a part to play, lines to deliver. I do not participate in the core of myth making; the nucleus of culture is formed out of the cryptic affairs of those families that rule the village. Their table talk, their trips to the mayor for urgent conversation behind closed doors, their quarrels among them- selves, their marriages and baptisms weave history out of their windows and into the streets. They keep alive the past in their prejudices and doubts, their stares at me as I pass slowly in my car. I am part of their mysterious culture-making, but only at the margins. I am what inspires their dread of the future; will there be more of me in the years ahead, and therefore less of them? Nothing of substance in their minds has changed in half a millennium. They dream of land, their heirs and descendants, the weather and the menaces imposed by Paris law makers.

I want them to remain in power, to have all the influence they need to save us from dissolution. Let them kick me out if they have to, I will go willingly, in handcuffs in the gendarme's van to board a flight for Houston. For now, I am tolerated by these elders on whose shoulders rest the burden of preserving this fading way of life. There is no alternative but to persevere. In an editorial in the *Herald Tribune* not long ago, William Pfaff tries to make sense of the reign of terror we live under from Muslim extremists. "The terrorist attacks on the West are a doomed reaction to a war that modern society has already largely won," he writes. "The modern world is the aggressor, determined – without even seriously thinking about it – to destroy the backward civilizations of everyone else, which it sees as discredited remnants of the past." Modernism has substituted "a material utopia for religious salvation."* I would say it has also substitued shopping for every other need, spiritual and personal we might feel. And the ancient world, Provence included, reels from the destruction.

The women come to the new village *épicerie* bearing a weathered shopping net for their provisions. They are like scrolls on which the winters have been written; in them lie many confessions of loneliness and endurance, of hard cold nights under the blankets with the wind gnawing at the roof tiles. They know the village as if it were their own bones and ligaments. They come and go like Zen masters, indifferent to this hour passing, as if it were mere grains of sand in a child's palm. The real story of the village is curves of many years, rolls of time following the tops of the hills out into the distance – where life and death merge and disappear.

The landscape calls out to a certain kind of dreamer in the world who comes along once in a great while and settles here. My friend Gustaf Sobin is an example; so is the poet Karin Lessing, who lives in Terre Blanche and writes in the solitude of a tiny office in the trees above her house. Sobin, Lessing, Louis Merveille, her late husband, practiced a kind of reserve and austere devotion that Provence demands, if it is part its dark tree limbs and allow an intimate glance into its heart. Visitors come and go, some of them impressed with the land and its history, others indifferent to it. But they leave after a while. There are others who feel almost pulled by the ancient heart of the place and try to sink roots. They buy a house, hire workmen to renovate it, move in for a time, get to know a few of the other foreigners, and eventually sell off at a nice profit, and move on. I have known quite a few of this kind, and have witnessed their struggle to stay on, to hold onto something too elusive to grasp, too vague to be seized by practical minds. They are intrigued with its powers and want to know why it holds some people for life. But the voices that lure us here are indistinguishable from the wind.

Even the familiar postcard of a Provençal windowsill with its pots of geraniums speaks of the region's aloofness, the impartiality of this lush country which lures as it refuses. The postcard, simple as it is, reveals the two hearts of beauty: the desire that beckons, the repulse of each suitor. There lay the principle of its own rarity and virginity, this candor of affection

---

* "Traditional Culture Strikes Back," 21 July 2005, p. 7

that withdraws at the first sign of advance. One may look, may approach and yet at some point the cold skin of virginity wards off the intruder, and ends an unfulfilled relation.

The true nature of Provence is a perfection of form and light no one can hold. Those who own some piece of it are no more in possession of Provence than the tourist passing in a camper. It's like holding a dove; it is not yours even when you cup it in your hand. It is only the dove again when you let it go. To own is to enter into a guardianship, to accept the role of custodian, and thus water lawns and trim trees, and tidy up gravel walks in a menial role. The rich are humbled by such tasks, even when they assign them to others. They must come out too with shears and rakes and fuss with the beauty they can only admire and assist. They are equal to the poorest gypsy on his ladder; they can look, they can love, they can do everything but control its life, its own creative will. When the English garden is planted, or the pool displaces the stone shed, things are not right. They bear the look of some other place, and there is a corresponding disappointment that will drive away the aggressive landowner, who will look for a more accommodating mistress.

One must come to the land as a humble petitioner for work as temple guardian or as water carrier, and forget that you own factories or run corporations, or own an acre of London real estate worth millions. All that is nothing here; you are only eyes and veins of blood, a guest of creation and no more. You may not meddle with, may not upset the balance, or things will unravel, and you will be left with your own sordid vanity heaped around you. The light will fall elsewhere, the beauty will slip away and you will find yourself unaccountably disconsolate and exiled.

Provence teaches ancient virtue, though this is not an age that listens well. Provence fades, and its delicate dream now seems almost an illusion. Those who are coming in and building, reshaping, turning vineyards into complexes and dry valleys into golf course communities, bring with them the weapons of a hostile philosophy. They try to imagine there is a Provence for them as well, and carve into the hills some altar to their own sense of worth. Provence comes no nearer to wealth than it does to fame or power; and yet all who succeed in Europe seem drawn to the place as a teacher, as a source of virtue. As the vale in which to grow young again. But it is all an illusion, a dim hope for those who have squandered their innocence. The land can do nothing but remain itself, lofty, detached from human life, reminding us how far we have wandered from the path.

Nature is the real story of Provence, a nature that has willingly conspired with man to grow a certain way unlike any other place in the world. The nature here is generous and extraordinarily fertile, even in droughts. The rock is alive and is the amorous bed of oaks that twist and writhe and make fabulous forms in the pliable, willing limestone. The briars and broom plants rise up tall and powerful in earth so arid even the nettles suffer and turn brown. This is the place where the natural world is more important, more full of character than the humans who serve it. The walls crumble but Hamlets full of passion rise out of their crannies as great shaggy hollyhocks delivering monologs out of their drooping blossoms. You cannot pass such flowers without looking them over, as if they were spirits. Of all the places I have known, this one makes being human seem superficial, almost irrelevant. The humanism that swept over the West three centuries ago and raised our consciousness above the natural world, did not take root here. The subject of attention is not us, but the aloof, indefinable force of creativity that churns in the earth and comes to us as endlessly malleable green forms. Human hands manipulate the power of life and wring food from it, or beauty. But the real splendor of Provence lies in what we cannot take from it. Like the night sky and full moon tracing the blue back of the Luberon, or the trickle of white fog cast by the Milky Way. We observe but shrug our shoulders; nothing can be pocketed of such wonders.

On my daily walks, I follow a one-lane road as it drops down among house-sized boulders that have rolled off the cliffs above me. How long ago they toppled, I can't say. The ground below me forms the bed of a dry torrent that once raged and kicked over trees, hurtled them to the bottom of the hill to the sand of the Calavon. I go along among oak saplings, beech trees, hickory, juniper bushes, here and there bare dusty ground and nettles. Jagged and ribbed rock rise behind the oaks, going straight up, pocked with caves. Great wedges of stone have been sheared off to form cold shadows where the boars leave their scat. On top of even the most precarious outcropping are new oaks, crowded together like school girls waiting for a bus. Birds everywhere, croaking, screeching, cawing as they fly off at my footstep. Behind my head, the drone of a bumble bee as it brings down a thin weed to fondle its pink blossom. Lady bugs walk the road ahead of me, long brown worms crawl elegantly along in the heat of the sun. A grasshopper informs me by its brown skin that the drought has broken through to August. The ground is cracked like tiles and the ants burrow deeper for moisture.

I stand ankle deep in weeds, the ground heaved up beneath me like a belly. I come here to do my yoga for a few minutes each morning. It is my excuse to worship the sun, which I do by holding my hands straight above my head, taking deep breaths of air as I bend from side to side. The birds observe me in silence; a jack rabbit rattles the brittle leaves nearby. I reach down and spread out my fingers on the ground before my feet. It is dry and crumbly ground peppered with tiny ants doing work. I pull up my foot and tuck it into my groin, hold up my hands in prayer and study the face of my village across the canyon. The farmers move through tarnished gold wheat fields in their tiny tractors, the snore of their engines coming thinly over the distance. The shutters are closed from the night before, but the kitchens are alive, preparing lunch. On my walk back I will smell onions sizzling in olive oil, garlic and red pepper wilting in pans for *ratatouille*. For now, all is peace and serenity. I am home. I dearly love this place.

Provence required that there be enough adversity in its beauty to dash the human hope that it could be mastered. Enough setbacks and the houses grew humble; enough misery and disaster and Roman pride was broken. It was a place of small, hard people who could endure its heat and dryness, and eke out a life. And what grew up finally was a bond between the two sides, a flexible relation between human guests and nature. It didn't always work, and there were repeated breaches in the contract, but in time, and time was the key, the human will wore down like a sandy ridge, and there was commerce, even fealty between them. No one can dabble in its ratios, or alter the subtle balance of rights; it is a relation that will die before it is changed.

Every region has its character; this one belongs to the ancient faith of the Ligurians and the Celts who followed. The hills were once darkly forested and gave rise to mythologies that impressed the Roman writers who came here. The ground was watched over by myriad deities; no stream or creek or crevice of hill was without some guardian spirit to placate and honor. It was the basis on which human accord was reached; talking to the spirits of the earth was essential if one were to scrape out a life here. The human spirit could not endure the adversities without another will to talk to; the land must be drawn into the compact, given its rightful place. Where the earth is resolute and uncompromising, religion grows best, thriving in bitterness and tragedy like the grape vine that flourishes in parched and rocky soil. Where the land is easy and forgiving, there religion weakens and the human ego replaces it. The great whisperers and talkers and prayers congregated here to petition for human succor; they were the first to see which gods resided here and gave them human names. The wind responded favorably, and the rains supported the first stirrings of planted seed. In Robert Graves' study of western religion, *The White Goddess*, he notes that the Celtic word for poet was *derwydd* or oak-seer, "the probable derivation of 'Druid.'" Those who could speak to the oak, or listen to it, reached the creator's mind hidden in these hills.

The true lovers are distinguished from the rest of us by their understanding of the vast, quiet force of land around them. They say nothing, claim nothing, but they're interested, informed, moved by attention to what stirs here season by season. Once, in a dull mood, I considered all the people I knew and sorted them into three kinds: those who understood people and nothing else; those who had a sixth sense about mechanical things, but not the living; and those with intuition about animals and plants, and contempt for the rest of life. There was rarely any overlap among them.

My grandfather spent his life making weapons at the federal arsenal at Rock Island. He understood metal and how it worked; he could talk to engines and levers and make them do things others couldn't. He had found the soul in cams and swivels and ratchets, but had no use for children or animals, who were stubborn and misbehaved. Wagon wheels were truer to his world than the gray nags that pulled his family over the prairies to New Mexico, where he proved a claim in 1910. Somehow the living flesh moved by a logic he couldn't grasp; the levers and gears of a rifle were more understandable than his own son, who tried to catch the moon.

We are fated with a certain love and understanding and live our lives accordingly. The gardener has no real love of the tiller he uses; he prefers the slow, unfolding will of a rose than he does the whirring and coughing of a motor. It troubles him that its own destructive tines will grind up roots and squash tulip bulbs and damage the loamy underworld he must break up each spring. The humanist lacks sympathy for either of these things; gardens are dirt with a few flowers in them, and machines are faithless inert contraptions. But a man or woman is a universe of motives and desires one may spend a lifetime contemplating. We make our lives out of these fated shapes of the heart, and grow up embracing only a fragment of the world. Provence calls a certain person to its borders who is moved by the deep mystery of the soil, by its powers to make life, and take it back again.

I know of one in particular, an American woman from California who grew up in a suburban house near San Francisco, under the ego of a lawyer-father, fell out with him early in life and drifted into the drugged stupors of Haight-Ashbury, where she settled briefly. She was there when Janis Joplin was just a girl knocking on doors to drum up an audience for her rock concert in the park. She remembered times when The Jefferson Airplane and other groups would sing for nothing to a few idlers.

She was a hippie selling beads for a living, a flower child. But one who didn't fall under the spell of a cult leader and cease to exist. She managed to escape before drugs became a hopeless underworld, landing in France, alone. She found a precarious footing in Paris selling bracelets in the streets. With the money she made, she went to Rome as a street peddler, drifted back to France to an abandoned village owned by a German and his American wife. She took one of the empty stone houses for a small rent and for teaching the couple's children. A year went by in this remote Stone-Henge world, under the autocracy of the German, who ardently followed a regime of ascetic living and exercise. What the two American women talked about, or thought, in those long, undisturbed nights of cold starlight and silence, one only imagines.

She told me how she once packed her knapsack and headed over the stony hills to another hamlet, even more remote and disused but for a hermit living there. When she found him, she spent the afternoon talking to the man, who sat at his table with quiet, respectful ease, listening to this young woman chatting. He showed no surprise or delight at human company; he had given himself over to some other reality by then.

Once a day, late in afternoon, a motorcycle wheezed up the long track to her hamlet to deliver the mail; the postman carried along a copy of the *Herald-Tribune* from Paris, and the mail. He would be treated to tea and biscuits, regaled with chatter from both women and the German, if he were not out on a trek. The sight of this face coming through one's thoughts and silent vigils was a deep exhilaration to her, she told me. It was difficult to let him go, to watch him disappear down the sandy track out into the world again, leaving behind silence and nightfall.

She left again, wandering northeast to Lourmarin, in the Vaucluse, a small valley town where Camus is buried, and set up once more in a stone cottage she rented for a year from her dwindling savings. She was looking for a patch of land to rent to begin a farm, her driving ambition. One day she wheeled her bicycle down the main street of the village observed by a young Frenchman, who watched with amusement as she struggled to tow a large branch behind her, her fuel for the night. He helped her drag it home and promptly fell in love with this willful American unafraid of work or solitude. He shared her interest in a farm and negotiated with his grandmother for the use of a rocky piece of hillside with a cabin on it. They moved in, bought a goat, asked a neighbor how to milk it, and . . . she felt the dark grip of earth reach out to her and pull her toward it.

The little field was not much to start with; after they proved to themselves farming was possible, they went further north to the Luberon valley, the *bassin d'Apt* and found an abandoned hamlet to repair over-looking a canyon full of meadows and a cold spring-fed lake. They rebuilt the little row of houses and took one to live in; the rest were rented out as *gîtes* in summer. She soon mastered the art of making goat cheese, which she supplied to all the local restaurants and *crémeries*, and sold the rest from a stall in the Apt market. Everyone knew her, not as the American, but merely as Linda, the woman who sold cheese. She earned the respect of villagers and farmers, and the juries that award medals for great cheese; no one thought of her as an outsider.

But the deeper change, the more interesting transformation, was in her own mind. She followed the long, tedious route of work, menial labor that included shepherding a herd of goats, milking them each day, washing the tubs and canisters and working the curd, pouring and turning the cakes, scrubbing them with salt water, curing and selling her product. She started a garden, raised pigeons and chickens, lived through the hard winters and long delayed springs. They raised two children, and by a kind of alchemical magic turned herself inside out, from a rootless suburban brat into a woman of the earth.

Her hands were rough and red from the cheese; knuckles prominent and wrinkled like a bird's claws. She is tall, loose-jointed, black-haired, a wide, American grin spread over crooked teeth, some of them capped in silver, eyes darting, a liquid-velocity of speech pouring from her mouth. Her voice is toned high with few notes, and when she drifts into French, the American accent comes with it, like stone under a clear creek. She has not turned against the human world, even by a little. She loves good company and a long chat at the table where wine is poured, and welcomes anyone to visit and taste cheese, admire the buildings her husband Claud has rebuilt, the land she loves. A walk with her down into the meadows includes fossil-hunting, short lectures on the flora, digressions off the little creek bed into brush where she shows you places to hunt *chanterelles* and *cèpes* in early fall.

Her knowledge of America has faded; it stops with 1969, when she left. Her past is a dry flower pressed into a book. Her speech drops a note lower when she talks of that distant time, that lost girl wandering the city, her memory of herself full of wonder and amusement, and pride.

Only by this humiliating path of daily labor can it be said she holds the land at all. Provence may come close to human speech, rising from the depths like a pond reflecting one's face, but what it says to the human soul is – nothing human matters. All things are bound together. All that is turns upon an axis beyond sight or vision or understanding, the radiant hub of something fertile and inexhaustible. The plumb-line of the creation is pure light, and from it comes all the green unfoldings of the earth. Labor alone brings one through the veil of sight or sound to the first tremble of living nerve and muscle in the rock – only by renouncing independence and ego does Earth awake.

But to spend an early evening chatting with her, none of these matters will arise. Her speech ripples and tumbles out touching nothing for long. Her speech is a kind of mockingbird's song satirizing talk itself, letting everything appear to gain importance as it springs from the mouth, whereas the hands rest quietly on the table, touching the stem of a wine glass with that tentative, primal motion of an animal. There, beyond all conversational powers, is the voice of life, resting in her hands.

The Christensen family now (l to r):
Maxine, Paul, Cedric, Cathy, and Signe.

Epilogue

ustaf Sobin died on 7 July, 2005. I was sent his obituary from several friends. He had suffered for three months from pancreatic cancer; friends with whom he had quarreled called him and reconciled. I was here, but not aware he was dying. I would have called as well. Instead, the news of his passing closed a garden gate and gave me the future without him. He had encouraged me to live in Provence back when I first met him. I felt lonelier sitting in the house thinking about our times together. The worm had turned.

Summer has followed summer in Provence for a lot of years. I have grown used to arriving in early May, riding the season to harvest, hovering over the empty wheat fields and picked cherries, the cut lavender, the grape vines loaded with purple bunches, the melon vines exhausted and browning in the fields days before leaving again. I would enter when spring had opened the ground and leave when fall was inching over the hills to close it up again.

It has taught me many things to live here, including slowing time, denying its rush against my bones. Last year we boarded a freighter, the *Marielle Bolton*, out of New Orleans bound for some port of Europe. It took thirty days to cross, thirty long days of flat summer seas, with only the Azores as a landfall after leaving Tampa. Time crawled, and it widened and opened vast trenches into the transparent air, in which to dawdle and dream, and float around in the elongated minutes of each hour. Books were read and cast aside; the wind was eaten by our eyes at the bow of the ship; sea turtles idled and back-washed their fins in a thousand feet of blue and creamy water. Sea nettles and Portuguese men of war bobbed alongside the hull, and porpoises came out to greet us and guide us in to Porto, and take us back out a few days later bound for Amsterdam, our last stop before boarding a train for Paris. That slow entry into Europe pleased me; no jet lag, but also, a rich and embroidered sense of the meaning of time, as it must have been understood five centuries ago. With leisure and a slow pulse, we arrived to spend a long and rambling summer, one of our best.

As creatures of a culture that has cast off much of its beliefs and given us malls and frantic consumption in their place, we long to believe in something, in any kind of spirit who might teach us to forget who we are. We ache to be bathed in some thermal spring where everything we knew might be cleansed of its selfish desires. A little sulfur and iron in the water, a bit of melted quartz to cleanse and rinse the blood and clear the mind. We preserve the few rituals we have, like eating meals together, taking walks at evening, studying the night sky in silence, spending time alone with our thoughts. But we need so much more that the land could teach us, the patient enduring earth that smiles back at the scorching, drought-prolonging sun. A willingness even to die when the rains are withheld or the ice comes early, this lesson so hard to accept through the great carapace of ego that is thrust on each of us. To stand still and drain one's thought down to the bones of the head, to stand empty to receive, that is the lesson of being here for prolonged periods. Simplify, undo the self's bindings, rest at the window, eat slowly, draw up the body into one's passive thought. Learn anything, but especially from the bees and the ants.

The house has long been finished. As much as I care to do to make it comfortable. It remains a rustic house, ascetic in its appointments. The *grenier* that had once been home to exotic spiders and a few scorpions has long been my study and my daughter's bedroom when she's home. Its walls are not straight or plastered but bald rock loosely mortared, with the beams dark with stain looming above. Freshly-painted French doors look down onto the little court between the houses. The door is now a row of plank shelves in the *cave*. I did much of the work myself, meaning I followed along behind Steven O'Grady, a young English friend who did all the serious work, while I did the stooping and grunting. Together we fashioned a reasonably faithful rendering of the room, giving it many more years of stable life.

Now we have light and cheerfulness and practicality. No longer the cobwebs and dust, or the mice to cart their shafts of hay into the loose stone for nests. The spiders, the long-legged fly-catching sort that vibrate when you come too close, have had to pack up and go elsewhere. The last scorpion of any size, which strolled up to my knee while I pounded concrete out of a threshold, got the butt of my hammer, I lament to say.

There, along the east wall, with its chink of light, stood a tentative pile of rubble and stone stuck together with a bit of lime and sand. It would have fallen down eventually if we had not chipped out the joints and repointed stones about to come loose. The wall came back slowly, with our prodding and hammering and our great trowel-loads of mortar (twelve parts sand, two parts lime, one part white cement, lots of water and stirring).

The work on the room began with a new roof, which took the better part of March to complete. We hired a village maçon to do the work, which is to say, we hired the *maçon* to find one old man and a young boy to do the hauling and fitting, while the *maçon* darted in once or twice a day to check the water in the pail and leave again. On other occasions, with other maçons we hired, it meant hiring Arabs from Apt to do all the actual work while the *maçon* held court at the village bar.

It was sad to see what *maçons* now preach in their trade: all the gnarled beams were pulled out because of supposed wood-worms. There were a few pits in the wood, little else. These came down and small, rather stingy square beams went in, very modern and clean pieces of yellow pine. They were no match for the oak that was carted off to some mysterious destination, which I rather think was Monsieur Chabaud's materials lot, where authentic Provençal articles are for sale at antique-store prices. The roof tiles were taken up, most with a few chips and lichens covering them from sixty winters of wind and rain. These too went off to M. Chabaud, I suspect.

But you will not sleep at night if you set out to get the better of a Provençal *maçon*. The rules will never change: the *maçon* is in business to outsmart you, whether you are native French or a foreigner. And he will. Even when he errs and gives you a small break on the price of brick or labor, he has got you bettered on every other front. The beams went down to Apt, the new planks came in; the old tiles disappeared, with their odd shapes and their lumpy, hand-made appearance, their imprint of the thighs on which girls had molded them. Now came the factory-made yellow tiles, all very plain and regular, like the age itself. Along one wall, the back one overlooking an empty lot, were a row of nude concrete blocks to ward off the sideways wind and rain from the Alps. Necessary, but ugly work. In the past, that border would have been cemented and shaped with great care by a trowel. Now, a bit of gray cement was slopped between blocks and the roof left as is. No one would see this naked side, it was thought, so why bother finishing it. The roof trash had been thrown down onto the lot behind, the shell of some former dwelling.

The New Provence emerges in such work. As in the daylight that came through large cracks of the wall where the new roof joined the house. Sloppy work for which I paid an outrageous price. It claimed most of my budget for the room. Hence, my own presence on the job with bucket and trowel and piles of sand, and a look of anxiety from day to day. Steve O'Grady and I went over the walls inch by inch, using scaffolds borrowed from the farmer at the head of the village. My younger daughter Signe, and my son Cedric, and Cathy were all there slinging gobs of mortar into the cracks, the proper mode of wall-filling here. You rear back with a ball of mud and let fly, and if you hit the target, there is a reassuring, thankful smack from the joint. The wall bows to you. Indeed, I felt like those blind men in the Sufi story who feel the sides and legs of a great elephant and cannot determine what it is. For two long, wearying weeks, Steve and I groped around filling in the cracks and gapes and wobbles of the four meandering walls, and finally stood back to admire the suddenly beige, amber, yellow, gray, iridescent undulations of the room. It had responded, it had risen from its grave.

Each morning I would rise, slip into my stiff sneakers and work clothes, grab the shovel and march up to the farmer's yard to get his wheelbarrow, then wheel it down to the village road and shovel in a load of sand. I would push my load through the *Grand'Rue* back to the *grenier* door, where Steve would haul up bucketfuls and throw them onto the bare floor for mixing. It felt good to greet my fellow villagers along the way, who secretly approved of my labor. Jackie, of course, found me amusing, but his father was more sympathetic. He agreed with me that the labor was hard on a man's back. Lime opens sores in the skin and dries out the hands until they are rough and cracked. To shake a *maçon's* hand is to grab a piece of splintery wood and give it a yank. When I looked at Giovanni's hands, they were clean, but they had turned to polished sandstone over the years. They were no longer just hands; they had become tools, weathered and beaten, scrubbed to a pale luster. They were the color of my walls, now that the lime had bleached the stone to a dusty cream color.

When the light streamed in off the opposite walls into the room, the stones glowed. I liked standing in the room amidst all the rubble and work buckets, just to observe this slow-changing glow as clouds blew in, or the sun tilted lower. It was a modest room, divided by a plaster wall. When work was done on the east wall, I looked up and realized some of the stones cut straight through the jumble on a slant, *an old roof line!* And on the next wall the line ran for six feet and stopped. So, another house had butted on at one time, overlapping by six feet. Someone else spotted another path of stone running at a different slant, a former roof from some other house. The main south wall, whose doors led into the hallway, bore the shapes of windows long-since filled in with stone or rubble. This wall once faced the cold mistrals, before the barn and hayloft had been built. And inbetween, there had been smaller houses, for the *ruelle* had been a private courtyard once used as a livery stable. My house, like the others on the north side of the *Grand'Rue*, had been built when the village had grown another ring, perhaps back in the early 16th century. The *Grand'Rue* had once traced the edge of the village, and houses opposite did not go up until the 18th century, when the last *enceinte* was razed.

Signe would now rest her head against the wall, and sleep beneath a venerable roof line. What would she dream about, I wondered? The pearl gray winter afternoons, the creaking silence, the smell of fires drifting on the wind? The white-robed penitents headed for the church on the hill above? Time hung over her in clusters of dark and light; the roof ticked with the changing temperature. It was cozy in that stone corner, a place to lay one's head, as if to cradle it on the lap of history. My other daughter, Maxine, got the second room, but it was dark and in the few years she remained at home, it wasn't ever her "room." She was glad to leave it behind, and it remained a junk room for years until I converted it two years ago into a dark room for my photography. Cedric had his room over the *Grand'Rue*, next to ours.

Now all three are empty for the most part. This morning, as I sat here in the "study," my name for Signe's room, she slept in her sleigh bed beside me. She was home for the summer, and this would always be her room.

My hands linger over the stonework where a window once stood; you could tell from the alteration of the stone where someone had filled it in. Had flowers once bloomed in it? I traced the ancient, buried sill under its crust of lime, wondering who might have trailed her fingers there one summery morning, when the weather had shifted and shutters could be thrown open to the sun. Sealed windows – blind eyes, memory that keeps its own silence. It was enough to caress such stone, and run my thumb along the shape of time – my piece of it. I would push my desk against this ancient window, now sealed more tightly with the peach-colored earth between its joints. I would stare back into it as I worked, there where someone had looked out to catch the starlight or to talk to neighbors. Three hundred years later I sat at a desk in the mid-air of this window, writing about the face that had blinked and smiled and drawn the window shut.

Friends had rallied to help me with the rebuilding of the *grenier*. At one point, I stood on a rickety ladder with half a plaster board on my head, while behind me stood Steve on another ladder, hammer in hand, tacks in his mouth, and to the right and left our other English friends Mary and Stuart, propping up the sagging panel with broom handles and sticks. Up it went, as we hammered furiously and got the thing in place. All of us milled about guessing the dimensions of the next piece to go into the ceiling. Friends, good ones on whom to lean for help. The sun warmed us all, and we ate big lunches together in the kitchen. I was *home*, I realized, looking at these faces bent close to solve the next problem together. What luck, what happiness to be tired, and aching, and struggling this hard upon a task. It was all to the good.

On late summer days I would drive around to other villages to photograph houses and gardens, or stroll the roadside woods looking for some peculiar oak to study, roots spraddled over two big boulders, leaning its long neck into the wind. I almost felt as if I were etching its dark body into my dreams. I had a field camera that took 4 by 5 inch negatives; the lens gulped light and copied the craggy, forlorn features of an oak onto film. Moss had grown on its north side, and it stood there with all the ferocity of a Galapagos turtle, head bowed, limbs scraggled and broken, weathering the years of mistral and drought. Even the log men left it alone, a grandpa gone in the teeth, too tough to saw into firewood. I loved such trees; they possessed the secret of life and held it tight in their clenched lips.

It suddenly occurred to me that I too was weathering and stiffening in this rocky paradise. My kids had grown up, each in their own ways. Maxine went down to Perpignan to study painting at an *école des beaux arts*, and finished up in Avignon. She teaches English to young artists there now, and has a child, Swan, now two years old. His father is a Moroccan, long resident in France and a wonderful cook. Her paintings are on exhibit in Tuscany, in Leonardo da Vinci's father's house. At twenty-nine, she has arrived; bilingual, already tasting success with her Goyaesque portraits and film animations, she may soon make it in the Paris gallery world.

Signe worked her way through several degrees at the Sorbonne-Paris IV, which supported her study at Brown University for six months. She decided last year to apply full time to Brown and was awarded a scholarship to complete her doctorate there in comparative literature. We greeted this good news with a bottle of champagne and a long dinner. Now she is a translator for a French research company, so the champagne keeps coming, our glasses tinkling over our jovial table. She leaves in a few weeks for Providence, and it has struck each of us that another door was shutting on French life as we knew it. She would cut her ties to Paris and only visit the next time, without student visa or apartment to go to.

Cedric graduated from a private *lycée* at Sophie Antipolis, near Nice and went up to Paris to law school. Two years later he switched to political science at the Sorbonne, but has since been admitted to the Fondation Nationale des Sciences Politiques, one of the grand *écoles* of Paris, alma mater to many French ministers. He will tote his leather brief case in those halls and emerge as a candidate for the administrative realm, if not here in France then in South America. More champagne and toasts this summer, and a sense that we have succeeded beyond our wildest dreams raising three American kids in Europe. As pioneers, much of what we did was guess work, and on my wife's part, sheer diligence and hope. But all three flourished in France and have become hybrid Americans, as much European in their ways as they are Yanks.

Cedric perhaps is the most rooted in this sunny coastal world of southern France. I bought him an expensive pair of sunglasses and when he put them on, he was indistinguishable from any handsome 22 year old who might be leaning against the pillars of the Grand Casino at Monte Carlo, or driving along the Croisette in Cannes. His girlfriend Pachu is a lanky southern brunette with lovely eyes, and a grace that seems distilled out of the umbrella pines and caleche walks of Cap d'Antibes, where she lives with her father.

I sometimes wonder what would have become of him had we stayed in central Texas and put him through the public schools, and sent him off to a state university. Would he have sat in a chair the same way, fingering his demi tasse in that nonchalant elegant way? Would his speech elide and slither from his lips in a tangy blend of Paris street talk and the odd word that betrayed his education? Would his palate have been trained to know good wine from bad, ripe cheese from green? His long fingers were graceful and at ease, brown from the sun, his mind crammed with travel and a gallery of oddballs and Paris stories. I can't help but feel that Cedric especially is the creation of our rash plan, a remarkable flower of our guesswork.

These days the house on the *Grand'Rue*, sticking out a little into the street so we can glimpse all the way down the curve and see the life of the town go by, is quiet much of the time. Thick amber sunlight spills onto the tile floor of our kitchen as I read the paper. The wind sighs in the upstairs windows, and lifts and lowers the curtains as if thinking of the past. Kids don't clamber up and down the steps or shut the doors or race to the phone when it rings. The wind talks to itself in the drapes and in the string curtain over the doorway. Cathy is upstairs reading, her slippers kicked off at the bottom of the stairs. She walks barefoot on the cool tiles, a girl from Cincinnati who has changed over the years of living here. Her friends are the weathered crones of the village, whom she looks after, drives to their doctor's appointments or makes sure they visit one another. Rose Saint Martin was her best friend for many years, who died this past winter. Another rickety sliver of a woman lives across the way and calls Cathy *ma fille*, her daughter, and kisses her cheeks at the doorway.

We could not have made it without good friends. Luc and Elizabeth Thomas made their farm our refuge many nights, when the plank table groaned under heavy bowls of stew and fresh salad, which we gobbled up with delicious brown bread, while Luc poured his father's wine into our cups and hauled up more bottles as the moon rose and set. Dogs barked in the cold night air, and their kids came and went in that cozy, warm nook of light among the silent vineyards on all sides of us. John and Frances Dawson lived opposite us on the *Grand'Rue* and Frances whiled away the after-dinner evenings telling us of her childhood in the village and of the branches of her family, rich uncles in chateaux and admirals who left behind their emblazoned swords for heirs to squabble over. Her best stories concerned Harry Bell, an American who had been injured in the Korean Conflict and who lived on his disability pension. He had come here in search of property and bought several small houses and land outside the village. The smallest house, his *étude*, lay empty for decades until it went on the market and I bought it. I found out the village still called it *La maison d'harry*, the name I use for it too. It has a large window gaping at the center of the Luberon, and a tiny downstairs room with fireplace, and *caves* below.

Shana and Ulf, our Swedish friends, ply us with ice cold schnapps and trays of marinated cod and salmon brought from Malmo each Christmas. Steve and Sue Simons, whose cheerful house in Caseneuve has been our second home for many years, where we have spent New Year's nights before his immense fire place sipping the fragrant, chewy wines of his inexhaustible cellar. My next door neighbors, André and Germaine Fulconis, whose house once belonged to the village notary, Germaine's grandfather. André is the village historian and biographer of his grandfather, an important artist, and friend of Fréderic Mistral and Violet le Duc, the architect and rebuilder of medieval France. Laurie and Kim Cutler have laid out Provençal lunches that lasted all afternoon and early evening at their great round table in the garden of an ancient mill. Dear friends all, each of us wind-polished and seasoned by life here.

So much to be grateful for. Such good earth to come back to each summer and Christmas, opening the house and turning on heaters, lighting a fire in the hearth and filling dark rooms with light. Kids showing up from Paris and Avignon with bottles of wine and now a grandson, conversation that goes deep into the night. Our hearts melt at the first scent of lamb in the oven and the nutty aroma of freshly poured armagnac. We are comforted by such ancient amenities and take our seats in the new room, where our table is luminous with platters and candles.

Have I broken the crust that conceals Provence at last? Perhaps, and yet, no matter how long I stare into the woods on my morning walks, that paradise I so desire to embrace coyly eludes me in its dappled sunlight. A silence presides over the darker woods, as if a breath were held at the sound of my approach. But isn't this like love? Fear mixed with anticipation, that possibility of embrace that hangs just beyond certainty, enough to bring every cell to a pitch of yearning?

About the Author

Paul Christensen is widely recognized as a major critic of contemporary literature. He is a distinguished memoirist and poet. His books cover a wide range of interests, from other writers to his own experiences living and teaching in Texas; he is also the author of seven book-length collections of poems and several hundred published essays. His scholarly work includes two acclaimed critical biographies of the poets Charles Olson and Clayton Eshleman, and an edition of the letters of Charles Olson and Edward Dahlberg. Christensen's memoir of his professional life on this side of the Atlantic, *West of the American Dream: An Encounter with Texas*, has become a regional classic. Many of his personal essays touch on aspects of his residence abroad with his family during and following the Cold War. Christensen's articles on modern writers and literary movements have appeared in numerous scholarly journals. Together with Rick Bass, he edited *Falling From Grace in Texas*, a collection of essays and creative work dedicated to exposing environmental degradation and to celebrating the natural landscape of the Southwest. Among his award-winning books of poems are *Signs of the Whelming, The Mottled Air, Blue Alleys: Prose Poems* and *Hard Country* (the last two were recipients of the Violet Crown Award from the Writers' League of Texas). His short stories have appeared in national journals and received honors from the Texas Institute of Letters and other professional literary organizations.

Christensen teaches modern literature and creative writing at Texas A&M University and lives part of the year in southern France. He is a contributing editor on French culture to the journal *France Today* and writes frequently for the political weekly, *The Texas Observer*. He was a NEA poetry fellow in 1991 and has twice been appointed a senior lecturer by the Fulbright Commission. He is a member of the Texas Institute of Letters.

Wings Press was founded in 1975 by Joanie Whitebird and Joseph F. Lomax, both deceased, as "an informal association of artists and cultural mythologists dedicated to the preservation of the literature of the nation of Texas." The publisher/editor since 1995, Bryce Milligan is honored to carry on and expand that mission to include the finest in American writing, without commercial considerations clouding the choice to publish or not to publish. Technically a "for profit" press, Wings receives only occasional underwriting from individuals and institutions who wish to support our vision. For this we are very grateful.

Wings Press attempts to produce multicultural books, chapbooks, CDs, DVDs and broadsides that, we hope, enlighten the human spirit and enliven the mind. Everyone ever associated with Wings has been or is a writer, and we know well that writing is a transformational art form capable of changing the world, primarily by allowing us to glimpse something of each other's souls. Good writing is innovative, insightful, and interesting. But most of all it is honest.

Likewise, Wings Press is committed to treating the planet itself as a partner. Thus the press uses as much recycled material as possible, from the paper on which the books are printed to the boxes in which they are shipped.

Associate editor Robert Bonazzi is also an old hand in the small press world. Bonazzi was the editor / publisher of Latitudes Press (1966-2000). Bonazzi and Milligan share a commitment to independent publishing and have collaborated on numerous projects over the past 25 years. As Robert Dana wrote in *Against the Grain*, "Small press publishing is personal publishing. In essence, it is a matter of personal vision, personal taste and courage, and personal friendships."

Welcome to our world.

Colophon

This first edition of *Strangers in Paradise*, by
Paul Christensen, has been printed on 70
pound non-acidic paper containing fifty
percent recycled fiber. Titles have been set
using Cochin type; the text in Caslon. The
first 10 signature sets to be pulled from the
press have been numbered and signed by the
author. This volume was edited by Robert
Bonazzi. Wings Press books are designed
by Bryce Milligan.